# EXCAVATIONS AND OBSERVATIONS IN ROMAN CIRENCESTER 1998–2007

## with a review of archaeology in Cirencester 1958–2008

This volume is dedicated to Alan McWhirr in recognition of his service and commitment to the archaeology of Cirencester

Alan McWhirr at The Beeches, 1971

# CIRENCESTER EXCAVATIONS VI
# EXCAVATIONS AND OBSERVATIONS
# IN ROMAN CIRENCESTER
# 1998–2007

## with a review of archaeology in
## Cirencester 1958–2008

EDITED BY

NEIL HOLBROOK

With contributions by
Phil Austin, Alistair Barber, Edward Biddulph, Paul Booth, Mark Brett, Wendy Carruthers,
Mark Collard, Cynthia Poole, S. Cosh, Kate Cullen, G.B. Dannell, Timothy Darvill, Derek Evans,
Rowena Gale, Teresa Gilmore, Peter Grace, Peter Guest, Ellen Hambleton, Annette Hancocks,
Jon Hart, Tim Havard, Katie Hirst, E.R. McSloy, D.S. Neal, Richard Reece, Fiona Roe, Ian Scott,
Ruth Shaffrey, Andrew Simmonds, Alex Smith, Jane Timby, David Viner, Sylvia Warman,
Martin Watts, Steve Weaver, P.V. Webster and AnnSofie Witkin

Cotswold Archaeology
Cirencester, 2008

Published by Cotswold Archaeology

ISBN 978-0-9553534-2-0

**Cirencester Excavations Series**

*I. Early Roman Occupation at Cirencester*
By John Wacher and Alan McWhirr (1982)
ISBN 0 9507722 0 8

*II. Romano-British Cemeteries at Cirencester*
By Alan McWhirr, Linda Viner and Calvin Wells (1982)
ISBN 0 9507722 1 6

*III. Houses in Roman Cirencester*
By Alan McWhirr (1986)
ISBN 0 9507722 2 4

*IV. Cirencester Anglo-Saxon Church and Medieval Abbey*
By David Wilkinson and Alan McWhirr (1998)
ISBN 0 9523196 2 4

*V. Cirencester: The Roman Town Defences, Public Buildings and Shops*
Edited by Neil Holbrook (1998)
ISBN 0 9523196 3 2

*Front cover: Mosaic from Chester Street (see Fig. 56); excavation of the Roman town wall footings at Trinity Road, 2002; timber-framed building at Gloucester Street (see Fig. 8); Alan McWhirr at The Beeches, c. 1971*

Cover design by Lorna Gray, Cotswold Archaeology
Typeset and printed by Alden Hendi, Oxfordshire

# CONTENTS

# FIGURES

# TABLES

# ACKNOWLEDGEMENTS

The investigations reported on in this volume have been funded by the following bodies and individuals:

*Angel Cinema, 2004–6.* This project was undertaken by Oxford Archaeology. It was generously funded throughout by Charles Church Ltd and their support has been greatly appreciated. The fieldwork was supervised in the field by Rob Tannahill with the exception of the recording of the manhole and service trenches in The Avenue, which was carried out by Robin Bashford. The fieldwork was managed for Oxford Archaeology by Steve Weaver, and the post-excavation programme by Alex Smith. Thanks are owed to all the contributors to the report. The illustrations were prepared by Edeltraud Aspoeck and Julia Moxham, except Fig. 40 which was drawn by Magdalena Wachnik. The text was edited by Alex Smith.

*Bingham Hall, 2002.* The work was at the request of Richard Ponting and on behalf of the Trustees of the Bingham Hall. The excavations were supervised by Tim Havard and managed by Cliff Bateman and Martin Watts.

*Foresters Arms, 2003–4.* The work was commissioned by Jazzy Developments Ltd. The fieldwork was supervised by Derek Evans and managed by Clifford Bateman and Martin Watts.

*Cotswold Mill, 1998–9.* The work was for Thomas & Co. and we are grateful to Hugh Thomas and Paul Carter for their interest and assistance. The fieldwork was supervised by Alan Thomas and managed by Dawn Enright.

*Stepstairs Lane, 2002–3.* The work was for E.G. Carter & Co. Ltd, and was co-ordinated on their behalf by John Christie, Peter Burrows and Chris Andrews. Advice of environmental sampling and analysis was provided by Vanessa Straker (English Heritage) and Keith Wilkinson. The excavation was supervised by Mark Brett and managed by Cliff Bateman and Martin Watts.

*Insula IX, 1999.* The work was funded and carried out by the *Time Team* under the direction of Mick Aston and Neil Holbrook. Katie Hirst produced a typescript report which was edited and prepared for publication by Neil Holbrook. We are grateful to John Gater of GSB Prospection for permission to reproduce the geophysical survey. The producers of *Time Team* generously provided an additional contribution towards the cost of publishing this report.

*Trinity Road, 2001–2.* The work was for Cotswold District Council through their main contractor Wrekin Construction. We are grateful to Christine Woodfield and her colleagues at the Council, and Neil Ainsworth of Wrekin Construction, for their assistance. The fieldwork was supervised by Jo Williams and managed by Martin Watts.

*Stepstairs Lane, 2003–5.* The work was at the request of E.G. Carter & Co. Ltd. on behalf of Jephson Housing Association. The evaluation was supervised by Tim Havard and the watching brief undertaken by Franco Vartuca, Mike Rowe and Kate Cullen. The project was managed by Cliff Bateman and Martin Watts.

*Old Tetbury Road, 2004.* The work was at the request of Nigel Warren of NC Architects for APC Construction. The excavation was supervised by David Cudlip and managed by Cliff Bateman, Mary Alexander and Martin Watts. Teresa Gilmore thanks Malin Holst for helpful comments on an earlier draft of the report on the human bone from both this site and the Former Cattle Market.

*Former Cattle Market, 2004–6*: The work was for Cotswold District Council, and we are grateful to Roy Stove for his help and support. The main contractors Ledbetter Construction provided much practical assistance on site. The watching brief was undertaken by various members of Cotswold Archaeology, including Derek Evans, Franco Vartuca and Sylvia Warman, and was managed by Mary Alexander and Martin Watts. Louise Loe of Oxford Archaeology kindly granted permission for the use of the report on the cremation burial discovered in the evaluation.

*157 Watermoor Road, 2000.* The work was for Mr Gordon Ritchie. It was supervised by David Kenyon and managed by Cliff Bateman.

*Queen Elizabeth Road, 1999.* The work was for Wilmott Dixon Housing Ltd and the Cotswold Housing Partnership. We are grateful to John Ingram and Len Lawrence for assistance. The excavation was supervised by Alistair Barber and Jonathon Hart and managed by Mark Collard.

*Stratton Watermeadows, 2003.* The work was for Thames Water Utilities and we are grateful to their consultant Mike Lang Hall for assistance. The watching brief was undertaken by Charlotte Wymark and managed by Mary Alexander.

All the work undertaken between 1998 and 2007 reported in this volume was undertaken as part of the planning system, and was monitored by Gloucestershire County Council Archaeology Service which provides archaeological advice on planning applications to Cotswold District Council. We are grateful to Charles Parry, Senior Archaeologist at the County Council, for his long-standing interest and help on our projects and support for what we are trying to achieve. A number of the sites were also designated as scheduled monuments, and we are grateful to various members of the South-West regional team at English Heritage for their assistance on these projects. The contribution of the numerous field and finds staff and external specialists who have worked on these projects over the last ten years is gratefully acknowledged.

In preparing their brief account of the last fifty years of archaeology in Cirencester, Timothy Darvill and Neil Holbrook are most grateful to the following individuals for their help and insights in stitching the story together: Christopher Catling, David Gaimster, Alan McWhirr, Richard Reece, Heather Rowland, David Viner, Linda Viner and John Wacher.

David Viner's essay was compiled in a personal capacity, bringing together observations and research interests extending back over many years of residence in Cirencester, and as such the comments and contributions of a great many people can only be acknowledged in general terms. They are all thanked, nonetheless. Richard Reece, Neil Holbrook and Linda Viner kindly read early drafts of this essay, providing much relevant help and food for thought in so doing. Jan Wills kindly provided additional information and Peter Broxton recalled his childhood at Rivercourt. The weekly contributions by Gerry Stribbling and Peter Grace in 'The way we were' columns in the *Wilts & Glos Standard* between 1990 and 2005 provided a great deal of useful information and photographic reference, which remains a valuable resource. A local newspaper, in this case established as long ago as 1837, still has a key role in providing such stimulus to local historical enquiry for all its interested readers.

The illustrations were prepared by Peter Moore, Lorna Gray, Jemma Elliott and Elizabeth Gardner of Cotswold Archaeology, with the exception of those relating to the Angel Cinema which were prepared by Oxford Archaeology. The illustrations and photographs reproduced in this volume are credited to, and reproduced by kind permission of, the following individuals and organisations: Cotswold Archaeology, Timothy Darvill, D.S. Neal, Oxford Archaeology and the Society of Antiquaries of London. The photographs accompanying David Viner's essay are all by David Viner, except Fig. 14a which is from Reece and Catling 1975.

Richard Reece commented on an earlier draft of this report and has been unstinting in his interest and support of our work throughout. Annette Hancocks and Martin Watts assisted with bringing this report to publication. The project archives and finds have been deposited at the Corinium Museum under various accession numbers, and microfilmed copies of the paper records will be deposited at the National Monuments Record in Swindon.

# 1. INTRODUCTORY SECTIONS

## ORPHEUS AND THE HARE: FIFTY YEARS OF CIRENCESTER EXCAVATION COMMITTEE AND COTSWOLD ARCHAEOLOGY, 1958–2008
by Timothy Darvill and Neil Holbrook

### Introduction

Much has changed in the nature and scale of archaeological endeavour in and around Cirencester since December 1958 when a small gathering in the rooms of the Society of Antiquaries in Burlington House on Piccadilly, London, formally constituted the Cirencester Excavation Committee as the lead body to organise and execute excavations in this small town in the heart of the Cotswolds. Few there present would have guessed that in 2008 there would be celebrations for its golden jubilee, still less that a later generation of archaeologists could have transformed the simple Committee into a not-for-profit commercial company and registered charity with a turnover of more than £3 million per annum and a workbook filled with more than two hundred investigations contributing to the education of the public each year. This brief history of Cirencester Excavation Committee (CEC) and its successors outlines the growth of a single organisation and tries to situate its development within the ever-changing social, political, economic and academic environment. Across Britain there are more than two dozen similar organisations that emerged within the same mêlée, some now exceedingly healthy and others less so. A more broadly based history of this fascinating period in the history of archaeology is urgently needed, and in writing this account we are acutely aware of treading lightly into new territory (see McWhirr 1988 for an earlier treatment of this topic in Cirencester). We are also conscious of the fact that neither of us was archaeologically active in the late 1950s and 1960s and, to paraphrase Andy Warhol, anyone who says they can remember it probably wasn't there either!

### Picking up the pieces: The aftermath of the Second World War

Although no bombs fell directly on Cirencester during the Second World War, post-War reconstruction works made a major impact on the appearance and size of the town. Housing was a priority and by the end of 1947 more than a hundred new homes had been built on the newly created estates at Chesterton and Beeches (Welsford 1987a, 162). Over the following decade other developments, both privately financed and council sponsored, took shape to provide for the needs of an increasing population. Opportunities for archaeological work were seized whenever possible. The installation of a large woodworking machine at Lock's Timber Yard on the west side of Victoria Road in June 1947 brought to light a fine mosaic floor. Work was halted and the floor was excavated by local volunteers and workmen from the Council (Clifford 1949). Similarly, the erection of a telegraph pole on allotments at Ashcroft revealed a mosaic that was investigated on a small scale by Dr H. Catling in 1951 (Reece 1976) and at Querns Lane House Richard Reece undertook excavations in 1955–6 to reveal part of the Roman building and intramural street (Reece 1956). Such a pattern of small-scale work was of course possible because of the well-established interest in the history of the town started off in Victorian times and consolidated by Buckman and Newmarch's *Illustrations of the Remains of Roman Art in Cirencester* (1850), Beecham's *History of Cirencester* (1887), and Haverfield's paper on Roman Cirencester published in volume 49 of *Archaeologia* (Haverfield 1920). Private collections amassed by Earl Bathurst, Thomas Bravender and the Cripps family showed the wealth of what lay below Cirencester's streets, and were brought together in a fine new public museum of Roman antiquities housed in Abberley House in Park Street (now the Corinium Museum) which was opened by Professor George Trevelyan on 28 October 1938 to much acclaim (Austin 1938). One of the star attractions in the museum was the Orpheus pavement with the god encircled by birds and beasts; it was found at The Barton on the north-west side of the town in 1825 and was for long held as an icon of the Roman town and typical of the 'Corinium School' of mosaicists.

At national level discussions on the impact and opportunities of post-War reconstruction on historic towns were underway long before the War ended. A conference on the future organization of archaeology was held at the Institute of Archaeology in the University of London from 6 to 8 August 1943 at which the need for archaeological work in towns such as Cirencester was explicitly recognised by Ian Richmond in his overview of Romano-British Archaeology (Anon 1944a, 13). One tangible indirect consequence of this meeting was the termination of the Congress of Archaeological Societies and the creation of the Council for British Archaeology, a move facilitated in large measure by the Society of Antiquaries of London (Anon 1944b, 173–4). Both bodies maintained a strong interest in the archaeology of historic towns and were influential in shaping public opinion, galvanising activity at all levels, and promoting the value of Britain's archaeological heritage to government. No surprise therefore that the radical and influential Town and Country Planning Act 1947 provided sweeping new powers for local authorities, introduced the practice of spatial planning for the control of property development, and included provisions for the preservation of trees, woodland and buildings of special historic or architectural interest (Sections 28–30). Roman Corinium also enjoyed a measure of legal protection since the whole of the town had been designated a scheduled monument under the prevailing Ancient Monuments Consolidation and Protection Act 1913. Although weak by modern standards, this simple measure placed upon owners of properties in the town the duty of informing the Ministry of Works of any plans to develop their land in any way, and in turn the Ministry had certain powers to control such works by investigating and recording remains in advance of their destruction.

The need for archaeological investigation and recording in Cirencester was sporadic through the early 1950s as post-War reconstruction gathered pace. The construction of a new sewer at Watermoor, for example, necessitated cutting through the Roman defences. The Ministry of Works granted consent for the works on condition that a full archaeological excavation of the trench was undertaken and this was carried out under the direction of Miss Mary Rennie in poor weather during February and March 1952 (Rennie 1957). It was the first detailed examination of the defences and showed their complexity, scale and long duration through the 2nd, 3rd and 4th centuries AD. It also demonstrated that there was no pre-Roman occupation in this part of Cirencester, which prompted Elsie Clifford to consider whether such activity should in fact be sought at nearby Bagendon (Clifford 1961, 2). Among those acknowledged as helping with the excavation and preparing the report were Sheppard Frere and Graham Webster, both of whom were later to play influential roles in the provision of archaeological services in the town. Indeed, five years later Graham Webster was leading investigations at Dyer Court on the south side of Dyer Street in advance of construction works for what is now the Forum car park (Webster 1959). The work was done at the behest of and with financial backing from the Ancient Monuments Branch of the Ministry of Works who treated it as an emergency excavation. Members of the then recently formed Cirencester Archaeological and Historical Society acted as volunteers, assisted by volunteers from across the county and students from the geography department at the University of Birmingham. Forty-eight separate trenches were excavated to reveal sections of a Roman street near the centre of the town and the basic structure and orientation of buildings to either side. Tensions can be seen in the final report on the Dyer Court work between the

Ministry of Works who felt that excavations should only deal with deposits up to 4 feet (1.2m) deep and Graham Webster who saw the opportunity of exploring the full depth of stratigraphy in this key central area of the Roman town. Clearly a compromise was reached as the section through the main street in Trenches 2, 3, 16, 18 and 20 show the lowest surface about 20 feet (6m) below the modern ground level with no less than 24 successive re-surfacings through the full stratigraphic sequence. It was an impressive piece of excavation and to judge from available photographs carried out without the aid of shoring!

It was undoubtedly increasing intelligence about planned development elsewhere in the town, and the need to provide a consolidated and rapid response to new proposals, that led local enthusiast Mary Rennie and the London-based academic Roman archaeologist Sheppard Frere to write to the Society of Antiquaries of London in Spring 1958 inviting the Society to take the initiative in forming a Cirencester Excavation Committee. Their fears were real, and while their letter worked its way through the committees in London, archaeology was springing from the earth in Cirencester. Groundworks for the construction of the County Health Centre in Parsonage Field, Watermoor Road, revealed part of a Roman building, which caused the Ministry of Works to take over the site from the contractors and commission an archaeological excavation there over three weeks in July 1958. Four men were employed to carry out the work under the direction of Miss Rennie, assisted by local volunteers and members of the Cirencester Archaeological and Historical Society, and uncovered parts of at least four buildings, the largest with remains of a mosaic floor of geometric design (Rennie 1971). Later in the same year groundworks in advance of the construction of bungalows on the corner of King Street and Victoria Road prompted the Ministry of Works to commission Rennie to excavate this site in less than ideal conditions through November and December (CE III, 194–201). Among the structures recorded was part of a heated octagonal room, probably an imposing winter dining room of a fine town house.

## 1958: Creating Cirencester Excavation Committee

The letter (Fig. 1) from Rennie and Frere was read to the Executive Committee of the Society at its meeting on 14 April 1958, and after some discussion it was agreed to consider the matter at a special meeting of the Research Committee before the November meeting of the Council, after discussion of the project by Mr Frere, the Assistant Secretary to the Society (Philip Corder), and the Chief Inspector of Ancient Monuments at the Ministry of Works (P.K. Baillie-Reynolds). The special meeting was duly held on 6 November 1958, and at Council on the same day it was resolved 'to approve the recommendation of the Research Committee that a Cirencester Excavation Committee be formed forthwith to conduct excavation within the Roman City, and that the list of names of Fellows and of institutions to be invited to form such a Committee, proposed by

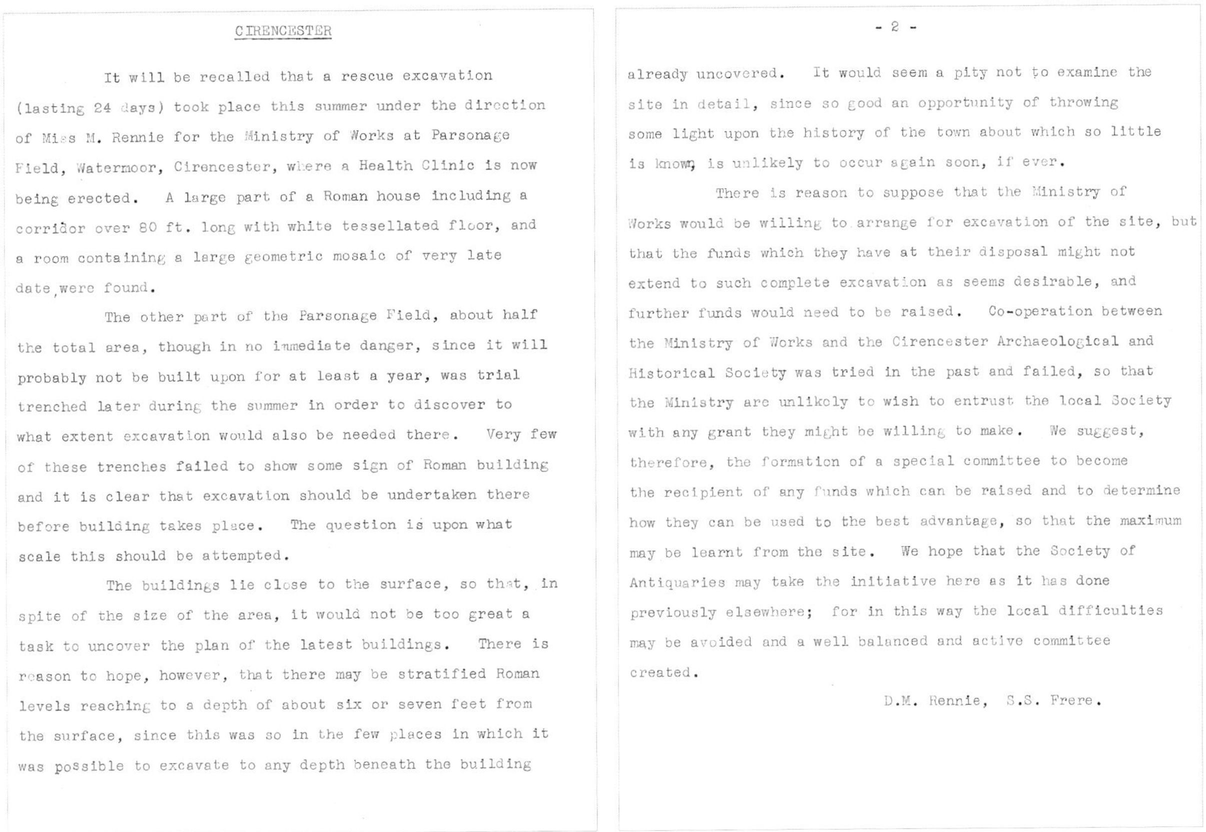

CIRENCESTER

It will be recalled that a rescue excavation (lasting 24 days) took place this summer under the direction of Miss M. Rennie for the Ministry of Works at Parsonage Field, Watermoor, Cirencester, where a Health Clinic is now being erected. A large part of a Roman house including a corridor over 80 ft. long with white tessellated floor, and a room containing a large geometric mosaic of very late date were found.

The other part of the Parsonage Field, about half the total area, though in no immediate danger, since it will probably not be built upon for at least a year, was trial trenched later during the summer in order to discover to what extent excavation would also be needed there. Very few of these trenches failed to show some sign of Roman building and it is clear that excavation should be undertaken there before building takes place. The question is upon what scale this should be attempted.

The buildings lie close to the surface, so that, in spite of the size of the area, it would not be too great a task to uncover the plan of the latest buildings. There is reason to hope, however, that there may be stratified Roman levels reaching to a depth of about six or seven feet from the surface, since this was so in the few places in which it was possible to excavate to any depth beneath the building

- 2 -

already uncovered. It would seem a pity not to examine the site in detail, since so good an opportunity of throwing some light upon the history of the town about which so little is known, is unlikely to occur again soon, if ever.

There is reason to suppose that the Ministry of Works would be willing to arrange for excavation of the site, but that the funds which they have at their disposal might not extend to such complete excavation as seems desirable, and further funds would need to be raised. Co-operation between the Ministry of Works and the Cirencester Archaeological and Historical Society was tried in the past and failed, so that the Ministry are unlikely to wish to entrust the local Society with any grant they might be willing to make. We suggest, therefore, the formation of a special committee to become the recipient of any funds which can be raised and to determine how they can be used to the best advantage, so that the maximum may be learnt from the site. We hope that the Society of Antiquaries may take the initiative here as it has done previously elsewhere; for in this way the local difficulties may be avoided and a well balanced and active committee created.

D.M. Rennie, S.S. Frere.

*Fig. 1* Letter from D.M. Rennie and S.S. Frere read to the Executive Committee of the Society of Antiquaries on 14 April 1958 proposing that a committee be established to oversee future archaeological excavation for Cirencester

the Research Committee, be adopted' (Society of Antiquaries Minute books).

The first meeting of the Cirencester Excavation Committee (CEC) was held at Burlington House, Piccadilly, on Tuesday 16 December 1958 with an agenda that included the election of officers, the election of an Executive Committee, co-options to the Committee, the appointment of a Director for the excavations, financial arrangements, and a programme of works for 1959. Professor Ian Richmond, then a Vice-President of the Antiquaries, was elected as the first chairman of CEC. Richmond was Professor of the Archaeology of the Roman Empire in the University of Oxford and the dominant figure in Romano-British archaeology at the time. He was widely respected, admired and, indeed, loved by colleagues and pupils alike, and had started work in Gloucestershire at Chedworth Roman Villa in the summer of 1958. Knighted in the Queen's Birthday Honours List in 1964, Richmond's influence on the affairs of the Committee was immense until his death at the tragically early age of 63 in October 1965. Capt. Stewart Gracie RN, a diligent and energetic Gloucestershire-based amateur archaeologist well known as the founder of excavations at Frocester in 1958 was made secretary, and Miss Katherine (Kitty) Richardson was appointed Director of excavations. The Society also made a series of grants from its research fund to support the work of the Committee, and in 1959 issued an Appeal Leaflet seeking one-off donations or a seven-year covenant with the Society that enabled the

recovery of income tax and directed the entire proceeds to the Cirencester Excavation Fund.

News of the establishment of CEC was widely reported and caused considerable local interest. Much emphasis was placed on its remit to focus on emergency excavations in advance of building operations (Anon 1959, 191), although the 1959 Appeal Leaflet (Fig. 2) takes a more holistic view by noting that 'no large scale excavation has, however, been undertaken and without it our knowledge of the history and development of this important Roman centre remains virtually blank'. From 1959 onwards meetings were held in Cirencester. Colonel W.A. Chester-Master was the first patron. As well as the officers already noted (Richmond, Gracie and Richardson), Ivan Sheppard of Lloyds Bank in Cirencester was recruited as the first treasurer. The Ministry of Works was represented by its Chief Inspector of Ancient Monuments P.K. Baillie-Reynolds and inspector J.R.C. Hamilton; Gloucestershire County Council was represented by Major-General F.V.B. Witts; Cirencester Urban District Council by J.E. Jefferies and J.W. Elliott; the Bristol and Gloucestershire Archaeological Society and the Society of Antiquaries by Joan Evans; the Cirencester Archaeological and Historical Society by G.B. Young; the Corinium Museum by Donald Atkinson, the Honorary Curator; Bristol University by Professor J.M. Cook; the Council for British Archaeology by W.F. Grimes; the Society for the Promotion of Roman Studies by Miss M.V. Taylor; and the Haverfield Trust

CIRENCESTER EXCAVATION FUND APPEAL

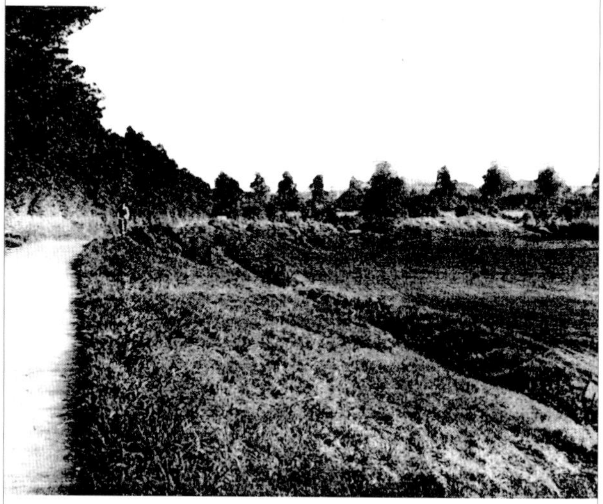

This view of the rampart which backed the Roman city wall at Cirencester is to be seen in Watermoor Recreation Ground, where is sweeps round to enclose the south-eastern quarter of the city.

THE CIRENCESTER EXCAVATIONS

CORINIUM, the modern Cirencester, was the largest town in Roman Britain after London, the tribal capital of the Dobunni and in the fourth century probably one of the provincial capitals. Sporadic discoveries and very limited systematic excavation have produced the remarkable sculptures, fine architectural remains and splendid mosaic pavements, now displayed in the Corinium Museum, and also evidence for a rectangular grid of streets centred about a large county hall. A beginning has also been made upon a study of the town defences.

No large scale excavation has, however, been undertaken and without it our knowledge of the history and development of this very important Roman centre remains virtually blank. The Society of Antiquaries of London, with the support of the Cirencester Archaeological and Historical Society and the Bristol and Gloucestershire Archaeological Society, is therefore sponsoring a systematic study of the town through excavation, taking as the first area the Parsonage Field in Watermoor, where remains of well-built houses were recently disturbed in erecting the County Health Centre. But there is more work to do. Further information is needed upon the town wall, the public and religious buildings and the cemeteries, including the military cemetery certainly associated with a fort established in the earliest days of the Roman occupation. Much would be found to enrich and amplify the collections of the Museum and the information gained would certainly throw much new light upon the way of life in Roman Britain and upon the history of the Roman occupation, which covers virtually a fifth of the long history of a town that has ever since remained a notable centre of Cotswold life. Too much of this period is at present dark, but both the initial military occupation and the evidence for prosperous activity in the fourth and fifth centuries give the site peculiar importance and promise.

The Excavation Committee is widely representative of local and national archaeological interests. Work will start in the Parsonage Field in May, 1959, under the direction of Miss K. M. Richardson, F.S.A. Donations large or small are earnestly solicited in order to enable the work to proceed upon the requisite scale, and a form of subscription is attached.

*Fig. 2* Fundraising brochure for the newly established Cirencester Excavation Committee

by J.N.L Myres. There were also eight private individuals: The Hon. W.R.S. Bathurst, Mrs E.M. Clifford, Philip Corder, Wilfred I. Croome, Sheppard Frere, Mrs Helen O'Neil, Miss Mary Rennie and Graham Webster.

The idea of an excavation committee as a community-driven means of promoting and organising archaeological work may at first sight seem rather strange, but as an organisational structure had a long history born of collegiate endeavour that in the first half of the 20th century was popularised for archaeology by Mortimer Wheeler. His enthusiasm for getting things done, his military mind, a commitment to a kind of autocratic democracy and a concern for what might nowadays be called 'inclusiveness' made the recruitment of a governing committee an ideal vehicle to carry forward his plans. In 1929 a Verulamium Excavation Committee was set up under the chairmanship of Sir Charles Peers to support and raise funds for Wheeler's ambitious investigations undertaken between 1930 and 1934. Locally, the Roman Research Committee for Gloucester was established on 12 January 1931 to provide a relatively informal collective of interested parties supporting a series of selected projects around the town starting with the excavations at the Crypt School in Brunswick Road (GRRC 1930). Wheeler, who had just completed two seasons of excavation at the Roman temple in Lydney Park at the invitation of Lord Bledisloe, was a member of the Committee (the only one not resident in the area) and his influence may be discerned in its creation. Both these organisations, and others across the country, focused on research projects, and in the main were fairly short-lived. However, after the Second World War some were reinvigorated and others newly instigated as the basic structure was sound and there was a new and clear need to involve both individuals and organisations in the common cause that was now focused on mitigating the impacts of development on the historic environment. Canterbury was the first in 1944, followed quickly by others such as Dover, Exeter, Gloucester and Lincoln. Much the same happened at St Albans in 1954 with the reconstruction of the Verulamium Excavation Committee, but the essential difference here was the independence of the organisation, a feature that soon came to define and characterise the emergent field of rescue archaeology, alongside alternative administrative solutions based in local museums or university departments (Biddle 1974, 108–9). Sheppard Frere was appointed director of excavations at Verulamium, and it was his pioneering experiences that allowed CEC to follow closely behind. Indeed, some of the barrows and buckets used in the early work of CEC were borrowed from St Albans, and one of Frere's most enduring contributions to excavations in both towns must be the steady supply of pipe-tobacco tins (Three Nuns was preferred at Cirencester) in which valuable and fragile small finds could conveniently be stored! John Wacher's later contributions on this score were similarly memorable.

The first excavation to be undertaken by CEC, between 4 May and 15 June 1959, was in advance of the anticipated development of the northern part of Parsonage Field on Watermoor Road for the construction of an old people's home. Four workmen were employed, Mary Rennie acted as deputy director to Kitty Richardson, and many of those who participated in earlier seasons either helped with the excavation or assisted with post-excavation analysis and reporting, the proofs of the promptly completed report being checked by CEC's chairman Ian Richmond (Richardson 1962). The excavations themselves were innovative in combining the tightly structured trenching characteristic of the Wheeler System with a desire to provide a full ground plan of the principal building that demanded a more open-area approach. It was an experiment typical of Richardson, who came to Cirencester as one of 'Wheeler's babes' having worked with Sir Mortimer at Verulamium in 1930–3, Maiden Castle in 1935–7, the hillforts campaign in northern France in 1938–9 and Stanwick in 1951–2. She was one of the first archaeologists to use mechanical dragline excavators to strip topsoil and empty deep features when she directed investigations at Boscombe Down West in 1949 (Richardson and Stone 1951). (Frere had pioneered the same technique in an urban environment in Canterbury that same year.) She was a lady in much demand, and after working at Cirencester in 1959 moved to London to work for the Council for British Archaeology as editor of the British Archaeological Bibliography, a role she continued until retirement in 1972.

The 1959 season had gone well and the Committee could now turn its attentions to a number of other impending threats. All the signs were that development would continue apace in Cirencester for a number of years to come, so it faced an enormous task. Richmond recognised the importance of replacing Kitty Richardson with someone well versed in Romano-British urban archaeology and it was envisaged that Sheppard Frere would direct the excavations. Frere had to withdraw at short notice, however, owing to other commitments, and Richmond invited John Wacher to take over. John had recently been appointed as assistant lecturer in British archaeology in the newly founded department of archaeology at the University of Leicester and had an impressive record of urban excavation. He had worked as a supervisor under Sheppard Frere at Canterbury and Verulamium and had directed his own excavations at Brough-on-Humber and Leicester in 1958 and at Catterick in 1959. His appointment established a strong link with Leicester University that continued for more than two decades. Richmond, Frere and Webster remained influential members of the Committee, and it was Frere who took up the Chairmanship upon Richmond's death in 1965. He was also instrumental in the decision to publish annual interim accounts of the work of the Committee in the *Antiquaries Journal* and to deliver an annual lecture to the Society in London, an approach that he had successfully developed in the seven interims published between 1956 and 1962 on his work at Verulamium. John Wacher's first excavation for CEC was an examination of the Verulamium Gate to the north of London Road along with a section of the Roman defences in the Abbey Grounds in advance of the construction of a housing estate (now Corinium Gate) on the east side of the town. This took place over seven weeks in March and April 1960 and began what many see as a 'Golden Age' of large-scale annual summertime excavations in the town that lasted pretty much continuously for fourteen years.

## 1960–1974: The Golden Years

Work at the Verulamium Gate and adjacent north-eastern defences yielded impressive results and stimulated an interest in urban defences that proved to be one of John Wacher's long-standing research interests through the rest of his career. The work also involved a notable early example of environmental archaeology, with a selection of mollusc shells collected and analysed by local cleric Canon L.W. Grensted (CE V, 46–7). The first interim account was duly published in 1961 accompanied by a plan of the Roman town which was little different from that produced by Haverfield forty years earlier (Fig. 3a; cf. Haverfield 1920, pl. XI). However, by the time of the second interim John had got his teeth into Cirencester and produced a new plan of the Roman town, complete with numbered insulae, which has formed the basis for all subsequent revisions (Fig. 3b). Richmond read and improved all the interim accounts up to his death in 1964, a process which all refered to as 'Ian-ising'. In John's second season, 1961, the programme of work had expanded to comprise three weeks at Easter and nine weeks in the summer. Excavations took place at Leaholme Gardens where traces of public buildings and an underlying military fort were discovered (Fig. 4). The discovery of the upper torso of a human skeleton in the top of the side ditch of Ermin Street proved to be especially influential as this was interpreted as evidence for the decline of town life at the end of Roman rule in Britain. As John Wacher colourfully records 'all traces of order had broken down: grass was literally growing in the streets and unburied bodies were left to rot in roadside ditches . . . we might wonder whether if this event was connected with one or other severe epidemics which occurred in the fifth or sixth centuries' (Wacher 1974, 313; but cf. Reece 1988, 124–5). The committee was able to support this work due to its vigorous and successful fundraising which collected £2,200, by no means an insignificant sum in the early 1960s.

Support in kind was always vital to the Committee, however, with dig HQs being set up wherever premises could be made available, including an old slaughterhouse off Dyer Street and the skittle alley of Watermoor Hospital Staff Social Club. Public access to the excavations was always considered important and from 1961 onwards the Archaeological and Historical Society organised guided tours of the trenches and assisted with the catering, as well as undertaking much of the advance planning such as finding accommodation and a suitable camp site. Throughout, the brand of archaeology promoted by CEC was a very public kind of archaeology in which people could join in with the work or at least see it happening. Col. W.A. Chester-Master assisted where he could as Patron of the

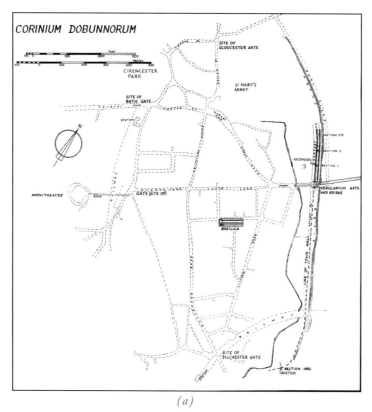

*(a)*

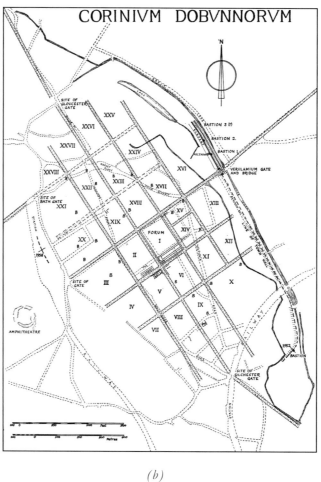

*(b)*

*Fig. 3.*    a. Plan of Roman Cirencester published in the first interim report in 1961. b. The greatly improved plan published one year later in the second interim report

*Fig. 4* John Wacher leading a site tour at the Leaholme excavations, 1961

Committee, and at his death in January 1963 was replaced by the equally enthusiastic Earl Bathurst who remained in post until the final dissolution of the Committee in 1989, although in later years he was often represented at functions and events by his son Lord Apsley. The role of the local council in the affairs of CEC was also an important factor in its success. For while Cirencester Urban District Council had no specific legal requirement to support archaeology in an historic town such as Cirencester there was clearly a great deal of local interest, moral support for idea of recording archaeological remains and more than a little recognition that tourism and what might now be called heritage was important to the economy of the town. Foremost among local supporters from early times was John Jefferies, sometime Chairman of the Council, and Derek Waring, the first Chief Executive of Cotswold District Council.

In 1962 work focused on excavations in Coxwell Street where traces of a possible theatre were found, the large Police Station site south of Market Place which revealed more of the street plan and buildings adjacent to Ermin Street, and at City Bank in the far south-western corner of the town. The first 'research' as opposed to 'rescue' excavations were undertaken in late 1962 and 1963 at the amphitheatre on the west side of the town, work that continued in 1966. In 1963 there were also excavations at King's Head Yard off the Market Place, two separate sites off Lewis Lane, Parsonage Field in Watermoor Road and in Watermoor Hospital Gardens. In 1964 trenches were dug at Lloyds Bank in Silver Street, at the Gaumont Cinema site on the corner of Victoria Road and London Road, at Ashcroft House in Querns House and in Chester Mews, while in the following two years sites such as the

northern defences off Spitalgate Lane and Dollar Street were investigated. All contributed to the emerging plan of the Roman town and it is instructive to compare the maps presented in successive interim reports through the 1960s. The period between 1964 and 1966 was dominated by another site, however, because in 1964 much of the pre-planned work had to be curtailed when the implications of proposed development on the site of Cirencester Abbey became apparent. After the first season at the Abbey in 1964 the Committee was acutely aware of the potential resources that might be required to complete the excavation, and the difficult decisions which would lie ahead in balancing the competing claims of the Roman and medieval archaeology of the town. John Wacher fell ill during the 1965 season, and retired from active fieldwork in Cirencester; Alan McWhirr and David Brown took over as joint directors of the excavations. Conscious of the importance of the discoveries being made at the abbey, the Committee invited David Brown, an Anglo-Saxon specialist, to direct the excavations there in 1966. David was brought up in the Cotswold village of Daglingworth and had started digging in Cirencester in 1960 during his vacations from Cambridge. He also dug with Frere at the samian ware production site at Lezoux in France. Alan McWhirr had also dug with Frere at Verulamium and with Wacher at Leicester and Catterick. His first connection with Cirencester had been as a supervisor at the Leaholme (basilica) excavations in 1961. At that time Alan was a school teacher in Leicester who dug in the holidays, a situation which continued when he became a lecturer in Environmental Studies at Leicester College of Education (latterly Leicester Polytechnic). In 1988 he joined the Department of Archaeology at Leicester University on a part-time basis and in a full-time capacity in 1995 to set up a distance-learning course in archaeology.

By 1967 the threat to the site of the Abbey had diminished, and David Brown withdrew from the Committee as he had just been appointed to a post working on the collection of Anglo-Saxon grave goods in the Ashmolean Museum in Oxford. Alan McWhirr therefore assumed sole charge of the excavations and through the later 1960s and early 1970s masterminded a series of high-profile projects closely tied to the rapid expansion of the town and the threats posed by major developments in its historic core. In 1967 this included work at The Station Yard beside Sheep Street, Watermoor School, and sites at Midland Road and The Sands in the south-east corner of the town. 1968 saw work at The Waterloo, 17 The Avenue and Victoria Road, all of which added yet more detail to the town plan and began to focus attention on the fact that occupation across the walled area of the town was uneven in its intensity and date.

Between 1969 and 1975 a number of small excavations were undertaken around the town, but the work of the Committee mainly focused on three classic excavations whose results still figure prominently in textbooks on Roman Britain. In 1969 plans for the construction of the Cirencester western relief road led to the start of excavations in the Bath Gate cemetery which were to carry on until 1974, while on the

*(a)*

*(b)*

*Fig. 5*   Excavation in the 1970s. a. The Beeches in 1971. b. Admiral's Walk in 1975

opposite side of the town excavations between 1970 and 1973 at Beeches Road (Fig. 5a) uncovered two very well-preserved town houses, one of which yielded the iconic hare mosaic which was rapidly adopted as the logo of the Corinium Museum, stealing attention from the Orpheus pavement and soon installed in a prominent place for visitors to admire the detail of its design. The final site involved the excavation of a strip through St Michael's Field between 1974 and 1976 in advance of a (thankfully never to be constructed) road link. The excavation was known as Admiral's Walk and uncovered the substantial remains of houses, shops and a part of a large public building, plus further evidence of early military activity (Fig. 5b).

All three of these large projects involved extensive open area excavations with teams of up to a hundred volunteers and students from Leicester working mainly through the summer months and living on campsites and in digs around the town. Alan McWhirr stayed with the Burton family who owned the rambling secondhand bookshop in Dyer Street which was always well stocked with archaeological volumes and made enjoyable browsing on a wet afternoon. A favourite haunt for supervisors was a rented house on the corner of London Road and Beeches Road that hosted many parties and deep debates about the archaeology of the town. The Twelve Bells and the Black Horse were favoured watering holes through the long summer excavations, although there were always a few diggers to be found in the Wagon and Horses, the Bear and the Nelson, easily recognised by their dirty knees and dusty shoes.

Throughout its Golden Years Cirencester was part of what became known as the digging circuit, and between 1960 and 1976 a number of up and coming archaeologists cut their teeth working in the town. In the early years some came here for what Alan McWhirr describes as 'an annual dose of archaeological masochism' because the excavations at Verulamium were now starting to wind down. All were eager for the opportunities and training afforded by a high-profile programme of excavation under the direction of the country's leading practitioners. Among the many people who worked on the digs during this period some went on to forge successful careers in academia (Timothy Darvill, Mark Hassall, Tony King, Henrietta Miles (later Quinnell), Martin Millett and Steve Roskams) and professional practice (Scott Anderson, Roy Canham, Chris Catling, Geoffrey Dannell, Rosalind Dunnett (later Niblett), Christine Mahany, Jean Mellor, Tim O'Leary, David Viner, David Wilkinson and Bob Zeepvat). Mention must also be made of the many site supervisors, assistant supervisors, finds assistants, photographers, illustrators and diggers (nowadays sometimes known as 'shovelbums') who made the excavations what they were. Many of them are named in the acknowledgements to the interim reports and the five published volumes of Cirencester Excavations, among those not already noted are: Annie Anderson, Anna Bachelier, Peter Bellwood, C. Birchell, Peter Broxton, Gavin Brown, Christine Butcher, Phillipa Cullen, Jim Derry, Elizabeth Dowman, Robert Downey, R.A. Fagence, Brian Gill, Peter Grace, Maggie Hewitt, Sheelagh Johnson, Gillian

Jones, Maurice Jones-Mortimer, Ian Lea, Helen McWhirr, Marion Owers, Tony Pacitto, Alan Parsloe, Alan Perkins, Mrs Petty, Tony Poole, Charmain Reed, John Robinson, Jennie Ruff, R. Rumens, Colin Shuttleworth, H. Smith, Sarah Smith, Merlyn Vyner, Anna Wacher, Eleanor Waite and Mark Webber. A wide range of experts in everything from amphorae to wall plaster has worked on material recovered from excavations in and around Cirencester and duly reported their findings in the published reports.

Richard Reece is another distinguished archaeologist, Cirencester born and bred, who has had an association with the archaeology of the town stretching back to his teenage years, when he directed his first excavation in the grounds of Querns Lane House in 1955. Richard rarely worked on the CEC excavations, but he undertook numerous small-scale investigations across the town, as for example the salvage recording at Oakley Cottage during the construction of a new petrol station in September 1960 (Reece 1962), and directed the final stage of excavations at The Beeches in 1973 after the main season had finished, which allowed a full building plan to be recovered. His greatest contribution to the work of the Committee was in identifying every coin that the Committee excavated, a monumental undertaking whose listings ran into the tens of thousands at the last count. His publication of this work in 1998, in conjunction with Peter Guest, put the town at the head of coin-reporting in Britain (CE V, 247–93).

Across Britain rescue archaeology was gradually changing as the 1970s unfolded. The early 1970s saw the creation of a number of new full-time professional archaeological units, at places such as Canterbury, Exeter, Lincoln, London and York, and some innovative approaches to recording. Enthused by the experiences of Tim O'Leary and Steve Roskams at the multinational excavations at Carthage and encouraged by innovative publications on stratigraphic sequences by Ed Harris, the 1974 supervisors working at Admiral's Walk – Rick Middleton, Tim O'Leary, Giovanna Vitelli, Chris Goodway and Timothy Darvill – experimented with the emerging idea of single context recording. Despite using miles of permatrace and reams of paper it proved to be largely unsuccessful, with many of the records proving unintelligible in post-excavation analysis. But it was through such experiments that the principles of modern urban archaeology were established and a revised and much improved version of the system has now become standard practice.

Public interest in archaeology in Cirencester remained high through the early 1970s. The summer excavations, especially those at The Beeches and Admiral's Walk, attracted thousands of visitors, both local residents and tourists from further afield, with August Bank Holidays being particularly popular and rather hectic. The AA provided signage to direct drivers into appropriate car parks. Queues formed to file around the excavation trenches. Members of the Cirencester Archaeological and Historical Society acted as guides, and prepared refreshments, galvanised and led by Miss D.M. Radway, Miss Joyce Barker and Mr

Kenneth Povah. Mr Povah was a retired school teacher and excellent artist who frequently used to sketch or paint reconstructions of what could be seen in the trenches in order to illuminate the tours he led. Collecting tins were always ready at hand to receive a few coins by way of a donation to excavation funds, and some bright supervisor invented the caption *The rattle of the tin says 'thank you'*. Throughout the 1960s and 1970s there were close reciprocal links with the Corinium Museum and, courtesy of successive custodians and curators Donald Atkinson, John Real and David Viner, a long-standing tradition of free entry for those working on the excavations on their days off or when rain stopped play.

Through the 1970s government support for archaeology in England was channelled through the Department of the Environment and focused on providing block grants to cover the core costs of established regionally based organisations. Some of the new archaeological units deemed necessary to cope with the rising tide of rescue archaeology were based within local authorities; others were set up as autonomous trusts. Cirencester was not deemed by the Department of the Environment to be a sufficiently large place to justify a full-time unit in its own right, and in 1973 the Committee for Rescue Archaeology in Avon Gloucestershire and Somerset (CRAAGS) was created to administer funds from the Department in the three counties. CRAAGS was responsible for excavations in Cirencester in 1976 at the Bath Gate cemetery west of Sheep Street and St John's Hospital in Spitalgate Lane, both directed by Roger Leech. The introduction of a second organisation into Cirencester might have made for difficulties, but in fact a good working relationship was maintained between the two bodies, and both sites were subsequently published in collaboration with CEC.

The last major excavation in the centre of Cirencester was at Admiral's Walk in 1975, with small trenches at 26 Dollar Street and beside the amphitheatre running in parallel. The following year involved some small-scale clearing up work supervised by Timothy Darvill and a small team of local diggers drawn from the pool of skill by this time well established in the town: among them Jason Townsend, Andrea Morley, Ann Chapel and Helen d'Carle. Bob Zeepvat, who had worked at The Beeches and supervised the Price's Row excavation, undertook a string of site observation projects during the construction of the town's inner ring road system, and recorded the replacement of the town's main sewer along Watermoor Road, Victoria Road, Dyer Street and the Market Place (Zeepvat 1979).

The need to publish detailed reports on what had become a substantial body of excavated material was well recognised, and a small post-excavation team that included Val Rigby, Linda Viner, David Wilkinson and later Janet Richardson and Caroline Ireland was established in two or three rooms on the ground floor of Powell's School building in Gloucester Street. Alan McWhirr, David Viner, Timothy Darvill, Nick Griffiths and others were regular visitors to help progress the work of publication. These gatherings traditionally involved numerous 'butter buns' bought from one or other of the traditional local bakers that flourished

round the town – usually Whiddett's, Viners or Anne's Pantry – washed down with copious amounts of tea and coffee.

The tenth and last interim report of Cirencester excavations, covering work between 1973 and 1976, was published in the *Antiquaries Journal* for 1978. But although large-scale excavations came to an end in the mid 1970s the period remained a vibrant one for archaeology in the town. With David Viner as its first full-time curator, the Corinium Museum was extended and completely refurbished in 1973–4, reopening to visitors on 26 November 1974 with the Duke of Gloucester as guest of honour. One of the early archaeological events held in the refurbished rooms was a research seminar organised by CEC in November 1975 on the archaeology and history of Cirencester, which dealt not only with the Roman period but actually devoted more space to the Saxon, medieval and later archaeology of the town. The papers, edited by Alan McWhirr, were published as British Archaeological Report no. 30 in 1976 (McWhirr 1976).

CEC's headquarters were variously (indeed tenuously) located in sundry offices, in Park Street from 1978, in Silver Street (above one of Cirencester's well-remembered greengrocers) from 1985 and latterly upstairs in Abberley House adjacent to the Corinium Museum. Post-excavation analysis and reporting were in full swing and an ambitious programme of publication was planned with financial support from the Department of the Environment and others. Initially it was hoped to produce a series of thematic monographs issued as reports of the Research Committee of the Society of Antiquaries, but the nature and character of publication was changing and as the first volume took form the decision was taken for the Committee to self-publish the reports by taking advantage of the emergent new computer-based technology. This latter too evolved: volume II had microfiche but volume III reverted in part to small print to negate the use of fiche. The first volume covered the early Roman occupation at Cirencester and was launched at the Corinium Museum on 31 March 1982, at Cotswold District Council's invitation and with Sheppard Frere in fine form as Chairman of CEC and most of the then committee in attendance, including Joyce Barker, John Jefferies and David Viner, who acted as the committee's Honorary Secretary for twenty years from 1978 to 1997. It was around this time that CEC installed its first computer in the Park Street office, an Apple IIE acquired at educational discount through Alan McWhirr's Leicester contacts, which made its way to Cirencester when Alan McWhirr and Timothy Darvill met in a lay-by on the Fosse Way somewhere near Stretton-on-Fosse to transfer the bulky cardboard cartons containing the computer and its peripherals from one car to the other in a manner that seemed slightly shady at the time and which today would probably have led to the arrest of both innocent parties.

## Changing times: 1976–1989

Post-excavation work and small-scale excavations characterised Cirencester excavations through the late

1970s and 1980s. Cirencester Excavations volume II on the cemeteries was published in late 1982 and volume III on the town houses in Cirencester in 1986. Both sold well and have joined the ranks of key volumes on Britain's Roman towns. But maintaining the momentum was difficult and in 1979 government funding for archaeology shifted from core-funding of established organisations to project funding for specific initiatives. CRAAGS and its later incarnation Western Archaeological Trust failed to keep in step with the changing pattern of archaeological endeavour and went into voluntary liquidation in March 1985. Gloucestershire in company with other parts of south-western England was left without a professional archaeological presence.

The new Ancient Monuments and Archaeological Areas Act 1979 established more robust approaches to the protection and conservation of scheduled monuments and in Cirencester the definition of the scheduled area shifted from blanket coverage of the whole town to precisely defined and mapped areas of mainly open ground occupied by car parks and parkland. The Roman amphitheatre was a Guardianship monument, but Cirencester was not included in the list of historic towns defined as Areas of Archaeological Importance in the 1979 Act. Responsibility for spatial planning and development control was focused in the hands of district councils as defined local planning authorities under the radical and controversial local government reorganisation in 1974 that saw the establishment of a new form of two-tier jurisdiction. Cotswold District Council became the district authority for Cirencester and eastern Gloucestershire. Some strategic planning responsibilities remained at county level and while many county councils established archaeological offices and Sites and Monuments Records (SMR) during the early 1970s, Gloucestershire was one of the last into the field with the creation of an SMR in Shire Hall in Gloucester as late as 1982.

Meanwhile, in Cirencester, CEC working closely with the staff of the Corinium Museum and Cotswold District Council were trying to maintain some archaeological presence. Timothy Darvill directed small-scale excavations in the kitchen garden of the Querns, in advance of the construction of a new ambulance station behind the hospital, in June and July 1978 revealing evidence of extensive Roman quarrying, and in 1980 excavated a small trench at the south end of Tower Street (2–8 Chester Street) which provided valuable new evidence from the military phases of the Leaholme fort as well as another view of the large public building at the north end of *insula* VI. This work also included the first use of a systematic programme of environmental sampling that provided a rare insight into the palaeobotanical materials from the Roman town. Around the same period David Wilkinson was employed by CEC via the Corinium Museum to undertake post-excavation work and to carry out watching briefs and small-scale recording excavations across the town, for example at Querns Hospital in 1981 and at the site of the town's first Tesco store, in Brewery Yard and at Watermoor Hospital. David also compiled the beginnings of a listed buildings recording archive for the museum, and did a substantial amount of work on the Cirencester Abbey volume preparation. In the mid 1980s Nick Turner and Chris Guy undertook other site observations, usually linked to Scheduled Monument Consent applications. David Viner clearly remembers all this as being essentially a holding operation, with much archaeological potential unrealised and indeed unrealisable given the funding and organisation structures then prevailing; 'it is something of an abiding memory that so much was achieved on a succession of unconnected grants, chased with a certain amount of nervousness in advance of each season' (Viner 2000, 31).

The Committee met annually with a gradually rotating membership. One of the items that cropped up on the agenda year after year was the need for a professional archaeological unit to cover the Cirencester area, but despite numerous threats of impending large-scale development in the Waterloo area, Forum car park, and Brewery car park and old Railway Station none seemed to get beyond the creation of outline schemes and the commissioning of desk-based assessments that gathered together existing information and established the case for further work. A breakthrough came when Cotswold District Council appointed Debenham Tewson and Chinnocks as advisors for the promotion of a large-scale town-centre development over the Brewery car park between Sheep Street, Castle Street and Cricklade Street. The scheme, generally known as the Corinium Development, was masterminded by Gerald Allison and was bold and ambitious. A development brief was established and a design competition took place between November 1988 and January 1989. Numerous presentations were made by prospective developers and an exhibition of proposals in the Corn Hall attracted much public attention. After much debate MEPC was invited to work up more detailed plans and co-operate with Cotswold District Council to draw up a formal agreement, apply for planning permission and gain Scheduled Monument Consent for the works. Archaeological evaluations were required as part of the initial works, and CEC were identified as the body to undertake the work.

## CEC to CAT 1989–1991

At a meeting of CEC in April 1989 it was agreed to reconstitute the Committee as a company limited by guarantee, a management structure based on a small Board of Directors, and seek charitable status in such a way that the Directors were also the Trustees of the charity. As part of the reshuffle Sheppard Frere retired from the chair after nearly twenty-five years, passing the baton to Professor Mike Fulford from the University of Reading who was already an established member of the Committee. CEC's legal advisor, Meryl Atkins, found a series of useful precedents and in discussion with Committee members drew up the documents that would establish Cotswold Archaeological Trust (CAT) and secure its charitable status. The Trust came into existence on 17 March 1989. The first meeting of the Board of Directors was held in the Corinium Museum on 14 April 1989 when Mike Fulford was elected chairman and Derek Waring appointed company

*Fig. 6* Casper Johnson and Graeme Walker under-taking one of Cotswold Archaeological Trust's first projects, a test pit evaluation associated with the proposed Corinium Development in 1989

secretary. The other directors named on the founding articles of association were Timothy Darvill, Carolyn Heighway, Alan McWhirr and David Viner.

Particularly important at this early stage in the life of the Trust was the help and advice given by Glenne Mitchell, a special projects officer at Cotswold District Council whose responsibilities included both the Corinium Development and the encouragement of new small businesses and community initiatives. He quickly recognised the potential of having a viable archaeological capability in Cotswold District and campaigned tirelessly to secure resources and support. CAT started trading just a few weeks after its first board meeting appointing Chris Gerrard as Field Officer and Director of Excavations, together with Graeme Walker, Casper Johnson and Alastair Barber as field officers and site assistants to undertake a programme of field evaluation for the Corinium Development (Fig. 6).

CEC provided a small sum of money to pay the first wage bill, and Cotswold District Council agreed to an annual payment for retained archaeological services to cover inquiries that came through the Corinium Museum and the Council's planning department. Setting up the Trust involved a degree of risk, and all the initial Trustees gave generously of their time to help ensure its success. Glenne Mitchell was also able to provide office accommodation on the upper floors of the Old Railway Station in Sheep Street at a peppercorn rent. A selection of desks, filing cabinets and office equipment established an operational base for the team and a home for the Trust which served through several cold winters and hot summers down to 1996 with CAT eventually occupying the whole building. (A Grade II* Listed Building, the station opened in 1841 and was briefly the boardroom 'at the end of the line' during Brunel's design and construction of the Great Western Railway westwards.)

The creation of CAT could not have come at a better moment. Not only was the Corinium Development fuelling a sense of hope and opportunity in the town but on a political front the appearance in November 1990 of Planning Policy Guidance 16 (PPG16) on Archaeology

and Planning (DoE 1990) formalised the need to integrate archaeological matters in both strategic planning and development control. Local planning authorities were not only obliged to have regard to the preservation of archaeological deposits as a material consideration when determining planning permission, but they were given powerful tools in the form of powers to request desk-based assessment and field evaluations to fully inform the decision-making process, and specimen clauses for providing devel-oper-funded mitigation programmes where *in situ* preservation was not possible. In the background there was also the emergence of stronger European Legislation promoting Environmental Impact Assess-ment that appeared as an EU Directive in 1985, implemented in July 1988 in the UK by Statutory Instrument 1199. Cotswold District Council quickly embraced the new order and tenders for work started to arrive through the CAT letterbox. As well as work for the Corinium Development, nearly a dozen projects were undertaken in the first year, including evaluations and watching briefs in Cricklade Street, Watermoor Nursery, St Michael's Field, Victoria Road, Churnside and Corinium Gate. By 1990 CAT was working on projects across southern England.

English Heritage, since 1983 the government agency for archaeological and heritage matters, was supportive of CAT's development and in 1989 commissioned an urban assessment of Cirencester, one of the first batch to be undertaken alongside work at York, Durham and Canterbury, published as *Cirencester: Town and Landscape* in 1994. This was a long and substantial job that developed a range of innovative thinking that did much to pioneer what has become known as the Event-Monument model of archaeological resource manage-ment and formalise the staged management cycle linking archaeological inputs to the decision-making process embedded in the English town and county planning system. Balancing the imperatives of com-mercial archaeology with opportunities for trying new approaches and large-scale research has been a char-acteristic of CAT's work throughout its existence. *Cirencester: Town and Landscape* also contains one of the best reference bibliographies for Cirencester's archae-ology yet produced.

Through 1990 and 1991 CAT expanded its work-book and its footprint in the region and, while the undelivered and eventually abandoned Corinium Development gradually faded into the background, the idea of improving the line of the A417/419 from Stratton north of Swindon though to Birdlip high on the Cotswolds swept onto the agenda with CAT engaged to carry out the desk-based work and field evaluations starting in 1990. It was a large job and stretched resources to the full. It also involved taking on additional staff not only for fieldwork but also for administration. The administrator was Michael Hobday who worked for CAT part-time while also continuing a passion for commentating on polo matches, a skill that earned him an acknowledgement in Jilly Cooper's 1991 'bonk-buster' novel *Polo*, and eventually took him away to pastures new. One of the big changes prompted by the work connected with the A417/419 improvements was a recognition that archaeology was deeply embedded in the wider field of environmental consultancy. It was not long before CAT was drawn into this world, engaged variously as contractor or subcontractor within multi-disciplinary teams often headed by companies such as Countryside Planning and Management, based nearby at Quenington, or Barton Wilmore in Reading or Frank Graham in Worcester. Other clients during these early years included the National Trust, Thames Water and Cotswold District Council, connections that served to reinforce the way in which contract archaeology was already moving outwards from the traditional heartlands of prehistoric, Roman and medieval remains into the realms of a broader historic environment that was as likely to involve remains from the 20th century AD as from the 20th century BC. It was the excitement of working in a wider environmental context that gave Chris Gerrard the opportunity to move to Countryside Planning and Management in early 1991.

## CAT and commercial archaeology 1991–2008

In 1991 Neil Holbrook was appointed as the full-time Archaeological Manager to take responsibility for the day-to-day activities of the Trust. Neil was an out-and-out Romanist who had previously worked on Hadrian's Wall and in Exeter. The financial viability of CAT was on a knife edge throughout his first year in charge, a product of the immaturity of the new market for archaeological services and the prevailing harsh economic conditions which led to a slowdown in construction activity. With the collapse of plans for the Corinium Development, construction in Cirencester was on a small scale and CAT had to compete for the contracts to undertake associated archaeological fieldwork. It was obvious that if CAT was to survive it increasingly had to look for work elsewhere in Gloucestershire and beyond, and its major fieldwork for the next couple of years was away from the town at places such as Kemble, Tewkesbury, Wantage and Witney.

The early 1990s were a struggle as the provisions of PPG16 began to find widespread acceptance and developers came to understand that archaeological costs had to be worked into overall development costs. But by 1994 the recession had eased, archaeological evaluations and development conditions were commonplace, and CAT was developing a client base which gave it a sounder financial footing. The publication that year of *Cirencester: Town and Landscape* also provided a stimulus for a new assessment of the outstanding work on the most important unpublished excavations undertaken by CEC. In December 1994 English Heritage approved a grant which culminated in the publication in 1998 of Cirencester Excavations volume IV, covering the Anglo-Saxon church and medieval abbey, and volume V, dealing with the Roman town defences, public buildings and shops.

By now CAT was developing something of a reputation for reviving stalled post-excavation projects, having published earlier in 1998 its second monograph on excavations undertaken at Kingscote between 1973

and 1980 in a volume concerned with Roman small towns in the Cotswolds (Timby 1998). Work was also ongoing which would lead to publication of the 1969 excavations at Bishop's Cleeve Anglo-Saxon cemetery and the work in 1971 on a Bronze Age burnt mound at Charlton Kings. The number of staff employed by CAT was steadily increasing and by 1996 the company was on the verge of outgrowing its offices in the Old Railway Station. When Cotswold District Council requested that CAT vacate that building a search was begun for new premises which culminated in a move to the Headquarters Building of the former RAF base at Kemble, six miles outside Cirencester, in the autumn of 1996.

The remainder of the 1990s was a period of steady growth for the Trust. CEC was formally dissolved on 28 February 1997 as with the publication programme substantially completed its work was effectively done. Later the same day a professional seminar was held in the King's Head in the Market Place to discuss and define new research themes that would give added purpose to explorations of the archaeology of Cirencester. Matters such as the prehistoric antecedents, the local road patterns, the emergence of public buildings in the town and the role of the defences were all reviewed and remain important, and partly unresolved, research questions.

By 2000 the hard work which had been put in during the first ten years of CAT's life was starting to pay off as it established itself as one of the top ten archaeological contractors working in the UK, with a publication record that put a number of its competitors to shame. It was taking on larger and larger projects and working over an increasing geographical area, including important work in the Bristol region and South Wales. Its expertise in urban archaeology was increasingly being deployed in Bristol where a building boom was taking place and land values were sufficient to finance extensive excavations in advance of development. The company changed its trading name to the shorter, snappier, Cotswold Archaeology on 1 September 2002 and in 2003 its annual income passed £1 million for the first time.

Through the 1990s and beyond there have been gradual changes to the structure of the Trust and the composition of its board. Timothy Darvill took over as chairman from Mike Fulford in May 1992, and Richard Drew became company secretary in 1998. Glenne Mitchell was elected a Director of the Trust in 1992, but his untimely death in 1999 robbed the Trust of one of its most loyal supporters. Of the original Trustees, Mike Fulford and Alan McWhirr stepped down in 1993 and 1998 respectively; the rest remain alongside others: David Newton (1990–); Mick Aston (1990–2004), Trevor Rowley (1993–2001), Desmond Godman (1994–), the late Michael Oakshott (1995–2004), Tom Hassall (1999–2002), Sue Herdman (1999–2005), John Rhodes (2004–), Richard Courtney-Lord (2004–), Chris Catling (2004–) and Leslie Jones (2004–). Over the years a number of senior staff have been recruited to build the archaeological and managerial experience: among them Mark Collard, Martin Watts and Simon Cox. A handful of the field staff recruited in the first year or two are still with the company, notably Alastair

*Fig. 7* Fifty years on. Cotswold Archaeology excavating Roman shops beneath the Corn Hall, 2008

Barber, Cliff Bateman and Richard Morton. The initial offices at Kemble soon proved too small and in 2003 CA moved to larger and more comfortable accommodation in Building 11 in the same Business Park, the new offices being formally opened by Henry Elwes, Lord Lieutenant of Gloucestershire on 17 March 2004.

Work in Cirencester over the last decade has been consistent, if small-scale, as is described further in the Introduction to this volume, although as we write excavations are ongoing in the Corn Hall which are the largest to have taken place in the town for thirty years (Fig. 7). As we approach the fiftieth anniversary of the formation of CEC in December 2008 it is a source of pride that Cirencester remains the home of one of the leading archaeological fieldwork companies in the country, with a staff of over seventy and income in excess of £3 million. Its has also succeeded in publishing over a hundred site reports in a variety of regional and national journals, and sponsors an annual public lecture held in Cirencester which regularly attracts an audience in excess of two hundred.

Despite all that has changed, we like to think that we have remained true to the original ideals of CEC and continue to be a centre of knowledge and expertise about the archaeology of Cirencester. In the Appeal Leaflet issued in 1959 (see Fig. 2) the new Committee anticipated the benefits of its proposed programme of fieldwork: 'the information gained would certainly throw much new light upon the way of life in Roman Britain and upon the history of Roman occupation, which covers virtually a fifth of the long history of a town that has ever since remained a notable centre of Cotswold life. Too much of this period is at present dark . . .'. Fifty years on one hopes that Sir Ian Richmond and his fellow committee members would have been pleased about what has been learnt about Roman Cirencester, and also that the wanton destruction of archaeological remains by development has been brought to an end. We have also made some advances in our understanding of the history and archaeology of the other four fifths of the town's history, although as always much more needs to be done. Outside of the minster church and abbey we still know precious little about the post-Roman and high medieval archaeology of the town. Cirencester also retains a fine stock of historic vernacular buildings but, as David Viner outlines later in this volume, there has been comparatively little research which builds on the results of the pioneering survey of Richard Reece and Christopher Catling published in 1974. Certainly much remains to be learned, but on balance we can be pretty pleased with what has been achieved in the last half century and look forward to new opportunities and fresh approaches that will take us towards our first century.

## Cirencester Excavation Committee

### Chairmen

Sir Ian Richmond 1958–1965
Sheppard Frere 1965–1989
Michael Fulford 1989–1992

### Patrons

Col. W.A. Chester-Master 1958–1963
Earl Bathurst 1963–1989

### Directors of Excavations

Katherine Richardson 1959
John Wacher 1960–1965
David Brown 1965–1967
Alan McWhirr 1965–1989

## Cotswold Archaeological Trust

### Chairmen

Michael Fulford 1989–1992
Timothy Darvill 1992–present

### Archaeological Manager/Chief Executive

Christopher Gerrard 1989–1991
Neil Holbrook 1991–present

## Cirencester Publications 1961–2008

### Cirencester Excavations Monographs

Wacher, J.S. and McWhirr, A.D. 1982 *Early Roman occupation at Cirencester* Cirencester Excavations **I**, Cirencester, Cirencester Excavation Committee

McWhirr, A., Viner, L. and Wells, C. 1982 *Romano-British cemeteries at Cirencester* Cirencester Excavations **II**, Cirencester, Cirencester Excavation Committee

McWhirr, A. 1986 *Houses in Roman Cirencester* Cirencester Excavations **III**, Cirencester, Cirencester Excavation Committee

Wilkinson, D. and McWhirr, A. 1998 *Cirencester Anglo-Saxon church and medieval abbey* Cirencester Excavations **IV**, Cirencester, Cotswold Archaeological Trust

Holbrook, N. (ed.) 1998 *Cirencester: The Roman town defences, public buildings and shops* Cirencester Excavations **V**, Cirencester, Cotswold Archaeological Trust

Holbrook, N. (ed.) 2008 *Excavations and observations in Roman Cirencester 1998–2007* Cirencester Excavations **VI**, Cirencester, Cotswold Archaeology

### Other site reports

Richardson, K.M. 1962 'Excavations in Parsonage Field, Watermoor Road, Cirencester, 1959', *Antiq. J.* **42**, 160–82

Cullen, P.R. 1970 'Cirencester: the restoration of the Roman town wall, 1967–68', *Britannia* **1**, 227–39

Zeepvat, R.J. 1979 'Observations in Dyer Street and Market Place, Cirencester 1849, 1878 and 1974/5', *Trans. Bristol Gloucestershire Archaeol. Soc.* **97**, 65–73

Leech, R.H. and McWhirr, A.D. 1982 'Excavations at St John's Hospital, Cirencester 1971 and 1976, *Trans. Bristol Gloucestershire Archaeol. Soc.* **100**, 191–209

### Interim Reports

Wacher, J.S. 1961 'Cirencester 1960: First interim report', *Antiq. J.* **41**, 63–71

Wacher, J.S. 1962 'Cirencester 1961: Second interim report', *Antiq. J.* **42**, 1–14

Wacher, J.S. 1963 'Cirencester 1962: Third interim report', *Antiq. J.* **43**, 15–26

Wacher, J.S. 1964 'Cirencester 1963: Fourth interim report', *Antiq. J.* **44**, 9–18

Wacher, J.S. 1965 'Cirencester 1964: Fifth interim report', *Antiq. J.* **45**, 97–110

Brown, P.D.C. and McWhirr, A.D. 1966 'Cirencester 1965', *Antiq. J.* **46**, 240–54

Brown, P.D.C. and McWhirr, A.D. 1967 'Cirencester 1966', *Antiq. J.* **47**, 185–97

Brown, P.D.C. and McWhirr, A.D. 1969 'Cirencester 1967–8: Eighth interim report', *Antiq. J.* **49**, 222–43

McWhirr, A.D. 1973 'Cirencester 1969–1972: Ninth interim report', *Antiq. J.* **53**, 191–218

McWhirr, A.D. 1978 'Cirencester 1973–6: Tenth interim report', *Antiq. J.* **58**, 61–80

### Other publications

Reece, R. and Catling, C. 1975 *Cirencester: development and buildings* BAR Brit. Ser. **12**, Oxford, British Archaeological Reports

McWhirr, A.D. (ed.) 1976 *Studies in the archaeology and history of Cirencester* BAR Brit. Ser. **30**, Oxford, British Archaeological Reports

Darvill, T. and Gerrard, C. 1994 *Cirencester: Town and landscape. An urban archaeological assessment* Cirencester, Cotswold Archaeological Trust

Holbrook, N. 2008 'Cirencester and the Cotswolds: The early Roman evolution of a town and rural landscape', *J. Roman Archaeol.* **21**, 200–19

## A RICH RESOURCE: STUDYING CIRENCESTER'S HISTORIC BUILDINGS
### by David Viner

### Introduction

The purpose of this study is to offer a brief assessment of achievements made and, it is also argued, opportunities overlooked in the study and interpretation of the upstanding architectural heritage of Cirencester since 1958. It is hoped that it may also serve as a stimulus for future action to continue the long tradition of archaeological endeavour in the town, as enshrined in the Cirencester Excavations series of five volumes published between 1982 and 1998, moving forward to incorporate study of the upstanding building fabric as integral to the overall archaeological record. It is salutary to note that no such study of any individual *extant* building has featured in any detail in the five preceding volumes in this series, which accurately reflects the nature of archaeological research in Cirencester and indeed elsewhere for much of the second half of the 20th century.

The town has a rich stock of buildings. In terms of listed building status, the total in 1971 was nearly 350, including 2 Grade I and 19 Grade II* (Leech 1981, 22). Following the re-listing survey undertaken in 1989–90 this total has risen to 366 listing entries (but many more buildings of course), a rich legacy indeed for future researchers, residents and visitors to inherit and seek to understand. Additional legislative protection is afforded by Conservation Areas, which in Cirencester have a distinguished pedigree, the original designation for the central town area dating from 1968, within a year of the Act introducing the concept. Watermoor followed in 1984 and two more in 1991. At the time of writing this assessment Cotswold District Council, as the local planning authority, was consulting on the future of such arrangements locally, in tune with the overall changes forthcoming nationally in the whole approach to protection of ancient monuments and historic buildings.[1]

However, many (including some of the finest) of Cirencester's buildings remain relatively little examined or understood. Private as well as public ownership imposes its own constraints, and much of the fabric is almost permanently hidden from view. Nevertheless, this collective resource forms one of the town's primary attractions for visitors, and there is a long-standing and well-established literature harnessed to the attractiveness of stone buildings, and to the role which Cirencester plays in its Cotswold hinterland, all of which is often offered with an appeal to a nostalgic charm underpinning much of heritage presentation in the Cotswold district. The town and district is not alone in that regard, as has been noted recently in an almost exactly parallel set of comments for historic Gloucester (Heighway 2006, 213), and arguably both have been much less successful in exploiting such tourism interest to develop detailed building study programmes than some other historic towns and cities elsewhere, such as Ludlow or Lincoln.[2]

**History of studying buildings**

In reviewing a period of some fifty years a number of very clear milestones are immediately identifiable, and these form the core of this study. A sense of the general state of the building fabric in the years following the Second World War is discernible without much difficulty in the pages of a photographic study published in 1951, Festival of Britain year (Jowitt 1951). In some thirty images, which now forms a specific archive in its own right, the town's principal historic buildings are featured, ecclesiastical and secular. They mirror something of the timeless quality captured three decades or more before by three photographers in a town history of 1924 (Baddeley 1924); their work remains admired in local archives today.

Subsequent visiting or resident architectural histor ians have contributed their own assessments, generally finding the town and its long history attractive to explore. David Verey, a Gloucestershire man and author of the original two county volumes in the Pevsner Buildings of England series in 1970, needed no encouragement to extol the virtues of a largely stone-built town, with much of its architectural heritage of 17th and 18th-century date (Verey 1970; Verey and Brooks 1999). He also maintained a particular interest in the work of individual Victorian architects, including Samuel Whitfield Daukes, who won the architectural competition for the Royal Agricultural College (1845–6), a significant building on the western edge of the town, and William Jay, architect of Watermoor House in 1825–7 (Verey 1973; 1976).

In admiring mode, Alec Clifton-Taylor probably did as much as any commentator since the 1950s to popularise traditional Cotswold architecture, both in the vernacular style and the classically polite, the region in his view offering 'English traditional architecture at its most *succulent*' (Clifton-Taylor 1988, 7). His essay on Cirencester, wisely republished as a separate volume by the town's Civic Society to celebrate its own twenty-first birthday in 1988, provides a good summary not only of the principal buildings with their architectural detailing described, but also the development pressures the town then faced.

Clifton-Taylor found the town coping well; 'on the whole planning here has been skilful' (ibid., 39), although a report undertaken by the Georgian Group shortly afterwards was far less sanguine, declaring the primary threat to the character of the town to be the erosion of the architectural detailing of the older buildings, and the poor standard of design and workmanship in the new work. This was in the context of a town with 'a rich architectural history', based upon 'a tradition of economic success that allowed a variety of well-constructed buildings to populate the town' (Frank 1990, 1). The combination of pressures large and small on the town's fabric was a particular concern of the late 1980s; a proposed large-scale development extending westwards from the Brewery car park across and beyond Sheep Street ultimately proved to be abortive, leaving a planning blight over several stand-alone historic buildings which still continues, not least to the town's former railway station of 1841 and to a lesser extent its former Memorial (originally Cottage) Hospital of 1873–4 onwards and the former Independent Chapel of 1833 (later Apsley Hall) opposite. Such projects generate their own literature, not all of which is gathered together as the archive it should represent, but two small studies make the point that development pressures can and indeed should trigger published historical assessment (Clews 1988; Viner 1988).

The Georgian Group report also served to highlight other factors which were impacting upon any wider appreciation of the town's built heritage. Although the core of the medieval and post-medieval town has enjoyed Conservation Area status since 1968, the report noted that 'while the more prominent buildings are well maintained, it is the Grade II and the Conservation Area buildings that are under threat. Obviously it is the group impact of *all* of Cirencester's buildings, both the grand and the more modest, which contribute to its unique character' (Frank 1990, 1). Minor alterations to doors and windows as well as the removal of interior fittings all erode character, reducing the diagnostic features which are essential to dating and interpreting any building's unique history. The accompanying, if brief, photographic survey listed some sixteen or so examples of such steady degradation and loss of historic character. Interestingly the need to compile a more detailed archival record of such activity was not mentioned, although some fifteen years previously the then chief executive of Cotswold District Council had expressed the hope that a thorough survey of Cirencester's historic buildings would be undertaken in due course as an essential ingredient in raising overall levels of appreciation (Waring 1976). Other than the welcome re-listing survey in 1989–90, no such comprehensive overview has been attempted.

## Town histories and photographic records

Over-arching town histories are few and far between, not least because of the effort involved as the range of documentation available continues to expand, and also as a reflection of fashion in historical study. Town historians still respect and defer to the standard detailed history published by K.J. Beecham as long ago as 1887, a thorough study of its own time, helpfully including the author's subsequent notes up to 1910 in the latest published edition in 1978 (Beecham 1887).

An equally substantial contribution, unfortunately not brought together into a single study, was the range of researches with a strong historical base undertaken by Revd. E.A. Fuller and published in some seventeen articles between 1874 and 1933, the great majority in the 1880s and 1890s in the *Transactions of the Bristol and Gloucestershire Archaeological Society*.[3] Fuller came to Cirencester as curate in 1854, before moving after two years to Colesbourne for eight years and thereafter back to Cirencester for a further six years. This was far from a moribund period in the life of the town's principal church as Bob Jennings' essay has shown (Jennings 1976), and Fuller's work, despite its often heavy style, contributes greatly to our appreciation of the town's more significant buildings, both ecclesiastical and secular. Like Beecham, Fuller provides a platform upon which all subsequent work can be assessed.

The publications of St Clair Baddeley and in the period under review Jean Welsford, Bob Jennings and others has enhanced the corpus, Jean Welsford's substantial contribution also including a presentation of historic photographs which reveal much about town houses and buildings now long gone (Baddeley 1924; Welsford 1987a; 1987b).[4] Photographic archives of streets and buildings have been built up from a number of sources and Cirencester is well served in this respect, not only in the Corinium Museum's extensive holdings but also in the local studies collection largely owned by the Trustees of the Bingham Library and lodged in that building until transferred, as a consequence of refurbishment and reallocation of space, to Gloucestershire Archives in 2007.[5] The Trustees' holdings also include a substantial collection of local topographical art, containing a range of illustrations recording town streets and buildings at various dates. One outcome of the complete re-cataloguing programme which the Trustees have sponsored has been a photographic volume linked to celebrating the philanthropic work of Cirencester-born Daniel George Bingham in the town (Viner and Viner 2004). The photographs used in this

study also reveal the state of the town's buildings and amenities in the early years of the 20th century (captured with considerable clarity in the work of J.H. Thomas and W.D. Moss) and act as a strong record of those buildings with which Bingham was closely associated, the Bingham Library (opened 1905), the Bingham Hall (opened 1908) and extensions to the Memorial Hospital, completed in 1913.

Such visual evidence also serves as a reminder of how much the central area of Cirencester was rebuilt, or at least given new facades, during the fifty or so years before the First World War. Photographs by Thomas, Moss and by F. Mortimer Savory capture much of this, including public and commercial buildings such as the new Corn Hall of 1862–3 in the Market Place, the refronting of the adjoining King's Head Hotel (1863–4) and the large new Wilts. and Dorset bank building of 1897. Another feature was the replacement of a number of medieval or late medieval timber-framed properties by rows of stone housing, often in a rather severe Cotswold Tudor-Revival style and at the behest and expense of the Bathurst family of Cirencester Park, the principal property owner in the town. Silver Street, Black Jack Street and considerable sections of Castle Street and Cricklade Street all provide good examples. Earl Bathurst engaged the London architect John Birch for much of this work, particularly in Castle Street (1896–7). Bingham's preferred choice was V.A. Lawson, whose original training as an engineer is reflected in much of his architectural work. Lawson's impact on Cirencester as a whole, including Watermoor, was considerable and deserves a specific study.[6]

## Methodologies

It is important to draw distinctions between the various methodologies by which buildings are studied, in order not to imply that little has been achieved overall in Cirencester. Detailed measured surveys of individual properties remain in very short supply, and this represents perhaps the greatest missed opportunity of the last few decades. The reasons for this are many, but a planning culture which does not appear to make full use of planning policy guidance, such as Planning Policy Guidance Note 15 introduced in 1994 (see below), inevitably sets the trend, and there are still relatively few detailed historical and architectural assessments compiled as part of the planning process. Increasingly, however, owner or occupier interest in individual properties is growing, often as part of the rapid expansion in family history research, and this at least bodes well for the future. Planning requirements to undertake even a photographic record (in the absence of anything more detailed) does not of itself place such material in the public domain, especially if it is not deposited in an appropriate archive.

While respecting the wider roles of Gloucestershire Archives and the National Monuments Record of English Heritage, the overall conclusion must be that the town still badly needs some form of archival focus around which this mass of disparate material can be gathered and promoted. Interestingly, such a project was developed at the Corinium Museum as part of a Manpower Services Commission job creation project during the mid 1980s, with a respectable list of small projects in a relatively short time, but this has not been subsequently advanced (Wilkinson 1985–6). It has a parallel, both in concept and in timing, with a similar project to register and create an archive of Gloucester's historic buildings, also housed in one of that city's museums. That too has value but no subsequent growth (Heighway 2006, 213).

This is not to say that the study of the history (as distinct from the detailed physical/structural recording) of Cirencester's buildings has been neglected, although such research is inevitably disparate, not always in published form and requires considerable effort to bring together into any cohesive record. The approach is far from systematic. The town also still awaits its volume in the Victoria County History series, sadly not envisaged for many years yet.

## Key projects

However, two projects stand out, published in consecutive years but independently prepared, which moved the published data on Cirencester's buildings forward substantially, and they remain important sources of reference. *Cirencester: the Development and Buildings of a Cotswold Town* (Reece and Catling 1975) resulted from a five-week survey in the summer of 1974, examining all buildings of pre-1922 date, using map regression analysis and providing a rough approximation of the date of their facades based on stylistic features.

A series of some ten styles was identified, based on a variety of details and materials, providing a framework around which any more detailed study of the town's buildings could be advanced. The growth of the town was assessed and some pertinent comments added on the whole issue of loss and retention and the criteria against which both are measured in the modern planning system. Interestingly only three of the 84 illustrated buildings have disappeared since 1974, although reference is made to the loss during the study period of another significant 18th/early 19th-century town house.[7] One particularly telling point concerns the town's earliest dated house, 10 Coxwell Street, which has an entrance arch of 1648 but has otherwise been subjected to such modernisation (externally at least, and one might suspect also internally) that 'has hidden or destroyed a building which could help us understand part of our surroundings' (Reece and Catling 1975, 61). Simply gathering together a list of dated buildings in the town, especially in and around Coxwell Street and concentrating on them would provide one particular focus.

A symposium in the Corinium Museum in November 1975 brought together a number of specialists pursuing the post-Roman development of Cirencester, and the resulting volume of essays (McWhirr 1976) exemplifies the eclectic nature of contemporary research co-ordinated to advantage. Joyce Barker's essay on the George/Powell family and Gloucester House in Dyer Street remains one of the few studies bringing inventory information to

bear upon a particular Cirencester building (Barker 1976). Rebecca Powell was (and in name remains) a substantial benefactor to Cirencester in the first half of the 18th century. Gloucester House was largely rebuilt including a new frontage *c*. 1780–90 for a subsequent owner and is still a significant building, associated in turn with several well-known Cirencester families, Cripps, Rudder, Plummer and Ovens.

Previous house studies, in each case by the property owner, had been the modest commentary on 33 Dyer Street, just across the road (Klitz 1969–70), and a more detailed examination of Langley's Mill in Watermoor, a mill site from at least the 16th century and surviving today as two cottages, nos 12 and 14 City Bank Road (Walls 1985–6). David Verey's interest in individual architects of the 19th century has already been mentioned; his study of William Jay clarified who was responsible for the design and execution of Watermoor House in 1825–7 (Verey 1976). Jay may well also have been responsible for Arkenside in Lewis Lane, demolished in 2006 (Fig. 15).

## Timber-framed buildings

A short but significant essay by David Smith on a surviving fragment of timber building at 49 Castle Street, recorded in 1975, is a reminder of the timber building tradition which at least perhaps to the public eye is otherwise rather lost behind, beneath or replaced by the ubiquitous stone building traditions of the Cotswold region in general and its market towns in particular (Fig. 8). He noted that 'periodically entire timber-framed buildings were constructed in the [Cotswold] towns as well as other buildings where a stone ground floor wall carried timber-framed walling at first floor level' (Smith 1976, 109). Both forms can be found in Cirencester, the Bear Inn in Dyer Street and the Fleece Hotel in Market Place (albeit the latter rather obscured by pseudo-framing) being good examples with jettied floors of the entire frame type. Neither building, as far as is known, has been subjected to any detailed structural analysis or recording.[8]

No 49 Castle Street, albeit largely rebuilt post-recording, exemplifies the frame on a ground-floor-wall type of structure, and stands in a probably subdivided burgage plot. Smith noted that a study of burgage plots in Cirencester had yet to take place, and would be of considerable potential value in understanding the growth of the medieval town. Such systematic documentary research still remains largely unattempted for Cirencester.

That said, the work of historical geographer Terry Slater, also during the 1970s, does provide a firm basis for understanding both the medieval town and the processes of growth in the 19th-century town, particularly in the relationship between estate ownership and suburban development (Slater 1976a; 1976b; 1978). Clifton-Taylor also noticed how the historic town was 'wedged between two large estates, the former Abbey lands to the north-east and the Park to the west', together acting 'as a straightjacket' (Clifton-Taylor 1988, 37). Expansion to the south-east was one inevitable result, and Slater shows how the area of

*(a)*

*(b)*

*(c)*

*Fig. 8*   Timber-framed buildings. a. 33–35 Gloucester Street b. 17–19 Gosditch Street. c. 6–8 Dollar Street. (photos 1970)

former nursery lands south of Lewis Lane was systematically developed from 1850 onwards, providing incidentally a rich resource of well-dated mid and later Victorian streets and houses extant today.

## 19th-century Cirencester

Slater's further study was the associated development of Watermoor on a scale and intensity which effectively gave it a status as almost an industrial railway suburb. He shows how the efforts of an improved dwellings

company, an associated form of building society, could respond to the housing needs of the time (Slater 1976c). With one notable exception (Loveridge 1977), it is regrettable that oral history recording opportunities came too late to capture much of the richness of oral record which was undoubtedly contained within Watermoor during the lifetime of the railway works (opened 1895, enlarged three times, closed 1925) and of the railway itself (closed 1961). A flavour can certainly be found in the best of the Midland and South Western Junction Railway studies (Bartholomew 1982) but more could still be done on the housing stock and its occupants.

The 19th-century town, which Slater noted had bequeathed a wealth of historical records (Slater 1976b, 145), not surprisingly has been better studied in relative terms. Its building stock is considerable, its rate of survival better, while at the same time subsequent development pressures, particularly during the period under review, have threatened a number of buildings regarded as significant to town life, even if redundant to their original purpose(s). Recording driven by such development pressure has included various specific-purpose buildings; two brief studies have already been noted, for the town railway station and the Memorial Hospital; both survive, if only in partial use (Clews 1988; Viner 1988). Other stand-alone buildings where *in situ* measured survey has been undertaken include the former agent's house/warehouse at the Thames and Severn Canal wharf off Querns Lane, recorded prior to demolition in 1975 (Viner 1976), and the former town lock-up, surveyed as part of its presentation by the district's museum service (Viner and Powell 1991; Price and Viner 1994).

## Planning process

A summary statement in 1981 examined the relationship between archaeology and planning in Cirencester as part of a countywide survey (Leech 1981, 17–25) and the following quarter-century has bought a number of changes to that relationship, specifically the introduction of long-awaited Planning Policy Guidance Notes, no. 16 *Archaeology and Planning* in 1990 (PPG 16), and more significantly for this study no. 15 *Planning and the Historic Environment* in 1994 (PPG 15). Together, these provided local planning authorities with a clear steer on archaeology and the built historic environment as a threatened and finite resource and a material consideration in the planning process. The result as noted by Jan Wills, Gloucestershire's county archaeologist, has been 'an unprecedented amount of archaeological excavation both in Gloucestershire and elsewhere', with the majority of archaeological work being triggered by this planning advice mechanism (Wills 2006, 233). The imposition of PPG 15, however, has proved less effective.

While PPG 16 may provide adequate funding for specific projects and tasks, it does not of itself allow for wider synthesis. However, in 1994 as part of a programme of work on urban areas of national archaeological importance initiated by English Heritage, a detailed urban archaeological assessment volume was published for Cirencester, containing extremely valuable essays on the growth and development of the town from Roman to post-medieval times (Darvill and Gerrard 1994). This also contains by far the most useful and comprehensive bibliography to this whole period under review. Now out of print, this volume is well worth consideration for an updated edition, in part at least.

**Archaeological organisation**

When Cirencester Excavation Committee's work was absorbed into the newly created Cotswold Archaeological Trust in 1989, it might have been hoped that the study of standing buildings would also benefit from increased opportunities, helped by the subsequent funding changes for archaeology. Given that the greater part of the new trust's work has inevitably been directly dependent upon development pressures arising from PPG 16, and the inevitable funding constraints which accompany them, there has been relatively little achieved on the town's upstanding building heritage by this or any other archaeological unit or organisation, a number of which have worked on a commercial basis in Cirencester since the 1980s. Such comments apply equally to voluntary groups and societies. Rather, the range of projects reported elsewhere in this volume is an indication of the nature of development-driven, PPG 16-determined archaeological work in an historic town such as Cirencester over the past decade or more.

An early opportunity for CAT came with the proposed rebuilding of a block of properties at 32–38 Cricklade Street, which although only of late Victorian date (these properties were entirely rebuilt in 1893) nevertheless provided an opportunity for study in the town's commercial heart (Gerrard and Johnson 1989). The architectural survey element was integrated with an archaeological watching brief, and became even more valuable when these replacement buildings themselves suffered a major fire on 10 January 2004, requiring another substantial rebuilding.[9] Plot development for this site also formed part of the subsequent urban archaeological assessment, and remains one of the few published examples of its type for Cirencester (Darvill

*Fig. 9*   30–38 Cricklade Street restored after the fire of January 2004 (photo May 2005)

and Gerrard 1994, 125). However, the site report clearly shows how little time was allocated for any form of recording, access being via a watching brief condition, resulting in little more than a salvage opportunity.

One of the few Cirencester buildings to be subjected to structural analysis in any depth prior to and during rehabilitation for new use has been 44 Black Jack Street (Turner 1995). This property was in a very run-down condition when acquired by the local authority as a linked development with the Corinium Museum next door. It proved to be a much-altered building with only fragmentary surviving evidence of 17th-century date, viz. a floor beam and a section of oak panelling (not *in situ*) dated to *c*. 1620. Although documentary research was unrewarding, enough was achieved to show structural evolution on the site, suggesting the property to be once part of a larger footprint and with a distinctive plan of a frontage building with a rear wing set at an angle behind, a recognisable feature in Cirencester streets.[10]

Surviving architectural features and fittings have long been subjected to attrition, especially in town centre properties where ground floor areas, once adapted for shops, have continued to be enlarged and modernised. This process seems only to accelerate in the main shopping streets, especially the Market Place and Cricklade Street, where little of pre-20th-century date must now survive at ground floor level. The fate of 32–38 Cricklade Street, twice comprehensively rebuilt in a little over a century, is perhaps an extreme example (Fig. 9). Upper floors, however, may offer better hope of survival, and building conversion some years ago brought the late 17th-century moulded plaster ceiling and contemporary upper staircase on the first floor of 7 Cricklade Street to notice; it remains otherwise unrecorded in detail (Verey and Brooks 1999, 274). Roof spaces are generally speaking a little explored and even less recorded area anywhere in Cirencester.

**Cirencester's principal medieval and later buildings**

Until recently it could still be argued that little if any detailed structural research had been undertaken on any of the major surviving medieval buildings in the town, ecclesiastical and secular. Several recent initiatives suggest an improvement. The town's most outstanding building, the parish church of St John Baptist with its adjoining Town Hall in the south porch, is currently subject to a detailed and phased improvement programme which has been some years in preparation. This has spawned some detailed research, principally by Warwick Rodwell with an appraisal of the church fabric and fittings (Rodwell 1997), to which can now be added a detailed study by Malcolm James of the south porch and Town Hall, in advance of necessary structural repairs (James 2006). This latter also serves as a record of the previous programmes of repairs to the porch especially in 1908–9. Without doubt there is enough material gathered here and elsewhere to merit a monograph on this fine building, linked perhaps to the programme of planned works. There is also a reminder in scale and significance of the previous major restoration programme to the church of 1865–7 (Jennings 1976).

The two surviving buildings most closely associated with the Abbey of St Mary, Cirencester have also been the focus of recent investigation. St John's Hospital in Spitalgate Lane, founded by Henry I in about 1133, survives as an arcade of the infirmary 'nave'; its refurbishment and landscaping during the 1970s allowed a limited amount of archaeological recording (Leech and McWhirr 1982). Roof repairs including tile and timber replacement in 2006 provided a long-awaited opportunity to commission some dendrochronology, and the results now available are believed to provide the very first dendro-dating successfully achieved for *any* building in Cirencester (Arnold and Howard 2007) which is both an achievement and a salutary reminder of how much has been missed in the town since such techniques became more widely available. Previously it was believed (or assumed) that the roof was largely of one phase, early medieval in date, but with some later inserted timber repairs. What is now known is that the principal surviving roof structure dates to the second quarter of the 15th century (the majority of the timbers being felled in AD 1436), but that it incorporates a number of early 12th-century timbers, presumably re-used.[11]

Nearby Spital Gate is the only surviving gatehouse of the Abbey of St Mary, and dates from *c*. 1180–90 (Fig. 10). It has been variously known as the Saxon Arch or (currently) Norman Arch, not least to avoid any confusion with the nearby street named Spitalgate Lane and with St John's Hospital a short distance away. Its relationship with and contribution to the life of Cirencester Abbey was recognised in the various detailed archaeological studies of the Abbey of St Mary, but these did not include any opportunity throughout that extensive programme to undertake any detailed investigative work on the arch itself or its adjoining (now linked) cottage. It does however grace the cover of the published archaeological report (CE IV).[12]

In January 2005 the town council's quiet management of this Grade I building changed dramatically with its proposal to sell off this historic asset into the private sector. The resulting storm of protest merits publication as an episode of community interest in its

*Fig. 10* Spital Gate, variously Saxon Arch and Norman Arch, *c*. 1180–90 (photo 2006)

own right, and various alternative solutions were offered. One preferred route, to convert the cottage attached to the gatehouse into a specialised holiday let by one of the nationally recognised agencies in this field, is (at the time of writing) in the final stages of feasibility assessment and presentation. It is to be hoped that the useful brief assessments so far prepared may be expanded into a fuller archaeological recording programme, including dendro-dating of the gatehouse roof and substantial pair of doors, surely one of the most significant opportunities in any standing building in Cirencester (Townsend 2006).

The Weavers Hall or St Thomas's Hospital in Thomas Street is recognised as 'probably the oldest secular building still in use' in the town (Verey and Brooks 1999, 268) dating from the will of Sir William Nottingham of 1483 to endow 'a certain house lately built by me in Cirencester' for the 'use profit and maintenance of 4 pore men' (Fig. 11). Its austere facade to the street, through-passage plan and mix of small window openings are indicative of a building of considerable archaeological interest, well worthy of detailed survey when possible. Documentation has been assessed but remains unpublished in any summary form.[13] Of similar or later date and also in Thomas Street is Monmouth House, on an L-shaped plan and with many diagnostic features of the 15th and 16th centuries. Modernised for office use *c*. 1989, this building nevertheless must be another prime candidate for detailed survey and dating in due course (Verey and Brooks 1999, 268). Dollar Street has at least two further examples. Not all medieval diagnostic features may be above ground, of course, and the admittedly tentative identification of as yet undated undercroft(s) forming cellars beneath 82 Cricklade Street in 1997 should be noted. Other than cellar vaults known to form part of the King's Head Hotel in the town centre, this discovery is believed to be the only one of its kind in a domestic property fronting one of the town's principal streets.[14]

## Cirencester Park

Home of the Bathurst family, Cirencester Park is celebrated as a pre-eminent historic parkland, listed

*Fig. 11*  Weavers Hall in Thomas Street, *c.* 1483 (photo 1998)

Grade I, and the glories of its landscaping often overshadow any study of the mansion house itself. That is a topic largely outwith the framework of this study except that, in terms of property ownership and close physical relationship with the town itself, Cirencester Park has long exercised a dominant and stimulating influence on a considerable part of the town's built heritage. A visit to Cecily Hill alone amply makes this point. More pertinent in terms of specific buildings and structures are the follies which adorn the parkland and have a significance of their own. Much research remains unpublished and the Park as a whole certainly deserves a thorough published landscape assessment; meanwhile James Lees-Milne's much-admired essay in 1962 remains the starting point (Lees-Milne 1962, ch. 1; see also Mowl 2002, 67ff). The Park also includes Cirencester's only 'building at risk' on the English Heritage register (and one of only seven listed for Cotswold district), a state of affairs which has continued far too long. It is recognised that Alfred's Hall of *c.* 1721–3 (completed by 1732) 'may well have been the first of all castellated follies' (Verey and Brooks 1999, 282).

In terms of other country seats and major houses in and around the town, the county of Gloucestershire has been extremely well served in the long-term research project by Nicholas Kingsley which produced three substantial volumes (Kingsley 1989, 1992 and 2001, the latter in co-operation with Michael Hill), and these discuss not only Cirencester Park but five smaller town and suburban houses.[15] In terms of detailed archaeological investigations of standing buildings of this quality, the work of Warwick Rodwell at Daneway and at Lodge Park, each for their respective owners, provides a model study (Rodwell 2000).

## Coxwell Street

For visitors a key focal point for the domestic architecture of the town has to be Coxwell Street, which together with neighbouring streets forms the core of the 'historic quarter' north and north-west of the parish church. Here is a stunning visual impression of a range of buildings, both vernacular and polite, which appear from external evidence alone to be of 17th and 18th-century date. Any research project on Cotswold stone town houses would and should have this street as a principal focus, not least because 'one sees that this part of the town has hardly been altered for three hundred years. There is more genuine survival here than in any other town in the Cotswolds'. Although this assertion by David Verey in 1970 was subsequently modified in the revised Pevsner edition, it still holds good.[16] Just one modest study can be added (Turner 1996) but perhaps more telling have been the co-ordinated efforts of the street's residents to produce some permanent record of their shared heritage, in this case as a Millennium 2000 project. Individual houses are noted, details sketched, an excellent set of photographs by Bryan Berkeley provided, and there is a list of present-day residents (Turner 2000). This study provides another springboard and the obvious location for more detailed work, perhaps on the Ludlow model.

There are good parallels of detailed record not so far away, including the buildings of Burford, another Cotswold stone town with a long history and a fine surviving and accessible architectural heritage (Laithwaite 1973). More recently the fruits of several decades of determined research on the vernacular building traditions in and around Stroud and nearby Chalford have been published in considerable detail (Paterson 2006). Both provide much food for thought in both approach and presentational form. No one looking at the vernacular architecture of the wider region would omit Linda Hall's excellent study of the rural houses of south Gloucestershire, which contains considerable parallel material to the construction of buildings in the urban context at Cirencester and other Cotswold towns (Hall 1983).

## Demolition and townscape

Loss by complete demolition, although episodic over this assessment period, is a concern, as the removal of any historic building, especially without record, must be regretted. Two particular periods of change stand out, the first being the comprehensive redevelopment of much of the south side of Dyer Street between the Bear Inn and Gloucester House during the early 1960s. A sweep of contiguous buildings dating from external evidence to the 18th and 19th centuries was demolished, one noteworthy for its columned facade, still remembered as a local secondhand bookshop.[17] The replacement large-scale block of shops and upper floor housing, *c.* 1964–5, partly arranged around the small Catalpa Square, has attracted much criticism for its overall dominant effect on the street scene and more recently for the state of survival of its material detailing.

A decade later the long-awaited construction of the Cirencester ring road, in two phases in the early to mid 1970s, substantially changed the character of Cirencester's outer ring and directly involved some demolition, although the associated redevelopment projects resulted in a greater loss, especially in Watermoor where the new road scheme had its most dramatic effect on the old layout. What remained of Cirencester Watermoor railway station, goods yards and former works disappeared, as did most of the town gas works. The long-used Swindon road route (on a Roman alignment) out of town across Kingsmeadow was truncated and re-routed, and so too the old line of Siddington Road. Victorian red brick and stone terrace housing in School Lane and Midland Road was almost completely cleared away and replaced, 'demolished without any record' (Reece and Catling 1975, 73, 75) (Figs 12–13).

Equally dramatic was the almost complete redevelopment of the former GWR railway yards, good sheds and sidings off Sheep Street to the west of the town, as the new road was driven between town and amphitheatre. The creation of the Phoenix Way office development has been expanded subsequently by additional housing and a large-scale supermarket development, with the result that only the station building itself remains, isolated in a public car park. The history of the Cirencester branch line from Kemble offers a detailed pre-clearance record (Bray 1998). Querns Hill was re-aligned, and at its junction with Querns Road the council depot (formerly the Thames and Severn Canal wharf) redeveloped, resulting in the demolition of its final legacy, the former agents house and warehouse, one of the few buildings at this time recorded by measured survey (Viner 1976). A further cycle of the most recent redevelopment on this western side of the town is beyond the scope of this study.

**Town houses, Streets, Courts and Places**

Other losses are worthy of note. Two substantial town houses fell victim to the road schemes. At the London Road junction with Grove Lane, the stone villa known as Beech Grove was demolished *c.* 1974 to allow the Eastern Relief Road to take off to the south; its name is remembered in a housing development nearby. Across the town at the foot of Querns Hill on its original alignment was no. 2, a substantial Victorian property, utilised as Chesterville private school between the Wars and later requisitioned for various wartime uses. The considerable programme of archaeological excavation which accompanied the entire ring road development is fully reported in the Cirencester Excavations volumes. Rivercourt, a house dated pre-1897 at 29 Beeches Road, was replaced by another housing block around the same time.

*Fig. 12*   Midland Road, demolished soon after this photograph was taken. The shop was on the corner with Chesterton Lane (photo August 1970)

*Fig. 13*   School Lane awaiting demolition with replacement housing already underway (photo August 1970)

For terraces of more modest housing in the town, two points need to be made, first the approach adopted and encouraged by Cirencester Urban District Council during the 1960s and the early 1970s to rehabilitate various groups of housing, usually as sheltered housing schemes, and especially in and around Gloucester Street. Elizabeth Place and Barton Court are good examples, both to the street frontage and in the backlands behind.[18] However, some considerable demolition did take place, as a small example in widening the corner of Gloucester Street with Gooseacre Lane (a pre-1825 route from the town), and very little of the structures subjected to modernisation were recorded in any meaningful way, not untypical for that time. Off-street terraces came under particular pressure for modernisation or clearance, Price's Row off Watermoor Road (demolished in 1973) being a good example of such clearance, as was Gordon Place in Dollar Street. The loss of such yards, courts, alleys, places and rows, and the character and social history which went with them – "cleared away in extremely determined fashion in the last thirty years" – was particularly noted (Reece and Catling 1975, 26).

Significant domestic buildings lost within the core of the town include Ashcroft House, standing on the corner of its own small estate, demolished in 1964 to enable housing development; in retrospect the terraced housing which replaced it seems today particularly mean in scale and quality by comparison. The Abbey House of *c.* 1774–6, second of the significant houses in parkland created on the site of the former Abbey of St Mary, was replaced by the present day block in 1966. Amongst demolished non-domestic buildings might be mentioned the former Primitive Methodist Chapel tucked away off Lewis Lane, a simple brick structure of 1851, noted as 'perhaps the earliest whole building [in the town] to stand in clear unashamed brick' (Reece and Catling 1975, 58). Its single-unit interior was used as a store prior to demolition in 1998 and the space is now car parking (Fig. 14). The large Congregational Church of 1887 gave way in 1971 to a supermarket development, very much of its time and place, opposite the earlier and larger Dyer Street scheme. These losses apart, the town still boasts a good stock of chapel buildings as indeed it does of school buildings and almshouses, the range and interest of each group meriting special study.

## What to keep?

More recent pressures upon development land have brought other changes nearby in Lewis Lane. Not without protest, the former Regal cinema, which first opened its doors in 1937, was demolished in July 2004 to allow one of the town's first examples of new-style, higher-scale courtyard housing development, designated as Bingham Close in honour of one of Cirencester's well-remembered benefactors. Its interior was digitally recorded for Cirencester Archaeological and Historical Society prior to final closure in autumn 2003.[19] The same development pressures affected the adjoining property, Arkenside (nos 44–46 Lewis Lane), variously a private school evacuated from Leigh-on-Sea, Essex during the Second World War and latterly a guest house, but originally a pair of houses of 1859, rare in Cirencester, and believed associated with the work of William Jay (Fig. 15). Outside the Conservation Area, and following an English Heritage decision not to list, the building was demolished in the summer of 2006, with an understanding that its materials would be reused elsewhere.[20] Such a decision inevitably raises a number of questions about the integrity and protection of the building stock in an historic town such as Cirencester, about what should be retained and what let go subject only to record, all points raised with feeling years before (Reece and Catling 1975, 28).

Many more buildings, especially of Victorian date, have of course been rehabilitated by conversion and as such have been subject to desk-based analysis, producing a potentially large amount of material of archival value. Examples include the conversion of the former town workhouse of 1836–7 into offices for Cotswold District Council (summary in Viner 1994), the succes-

sive alterations, including a comprehensive refurbishment of the former brewery storage buildings off Cricklade Street as the town's arts centre, and the creation of apartments from the former town waterworks of *c.* 1898 in Lewis Lane and the former Cole's Mill behind.[21] Future historians must hope that architects, both in private and public partnership, as well as local authority planning officers will consign such records into safe long-term care as a permanent record of change. One good example of this is the deposition of the papers of Thomas Fulljames, surveyor, architect and civil engineer, whose practice

*Fig. 14*  Primitive Methodist Chapel of 1851, off Lewis Lane, photographed in 1974 and during demolition in April 1998

*Fig. 15*  Arkenside, nos 44–46 Lewis Lane of 1859, demolished in 2006 (photo 2004)

as Fulljames and Waller built the Royal North Glos. Militia armoury in Cecily Hill in 1854–6 (Carne 1995), described as a theatrical mock castle but designed with conviction (Verey and Brooks 1999, 259).[22] One might also add George Gilbert Scott's Holy Trinity church for Watermoor, a 'fine, thoroughly characteristic building' of 1847–51 (ibid., 256; Clack 2001).

Such examples, although undoubtedly popular in the public mind, often Victorian in date and mostly buildings constructed for community use, are nevertheless not necessarily central to the core need to understand the mass of private, *domestic* architecture in the town, which potentially also offers a longer date span for study. Much of Cirencester's building stock, at least in the historic core of the town, is either of 17th or 18th-century date or has antecedents of that date. More detailed research would undoubtedly extend this date range earlier. In that regard it is a typical Cotswold market town, presenting a series of diagnostic architectural features which have been much commented upon and no less admired. Indeed Cirencester can and should be studied in its Cotswold context, as numerous writers seek to do. An excellent reprise of this, as well as of the appropriateness of materials, is also one of the few Cotswold studies to contain any specific building plans (Hill and Birch 1994). Another model volume is the detailed study of the stone buildings of the neighbouring Banbury region (Wood-Jones 1986) and it is to be regretted that the companion study for the Cotswolds in this admired Manchester series was never published (Worsley 1956). It might well have spawned more directed local work.

## Research potential

It has to be said that it is in this core area of studying, recording and thereby better understanding the *domestic* architecture of the stone buildings of Cirencester where the greatest opportunity has been missed, and arguably continues to be missed. There are a number of factors at work here. First, the continuing economic vibrancy of the town effectively ensures that very little property is neglected and much of it is subject to periodic improvement. This can (and does) carry with it the potential for loss of detail, minor but accumulative, as well as loss of form and previous function in interior layout, plus various threats to external presentation. On the other hand, a periodic injection of capital should ensure a building's survival.

The successful imposition of planning controls (or lack of commitment to do so) with particular reference to the recording elements contained within PPG 15 has already been mentioned. It is reinforced from official sources too: although PPG 15 'provides much important advice on the management of the built historic environment, some aspects, especially the opportunities to secure the assessment and recording of historic building in advance of development, have not been implemented as widely as they might have been' (Wills 2006, 233). Statistical information backs this up; between 1982 and 2006 only 27 building recording reports are listed for Gloucestershire on a nationwide database compared with 116 for Oxford-shire, 114 for Worcestershire and 29 for Wiltshire.[23] Of these only about half a dozen appear on the Gloucestershire SMR for Cirencester. Some counties are clearly better resourced than others to make use of the Guidance opportunity.

The resource issue apart, there are various reasons for such a low imposition rate. These include various, almost cultural, differences of professional approach between archaeologists and conservation officers, a divide into which building recording inevitably falls. The former group are now well used to (and fully supportive of) the principle that the applicant funds the work; the latter seem much less willing to request work requiring applicant funding. The primary evidence which archaeologists see in any building may be cast for the conservation lobby in terms of the aesthetics of the architecture and the appropriateness of the repair, in which recording may be less of a priority. Forthcoming legislative changes may bring greater consistency, although resource issues will doubtless remain paramount.

Some recording may not of course be accessible or captured in the record. There are issues of privacy and security too; owners might well find access requests for primary building recording in any form unattractive, and certainly on a piecemeal basis rather than as part of some co-ordinated programme of research which is not necessarily development driven. This latter does not exist for Cirencester's buildings and this is probably the greatest failure of the entire period under review. However, the work of Reece and Catling and of Slater, the symposium organised by McWhirr and the essays in *Cirencester: Town and Landscape* for the early to post medieval periods all provide a firm springboard (Darvill and Gerrard 1994, 43–144).

## Townscape today

At the time of writing major refurbishment works are in progress on the combined and adjoining sites of the King's Head Hotel and the Corn Hall in the very heart of Cirencester, a project which represents a significant upgrading of town centre community facilities by a private development company. Associated archaeological excavations are underway, especially within the Corn Hall building itself, which represents the first major opportunity in such scale and depth in the town centre for more than a decade (see Fig. 7). The standing buildings do of course represent more than development of Victorian date. While facades to the Market Place of both the King's Head and Corn Hall are clearly of their time, the hotel certainly has medieval antecedents, especially set back from the street frontage, and also includes the former town Assembly Rooms of the late 18th century, externally austere as that structure might seem today (Fig. 16). While it is too early to anticipate the results from the programme of building recording and analysis, it must be hoped that the records made of this central site in the town centre will be available in a format which allows inclusion within an established archive.

Methods and traditions of physical conservation of buildings form another strand to any study of

*Fig. 16*  Rear of buildings fronting the Market Place including the King's Head and Corn Hall with former Assembly Rooms of late 18th-century date on the left (photo March 2008)

surviving architectural fabric. The Georgian Group's report in 1990 cited some examples of poor choices of material in this regard, including several examples in Gloucester Street, an area of the town with a rich assemblage of domestic vernacular buildings and continued pressure for modernisation and improvement. Here also at 33–35 Gloucester Street is a fine timber building noted by Smith for its 'uninterrupted line of first floor jettying between stone gables [which] suggests this was originally a single domestic unit occupying the entire façade of a burgage plot' (Smith 1976, 109). Its external finish is also noteworthy and appropriate for this level of listed building (it is listed Grade II*) in limewash, the revival of which technique has been a long-term campaign in the town by local craftsman and recognised specialist Rory Young (Young 1991). More recent work on a group of three houses at nos 3–7 Park Street has further enhanced public appreciation of this facade treatment.[24] Earlier a detailed two-year long conservation project for Lloyds Bank of its imposing building of *c*. 1720/30 in one of the town's main streets had been the subject of professional debate about materials and the Society for the Protection of Ancient Buildings' philosophical approach, bearing in mind the scale, quality and setting of this fine Palladian former wool merchant's house, a bank as early as *c*. 1790.[25] The project did take into account earlier comments about important window detailing (Clifton-Taylor 1988, 31–2).

## Presentation

The physical signposting and on-site interpretation in whatever form of virtually all of the town's principal ancient monuments, historic sites and many of its buildings is another issue, remaining capable of considerable improvement. This fact alone may be symptomatic of the general argument here, that research and dissemination of knowledge to the community at large about Cirencester's built environment of ancient monuments and historic buildings has not always been as fully developed as possible. Schemes to erect plaques on individual buildings or at locations of historic

interest have been fostered by various bodies at various times, usually to different designs, and however welcome leave a sense of a task unco-ordinated and incomplete. Cirencester Civic Society's programme has been the most noteworthy and determined.[26]

It is accepted that the major excavated monuments in the town are either largely buried from view (other than the Roman amphitheatre and a section of town wall, very little of Romano-British date is visible), and/or have been so denuded historically by robbery of their reuseable stone that they are marked only symbolically on the surface. The site of the basilica is one such; that of the former Abbey of St Mary also demonstrates this clearly, the outline of its principal church structure forming a feature (often overlooked) in the Abbey Grounds public park. Although the story of the creation of this park as a public amenity since the 1960s is beyond the scope of this study, it remains a remarkable achievement for a town council of the size of Cirencester. Certainly the effects of vandalism in particular have rendered site visits by interested members of the public, especially to the surviving upstanding section of the Roman town defences in the Abbey Grounds and/or the Roman amphitheatre off Cotswold Avenue as inevitably disappointing experiences. Heritage presentation, in the face of considerable constraints, remains very much an issue on such open, unstaffed sites in public places.

## Conclusion

In summary, sadly, it can be seen how little has been achieved in terms of recording and thereby better understanding Cirencester's upstanding historic buildings, and at the same time how much potential has clearly been missed during the period under review. This serves as a contrast to the extensive archaeological fieldwork and excavation activities in the town since the formation of Cirencester Excavation Committee in 1958, albeit much of that was inevitably focused upon the Romano-British town. With the benefit of hindsight, and ignoring the ebbs and flows of economic climate, it is of course easy to be critical and to a degree self-satisfied with what *has* been achieved. However, the fact that Cirencester has only recently acquired its first dendrochronological dates from a historic building, coupled with the still relative paucity of measured survey of any kind, and the very small number of examples of any comprehensive analysis of individual buildings, groups of buildings, ownership patterns or plot layout is disappointing. This ought to be testament enough to the continuing need to achieve a better understanding and improved interpretation, presentation and enjoyment of the town's rich legacy of historic buildings. Future opportunities, as the report of one of the first of Cirencester's post-War archaeological projects clearly stated almost fifty years ago, 'should be grasped more firmly' (Webster 1959, 58).

## Notes

1.  Cirencester: Conservation Area Character Appraisal and Management Plans, draft for consultation March 2008.

2. A programme of study in Ludlow by the Ludlow Historical Research Group produced three papers, summarised in Lloyd 2001. The Survey of Ancient Houses in Lincoln series produced three volumes between 1984 and 1990.

3. These are most conveniently listed in Darvill and Gerrard 1994, 206–7.

4. R.W. Jennings, e.g. in a series of articles on Cirencester 1750–1850 published in *Wilts & Glos Standard* in 1975.

5. Glos. Archives ref D10820.

6. Research by Rory Young, Linda Viner and the writer was presented in Viner and Viner 2004 and in a series of lectures celebrating the centenary of the Bingham Library during 2005.

7. Reece and Catling 1975, 28 for 26 Dollar Street (records and archives held in Corinium Museum); the losses were the Primitive Methodist Chapel in Lewis Lane (Fig. 14); the gas works in Watermoor and Rivercourt in Beeches Road.

8. For the potential of the Bear Inn, see Jowitt 1951, pl. 16. Notes and a record were made when 6–8 Dollar Street, including its jetty, was restored (Wilkinson 1985–6).

9. *Wilts & Glos Standard*, 15 January 2004, 1, 3, 5. Compare also pre- and post-1892/3 photographs of these buildings in Viner and Viner 2004, 116–7.

10. Report summary in *Trans. Bristol Gloucestershire Archaeol. Soc.,* 114, 1996, 171.

11. For a summary see also *Vernacular Architecture*, 38 (2007), 109.

12. See also the three articles by A.K.B. Evans cited in the bibliography of CE IV on p. 170. Stukeley's drawing of the Spital Gate in 1721 is shown in Darvill and Gerrard 1994, 110.

13. Linda Viner, unpublished research for the Trustees of the Cirencester Weavers Company; typescript records in the possession of the writer.

14. See *Wilts & Glos Standard*, 16 April 1998, 13. Alternatively these cellars may be post-medieval in date.

15. For Cirencester Park see Kingsley 1989, 76–7 and 1992, 100–3; for Abbey House see Kingsley 1989, 44 and 1992, 44–5; for the Querns see Kingsley 1992, 201–2; for Chesterton House see Kingsley and Hill 2001, 273; for Oakley Hall see ibid., 288; and for Watermoor House see ibid., 297.

16. Verey 1970, 175–6; Verey and Brooks 1999, 266. See also *Wilts & Glos Standard*, 1 June 2000, 17.

17. A photographic record is in the English Heritage National Monuments Record, Swindon, which also houses other records from this period of change in Cirencester, including 1–5 Gosditch Street and 26 Thomas Street.

18. But not without some criticism of scale and materials used; see Frank 1990, 8–10 and *Wilts & Glos Standard*, 21 February 2002, 15.

19. By the late Linda Walls for CAHS; copy held by the writer.

20. See Verey 1976; *Wilts & Glos Standard*, 20 July 2006, and correspondence file held by the writer.

21. Henry Cole & Co Ltd (Cotswold Mill), Lewis Lane, Cirencester, manuscript report by Linda Viner for Ivor Jones Associates, 1997.

22. For the visual impact of this building on Cecily Hill at the approach to Cirencester Park see Darvill and Gerrard 1994, fig. 48.

23. Archaeological Investigations Project, funded by English Heritage and housed at Bournemouth University, has a website http://csweb.bournemouth.ac.uk/aip.

24. See *Wilts & Glos Standard*, 8 June 1990 for 33 Gloucester Street.

25. *SPAB News* 1989, vol. 10, no. 3, 13–17 and vol. 10, no. 4, 4–5, 7.

26. Cirencester Civic Society's scheme from 1998, ably led by the late Michael Clarke, has proved the most far-reaching with some 41 oval blue plaques planned, but completion and a further phase were thwarted by procedural requirements regarding listed building and landowner permissions.

## INTRODUCTION TO THE EXCAVATIONS
### by Neil Holbrook

The remainder of this volume is primarily concerned with the results of archaeological work done in Cirencester between 1998 and 2007 by Cotswold Archaeology. In addition it includes work on the site of the forum by Oxford Archaeology and some previously unpublished observations by Peter Grace in Victoria Road in 1960 and at Coxwell Street in 1969 (Fig. 17). The latter were undertaken outside the auspices of Cirencester Excavation Committee, but produced worthwhile results deserving of wider dissemination.

While this report forms volume VI in the Cirencester Excavations series initiated in 1982, it differs from the earlier monographs in a number of important respects which reflect the changing way that archaeology is practised in England. Unlike previous reports this volume does not contain the results of any extensive excavations within the Roman town, but rather is a collection of smaller investigations. This is a product of the application of the guidance enshrined in *Planning Policy Guidance Note 16: Archaeology and Planning* (1990) which states that in a development context there should be a presumption in favour of the preservation *in situ* of important archaeological remains. Indeed a significant aspect of the work of Cotswold Archaeology is now devoted to devising solutions which allow development to proceed while ensuring that the vast majority of archaeological remains on a site are preserved. This is most frequently achieved by engineering designs which permit structures to be founded on concrete rafts above the top of archaeological levels, or else on a small number of concrete piles. It is now possible to construct many types of building on foundations which disturb less than 2% of the area of archaeology beneath their footprint (English Heritage 2007). The indiscriminate destruction of archaeological deposits in the town in the 1960s, 1970s and 1980s has thus thankfully been brought to an end. While that threat prompted a number of now classic excavations, we should not forget that Cirencester, like many other historic towns in Britain, suffered a number of depressing incidents where important remains were lost with little or no record (see for instance Sheppard Frere's succinct assessment of the missed opportunities at Minerva Court in Tower Street; *Britannia* 19 (1988), 465–7). There has therefore been considerable progress in the management of the archaeological resource in Cirencester in the last twenty years, although a number of

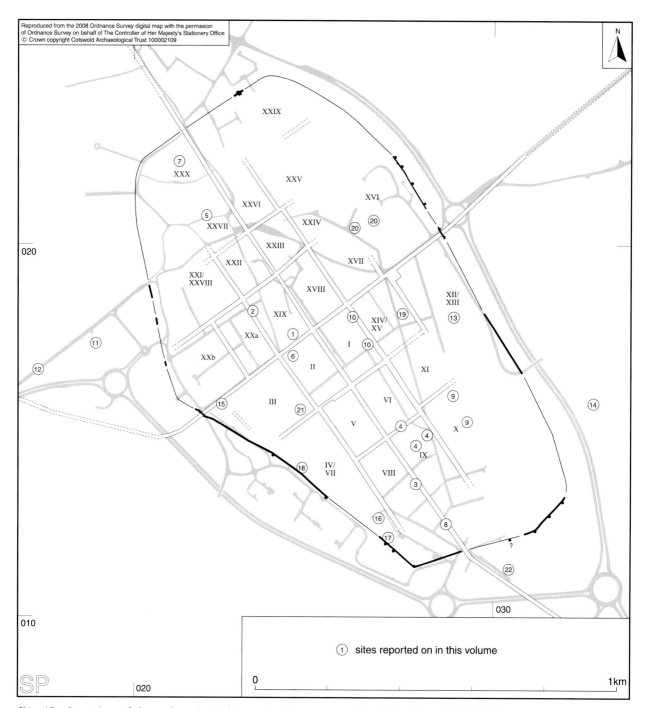

① sites reported on in this volume

0                                                                                     1km

*Fig. 17*   Location of the archaeological investigations reported in this volume (1:10,000)

1. Akeman Court; 2. 3–7 Ashcroft Road; 3. Bingham Hall; 4 Chester Street; 5 Corinium Museum; 6. Cotswold Mill; 7. Coxwell Street; 8. Foresters Arms; 9. Grammar School Field; 10. Lewis Lane; 11. Former Cattle Market; 12. Old Tetbury Road; 13. 57 Purley Road; 14. Queen Elizabeth Road; 15. 33 Querns Lane; 16. Stepstairs Lane excavation; 17. Stepstairs Lane watching brief; 18. Trinity Road; 19. 23 Victoria Road; 20. Waterloo Car Park; 21. 26 Watermoor Road; 22. 157 Watermoor Road.

important issues remain to be resolved, not least whether the preservation *in situ* of archaeological remains by the methods outlined above does actually achieve its aim. Are archaeological deposits beneath structures built in the last ten years really being preserved for investigation by future generations of archaeologists, or is this more a case of pragmatism given that the cost of archaeological excavation in Cirencester can render many types of development

uneconomic? Certainly archaeological excavation in Cirencester is not a cheap operation. Even relatively small investigations by the standards of those undertaken in the 1960s and 1970s frequently reveal complex deposits which require considerable skill in their excavation and interpretation. They also produce large quantities of artefacts that require conservation, study and reporting. The effect of archaeological costs on the economics of development in a small market town such as Cirencester should not be underestimated. Doubts are also beginning to be expressed about the feasibility of achieving preservation *in situ* of many types of archaeological deposit as the indirect effects of development are better understood, and this is now an active research topic (Nixon 1998; Davis *et al.* 2004; English Heritage 2007).

Inevitably the effect of this policy of preservation *in situ* has been to limit the number of investigations which have the potential to substantially increase our knowledge of the Roman and later town. Nevertheless, as this volume shows, there has been a steady accumulation of new information over the last decade. Another way in which the archaeology practiced in Cirencester in the last two decades differs from that previously is that Cotswold Archaeology is not the only archaeological organisation that works in the town. The market in archaeology has led to a number of other contractors working in and around Cirencester, and they will (it is to be hoped) publish their work in their own way. A search of the listings of the Archaeological Investigations Project shows that 262 fieldwork investigations of one sort and another were carried out in the parish of Cirencester between 1989 and 2005, of which 164 (63%) were by Cotswold Archaeology. Competition need not be a bad thing as long as standards are maintained, and differing approaches can be instructive. Nor is co-operation between different archaeological companies impossible, as the inclusion of a site excavated by Oxford Archaeology in this volume shows.

The demands of undertaking archaeology within the planning system necessitate that reporting is undertaken promptly, so that information is available upon which a planning application can be determined, or to permit the discharge of a condition of a consent. For pre-determination works typescript reports are produced, part of the ubiquitous 'grey literature'. For post-determination excavations which produce significant results the approach that has been adopted by Cotswold Archaeology, and agreed with Gloucestershire County Council Archaeology Service which provides advice on planning applications to Cotswold District Council, is that a typescript report is produced in a style which will facilitate its inclusion in a future publication such as this volume. Detailed reporting of individual groups of artefacts and ecofacts from each site has the potential to be unduly repetitive. Consequently we have adopted an approach that appraises the significance of each assemblage in terms of its contribution to the current state of knowledge of a particular class of material in Cirencester, or indeed more widely. Accordingly all classes of material recovered in an excavation are assessed, and this is included as an appendix in the typescript report. Where an individual item or group of material is considered to be worthy of more detailed analysis this is undertaken and the results are published here. Readers can therefore be confident that all the material recovered from the excavations reported in this volume has been assessed, and if it is not mentioned in the site reports it is because it has not been deemed to

be of sufficient importance to warrant this treatment. If readers wish to consult the assessment reports a copy can be obtained from the Gloucestershire County Council Sites and Monuments Record. There is no obligation under the planning system to disseminate the results of grey literature reports relating to evaluations and other small-scale projects more widely, but nevertheless we have taken the opportunity to include in this volume summaries of the more significant results which have derived from projects of this kind.

One final way that this report differs from the earlier volumes in the series is that it is the first to be produced without any financial support from English Heritage or its predecessors. All the investigations reported herein have been fully funded as a requirement of the planning process by bodies or individuals acting in the role of developer. A problem inherent in this system, however, is that there is no funding available for synthesis beyond that appropriate to an individual site, and yet this is manifestly necessary to create a volume such as this. The costs of drawing together the individual site reports have therefore been met by Cotswold Archaeology as part of its educational work. We also consider it appropriate to mark the fiftieth anniversary of the creation of an organised archaeological presence in Cirencester with another volume in the Cirencester Excavations series. In some cases we would have preferred to engage in a higher level of synthesis and research than has proved possible, but despite these restrictions we believe that this volume makes a valuable contribution to knowledge of the archaeology of the town.

While publication of artefacts in this volume is unashamedly selective, it remains important that the basis for the proposed chronology for each site is presented in sufficient detail to allow the reader to interrogate and evaluate the dating proposed. Each report therefore contains, where relevant, sections which outline the dating evidence which underpins the site phasing. These have been prepared by E.R. McSloy and adopt the format and approach used in Cirencester Excavations Volume V. Samian identifications are by G.B. Dannell and P.V. Webster. The coarseware pottery references derive from the Cirencester fabric series developed by V. Rigby, J. Keely and N. Cooper, which has been described and discussed in previous volumes. References to this series in the dating evidence sections are prefixed by the letters TF (type fabric) and references to Ceramic Phases refer to the scheme devised by Cooper (CE V, 324–41). In the coin lists CK refers to Carson and Kent 1960 and HK to Carson *et al.* 1960. Contexts followed by n.i. are not illustrated on the plans or sections. References in the text to CE I to CE V refer to previous volumes in the Cirencester Excavations series, and Cotswold Archaeology is abbreviated as CA throughout.

Neil Holbrook
*Corinium Dobunnorum*
April 2008

# 2. THE STREET SYSTEM

During the preparation of this volume a new plan of the Roman town has been prepared (Fig. 18). Previous investigations have been plotted onto a digital Ordnance Survey base which has resulted in accuracy not previously possible. One of the main results of this process has been the recognition that various

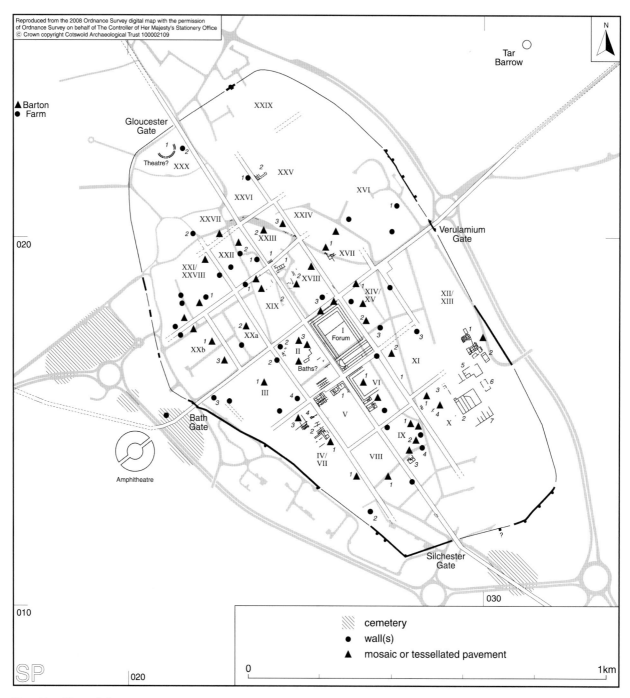

cemetery

● wall(s)

▲ mosaic or tessellated pavement

0 ——————————————————— 1km

*Fig. 18* Plan of the Roman town (1:10,000)

sightings of metalling on what is ostensibly the same street do not always align on a consistently straight alignment. It was recognised previously that the process of reconstruction of the town plan on the drawing table, which of necessity requires a 'joining of the dots' between comparatively few direct observations, has a tendency to create a plan which displays greater regularity than may have actually been the case (CE V, 19). The street grid as now depicted is no longer perfectly orthogonal, and certain streets evidently included dog-legs or changes of alignment (for instance Street C between observations C.1/6 and C.2 and Street J between J.1 and J.2/3). The irregularity now apparent in the street plan seems more credible, and bears comparison with towns such as Silchester and Caistor-by-Norwich where aerial photography and geophysics permit an accurate street plan to be traced across the whole of the walled area (Bewley and Fulford 1996; *Current Archaeology* 216 (March 2008), 7). In Cirencester the extent to which streets divided up the whole of the walled area is still unclear, especially in the north-east, north-west and south-east quarters where relict or active river courses may have disrupted attempts at unified planning. For instance two investigations have failed to detect Streets K and L in their anticipated locations and so *insula* XVII may never have been fully defined by streets on all four sides (Fig. 19).

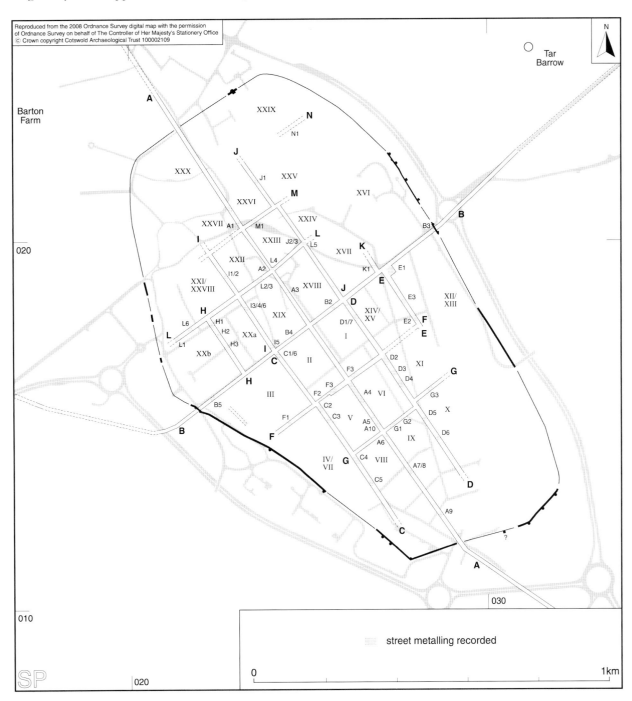

*Fig. 19*   Key to the labelling of the streets (1:10,000)

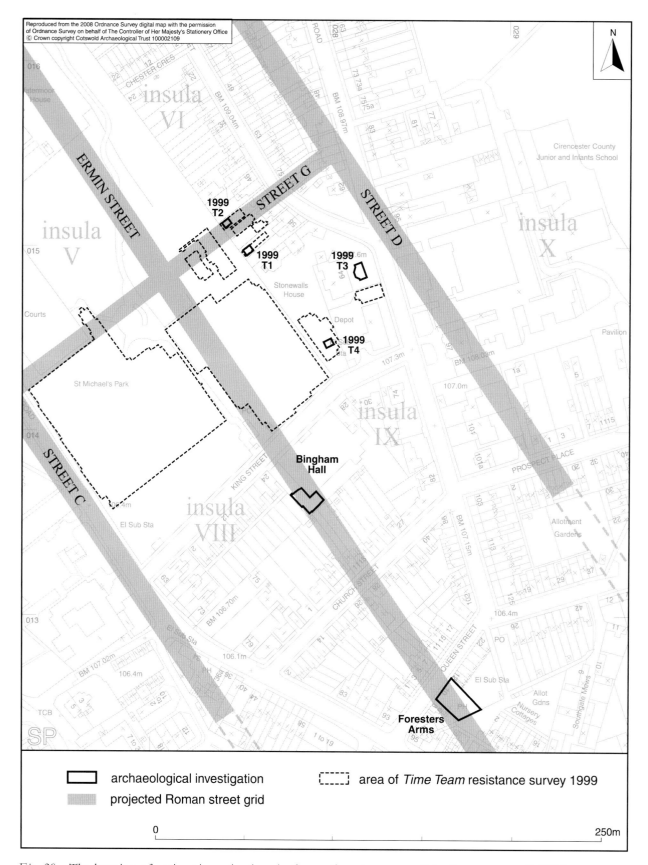

Reproduced from the 2008 Ordnance Survey digital map with the permission of Ordnance Survey on behalf of The Controller of Her Majesty's Stationery Office © Crown copyright Cotswold Archaeological Trust 100002109

| | archaeological investigation | | area of *Time Team* resistance survey 1999 |
|---|---|---|---|
| | projected Roman street grid | | |

0                                                                                                250m

*Fig. 20*   The location of various investigations in the south-eastern part of the Roman town (1:2000)

In this chapter two excavations which examined the course of Ermin Street as it passed through the south-eastern part of the town are reported, followed by short gazetteer entries of other smaller investigations which have taken place since the publication of CE V. The nomenclature adopted follows on from that introduced in CE V, with each street ascribed a letter and each separate investigation a number. Thus, as the excavations at Bingham Hall are the eighth separate investigation of Ermin Street (Street A), the investigation is numbered A.8. The locations of the investigations are marked on Fig. 19.

## BINGHAM HALL, KING STREET, 2002
### by Tim Havard and Martin Watts

### Introduction

In March 2002 CA carried out an excavation prior to the construction of a small extension to the Bingham Hall in King Street (see Fig. 17, no. 3 and Fig. 20). The metalled surface of Ermin Street was identified during the construction of Bingham Hall in 1908, and again in December 2000 in a small trial trench within the

proposed development area (CE III, 193). The entire footprint of the development, covering an area of approximately 130m², was machine-excavated to the top of archaeological deposits, which in places was only 0.3m below the existing ground level. Where unaffected by modern service trenches, Roman street metalling survived across the eastern half of the site, and a 1.2m-wide trench was positioned to give the best possible section across Ermin Street (Fig. 21, trench 4). Machine excavation also exposed Roman structural remains along the western side of the site, aligned almost exactly along a proposed foundation for the development. A second trench was laid out to examine this wall and any other associated deposits (trench 5).

The trenches were hand-excavated to no deeper than was required for the foundations. Removal of street surfaces was difficult due to their highly compacted nature and had to be undertaken mostly by means of a pneumatic drill. This made it difficult to discern distinct street surfaces, particularly in the later layers where

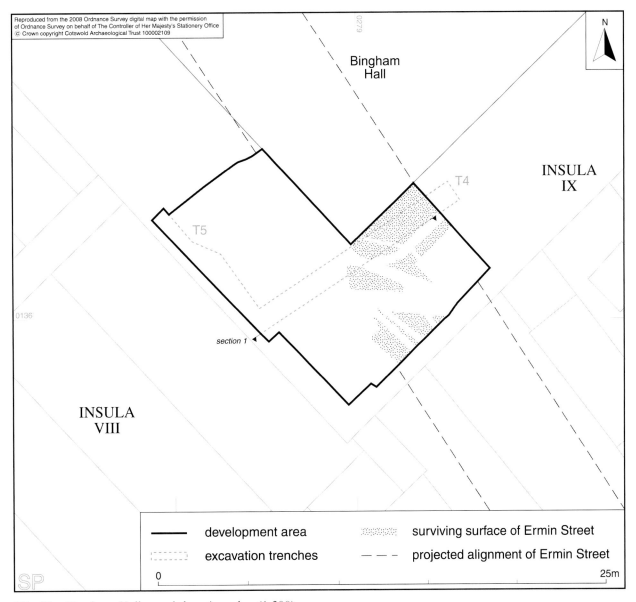

*Fig. 21* Bingham Hall trench location plan (1:200)

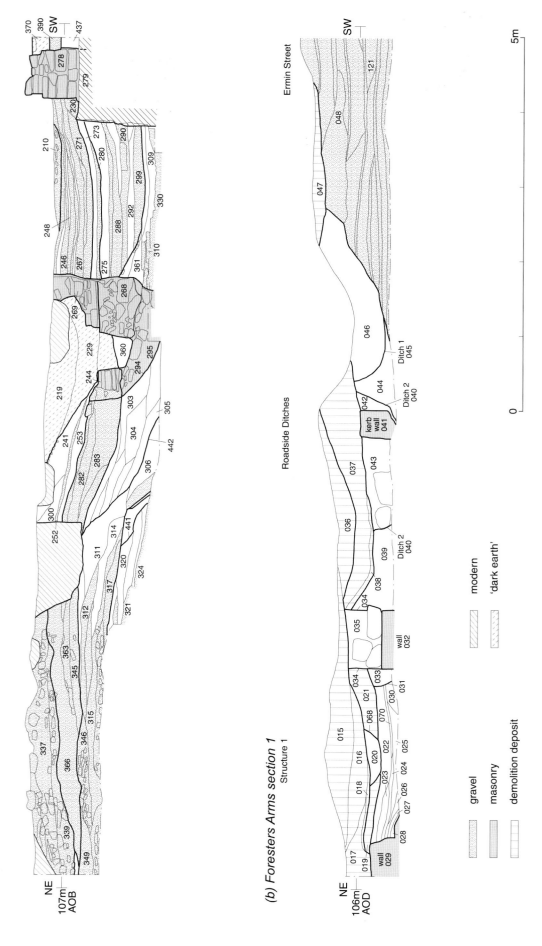

(a) Bingham Hall section 1

(b) Foresters Arms section 1
Structure 1

gravel

masonry

demolition deposit

modern

'dark earth'

*Fig. 22*   Sections at Bingham Hall and Foresters Arms (1:50)

deposits appeared to blend in to one another, as if patchwork repairs rather than full scale resurfacing had occurred. As natural deposits were not reached in either trench, this resulted in two substantial but incomplete sections, one across Ermin Street (Fig. 22a) and the other along its associated street-side development (trench 5). A watching brief was also maintained during the construction of the building foundations but this did not provide any additional information.

## Period 1: Early street surfaces and portico (late 1st to early 2nd century AD)

At the base of trench 4, two layers of street metalling (321 and 324) were exposed but not excavated at a height of between 105.9m and 106.2m AOD. These were sealed by layers of street-washed silt (e.g. 320), which together with the camber of metalling 324 suggested that these deposits lay at the edge of the street next to the side ditch. The build-up of silt suggests maintenance was intermittent, although the side ditch (441) was well defined. A further episode of re-surfacing and silt deposition was also apparent.

To the south-west of Ermin Street, the earliest identified surface (310, 330), at 105.9m AOD, corresponded in height with the earliest street metalling. The surface comprised irregular limestone slabs laid flat, and was sealed by several layers of silt (e.g. 309, 361), echoing the build-up of silt over the corresponding street. The rising up of these silt deposits towards the north-east indicated that a stylobate wall had been present, and therefore this earliest floor surface identified lay within a portico. However, due to later rebuilding no direct evidence of the portico survived.

### Dating evidence

Period 1 dating derives from deposits, principally 309 and 310, associated with the earliest road metalling. Dating is exclusively from pottery evidence, which includes three sherds of South Gaulish samian of Flavian date. Local finewares are restricted to single sherds of mica-dusted TF 54 and a probable flagon of North Wilts oxidised ware TF 9. Coarsewares comprise mainly reduced wares, particularly Savernake and local types, some with clay rustication. Though restricted in quantity, the assemblage is comparable in composition to Ceramic Phase 2 and probably dates to the late 1st to early 2nd century AD.

Layer 309: *Pottery* (15sh./204g). *Samian*: SG Drag. 36, Flavian. *Coarsewares*: TF 6, 5, 17, 9, 52.

Floor 310: *Pottery* (13sh./84g). *Samian*: SG Drag. 27, 29, Flavian. *Coarsewares*: TF 6, 5, 17, 9, 52.

## Period 2: Building 1A and the broadening of Ermin Street (2nd to late 3rd/early 4th century AD)

### Building 1A

In trench 5 the earliest remains related to Building 1A, which fronted Ermin Street, and to open areas either side of Building 1A (Fig. 23a). Up to six courses of dressed stone from the side walls (378 and 436) of Building 1A were recorded, but its front wall had been entirely replaced by later rebuilding. Internally,

the earliest recorded floor, of compacted clay (430, n.i.) stood at a height of 106.5m AOD. This was replaced by three successive surfaces of smooth limestone slabs, each surface bedded on a thick layer of compacted sandy silt. Each successive surface raised the internal floor level by approximately 0.2m; the final floor surface of Building 1A lay at approximately 107.2m AOD.

To the north-west of Building 1A a sequence of deposits that appeared to represent a courtyard was found. Three successive layers were again recorded, the levels of which broadly correlated to the interior surfaces of Building 1A, although robbing of wall 378 and later truncation had destroyed any direct relationships. The uppermost make-up layer comprised compacted limestone fragments and gravel, and was overlain by a well-constructed surface (393, n.i.) of compacted gravel with crushed tile, lying at *c*. 107.2m AOD. The similarity of surface 393 with the walkway surfaces within the portico in trench 4 suggests it was external rather than internal.

To the south-east of Building 1A was a series of silt deposits (including 406 and 411, both n.i.) that appeared to have been dumped against wall 436, although later construction had removed any direct relationship. Unlike those to the north-east, these deposits bore no relation to the levels of the internal surfaces of the building. They were overlain by several thin layers of silt, clay and gravel (including 437, n.i.) that were rich in charcoal and waste fragments of copper alloy, the uppermost of which sloped gently down from a height of 107.1m AOD adjacent to Building 1A. It seems likely that this was an open area, perhaps not directly related to Building 1A, with some scattered metalworking waste, but not enough to indicate an industrial function.

### Ermin Street

Two distinct phases of Ermin Street were apparent within this period. During the first phase, the level of Ermin Street gradually increased as repairs and general resurfacing was undertaken. The re-surfacing (e.g. metalling layers 312, 315, 317) was undertaken directly above previous street surfaces, with a gentle camber allowing rainwater to run off into a broad side ditch up to 2.5m wide (allowing for a stylobate wall *c*. 0.5m wide). The north-eastern edge of this phase of Ermin Street, which was at least 5m wide, lay beyond the trench. The last resurfacing of this phase (metalling layers 346 and 349) elevated the level of the street to approximately 106.8m AOD. Following this, the side ditch was allowed to fill up with silt (306, 311) and despite the ditch being redefined (442) it filled up with silt once more (e.g. layers 303, 304, 305).

The infilling of the side ditch may have been deliberate as it allowed for the construction of street surfaces above it. The street level above the infilled earlier ditch was rapidly raised with the deposition of layer 283, up to 0.4m deep. An iron linch-pin was recovered from the earliest metalling of this phase, layer 345 (Fig. 24, 2). The final surface of this phase stood at approximately 107.2m AOD. It is unclear whether this was a general broadening of Ermin Street or a slight realignment, as there was no clear evidence for the edge of the street or a side ditch to the north-east within this trench (Fig. 22a). To the south-west the side ditch must have been considerably narrower, perhaps only 1m wide, but later rebuilding had again removed all evidence.

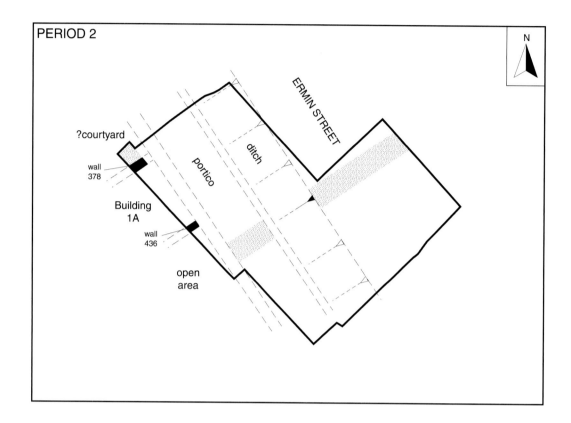

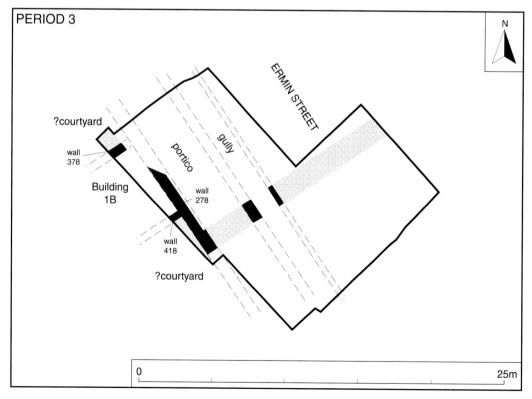

*Fig. 23*   Bingham Hall. Development of the building, portico and street (1:200)

### The portico

Floor levels within both Building 1A and the portico rose throughout this period, probably in response to the increasing street level from episodes of re-surfacing. Like the street surfaces, successive floor surfaces within the portico, such as surfaces 299, 290 and 288, were interleaved with thin accumulations of silt, including layers 292 and 275. The later floor surfaces sloped away from the adjacent building, no doubt to assist with the run-off of water. The largest accumulation of silt within this sequence, layer 275, may have accompanied the infilling of the adjacent side ditch. The uppermost walkway surface of this period stood at about 106.5m AOD. As with the underlying floor surfaces, all would have lain within a portico, with wall foundations on one side and a stylobate wall on the other but, as previously, all evidence of these structures had been removed by later, direct replacements.

### Dating evidence

*Building 1A.* Only small quantities of pottery are associated with the construction of Building 1A. A sherd of Central Gaulish samian, dateable to the Antonine period, is the only artefact from the early floor levels within the building. Pottery from the construction of wall 378 comprises Flavian samian and late 1st to 2nd-century AD coarsewares, quite possibly derived from earlier deposits. Dating evidence from the open area south-east of Building 1A includes Antonine (Central Gaulish) samian, Dorset Black-Burnished ware (TF 74) and a South-West white slipped ware (TF 88) flagon of probable 3rd-century date (CE II, MF 1 D05). This material is comparable to Ceramic Phases 5 to 6 (*c.* AD 200–300).

Layer 406: *Pottery* (3sh./48g). *Samian*: CG Drag. 33, Antonine. *Coarsewares*: TF 74.

Layer 411: *Pottery* (9sh./130g). *Samian*: CG Drag. 35/36, 2nd century. *Coarsewares*: TF 88 (flagon).

Layer 430: *Pottery* (1sh./2g). *Samian*: CG Drag. 18/31, Antonine.

*Ermin Street.* Pottery from the road surfaces comprises mostly broadly dateable types or derived (residual) material.

Layer 305: *Pottery* (9sh./416g). *Samian*: SG Drag. 15/17R, pre-Flavian. *Coarsewares*: TF 17/98, 40, 6, 9.

*The portico.* Material from the layers of silt within the portico floor surfaces includes a single worn coin of Vespasian (AD 69–79) from layer 275. The pottery, including one sherd of South Gaulish samian, is very similar in character to material from Period 1 deposits and is consistent with a date before *c.* AD 130/150.

Layer 275: *Coin*: Worn *as* or *dupondius* of Vespasian (AD 69–79).

Layer 292: *Pottery* (25sh./299g). *Samian*: SG Drag. 29, 1st century AD. *Coarsewares*: TF 17, 6, 9, 5, 40.

## Period 3: Building 1B and reconstruction of the portico (mid 4th century AD)

### Building 1B

Considerable alterations were carried out to Building 1A to create Building 1B. The north-eastern wall, which also formed the inner wall of the portico (wall 278), was completely rebuilt from the foundations (279)

upwards (Figs 22a and 23b). The south-eastern wall (436) was demolished and partly robbed (424, 427, both n.i.) to below floor level and a new wall (418) was built immediately adjacent. Fragments of a Roman lock-plate were recovered from associated deposit 413 (n.i.) (Fig. 24, 1). The interior floor surface of Building 1A was retained and extended over the remains of wall 436. The north-western wall of Building 1A, 378, also appears to have been retained. Up to seven courses of stone survived *in situ* from walls 278 and 418, both of which stood on pitched stone foundations.

### New portico and roadside gully

The rebuilding of the inner wall of the portico, 278, was accompanied by a further reconstruction of the stylobate wall in what was probably wholesale rebuilding of the entire portico. Any evidence for previous stylobates and roadside ditches was removed with a broad construction cut (294), the base of which was consolidated with large pieces of limestone (295), quite possibly from the demolition of the earlier portico, forming a foundation layer for new construction. The foundations of the new stylobate wall survived (268), as did the retaining or counterscarp wall (244) for a narrow gully that replaced the wide, side ditch of previous periods (Fig. 22a).

### Dating evidence

*Building 1B.* Only modest quantities of pottery can be associated with this period. Pottery from robber trench 427 produced a coin of AD 330–5. Deposits associated with the construction of wall 278 produced a small quantity of pottery including Oxfordshire whiteware mortaria (TF 90, Young form M22) and colour-coated ware TF 83, suggesting a date of after *c.* AD 250/270.

Layer 424: *Coin*: Constantine I (AD 330–5); *Pottery* (6sh./56g). *Samian*: CG Drag. 18/31, Antonine. *Coarsewares*: 74, 98.

Wall 278: *Pottery* (5sh./238g). *Coarsewares*: TF 83, 90, 98, 104.

*New portico and roadside gully.* A coin of Constantius I (AD 293–306) was recovered from the foundation rubble 295 for the stylobate wall. This deposit also produced a relatively large group of pottery, including TF 83 and 103 indicative of a date after *c.* AD 300 (Ceramic Phases 7–8).

Foundation layer 295: *Coin*: Constantius I (AD 293–306); *Pottery* (38sh./483g). *Coarsewares*: TF 104, 118, 98, 35, 6, 83.

## Period 4: Rising street and floor levels and rebuilding of the portico (mid 4th century AD +)

### Building 1B and possible courtyards

The internal floor level of Building 1B was raised by up to 0.15m, again with the deposition of compacted silt and the construction of a new surface. To the north-west, sandy gravels were laid to bring the level of the probable courtyard up to a similar height, and this was mirrored to the south-east of Building 1B with a substantial deposit of compact gravel (390) laid within the open area. A surface was established on top of this deposit. The similarity in the new surface levels either side of wall 418, at approximately 107.3m AOD, suggests that the former open area was now more directly linked to the building than previously, and was probably another courtyard.

### Ermin Street

Further resurfacing of Ermin Street was undertaken after the creation of the narrow side gully, with both metalled layers (252) and silt accumulations overlying the top of the counterscarp wall 244. The top of the uppermost surviving metalled surface, 337, was located at 107.5m AOD. The presence of substantial silt accumulations such as layers 300 and 241 may indicate that the alignment of the street shifted back towards the north-east during this period. Final silting of the gully, which must have been regularly cleaned, was represented by deposit 360.

### The portico

At least seven episodes of relaying or repairing the portico floor were undertaken before the stylobate wall was again rebuilt (Fig. 22a). Deposit 230 was probably placed to deflect water away from the wall foundations. Successive floor layers displayed the same slight slope as earlier walkway surfaces, with localised repairs such as layers 271 and 246 perhaps suggesting increased wear. The stylobate was rebuilt (269), reusing part of wall 268, when the floor surface had reached 107.1m AOD or higher. It is possible that metalled surface 210 also pre-dated this reconstruction of the stylobate wall, but truncation had removed any stratigraphic relationship.

### Dating evidence

*The portico.* Only one layer, metalling 210, produced significant artefactual material. Three coins, all House of Constantine copies, were recovered, together with small quantities of pottery. This material is suggestive of a mid 4th-century AD or later date.

Layer 210: *Coins*: ?copy, Constantinopolis (AD 330–335); House of Constantine copy (AD 335–7); House of Constantine copy (AD 335–41). *Pottery* (10sh./69g). *Coarsewares*: TF 104, 105, 98, 83.

### Period 5: Late Roman/post-Roman activity (late 4th century AD +)

Evidence for late Roman and/or post-Roman activity was restricted to a demolition layer (383, n.i.) within Building 1B, a few features including a stakehole and two pits, and deposits of dark earth (including layer 370) overlying all archaeological remains to the south-west of the portico (Fig. 22a). Dark earth deposits were also recorded infilling the upper parts of the roadside gully (e.g. 219, 229), which had been enlarged through the removal of part of the stylobate wall prior to a modern pipe trench being cut through these deposits.

### Dating evidence

The pottery is a mix of early and (mostly) late Roman material. The late Roman groups are similar in character to those from the preceding period, comprising mostly local coarsewares copying Dorset Black-Burnished ware, but also including Oxfordshire products and, in the case of demolition layer 383, sherds from a South-West brown slipped ware (TF 105) scale-decorated beaker. The 'dark earth' filling the final roadside gully contained two residual coins of Constantine I.

The absence of material from the second half of the 4th century, such as House of Valentinian coins, late Roman shell-tempered ware (type 115) and the latest vessel forms in Oxfordshire colour-coated ware (TF 83), may be significant. Such material is abundant in 'latest Roman' contexts elsewhere in Cirencester, and its absence may indicate that Roman activity may have tailed off in the immediate area by the AD 360s.

Demolition layer 383: *Pottery* (18sh./69g). *Coarsewares*: TF 74, 82, 105.

Dark earth 229: *Coin*: Constantine I (AD 318–24). *Pottery* (11sh./138g). *Coarsewares*: TF 9, 83, 84, 17/98, 104.

Dark earth 219: *Coin*: Constantine I (AD 318–24). *Pottery* (7sh./151g). *Coarsewares*: TF 104, 106, 17/98, 95/98.

### Discussion

The project provided an opportunity to excavate a section through Ermin Street and its south-western side ditch, and also to gain some information regarding roadside development to the south-west of the street in this area. The requirements of development meant that natural deposits were not exposed, but a sequence of at least eleven successive street surfaces was recorded, lying between 105.9m and 107.5m AOD, and dated to between the late 1st/early 2nd century and the mid 4th century AD.

The expansion of Ermin Street over the earlier and much broader side ditch in the latter part of Period 2 was clearly deliberate, and probably represents a broadening of the street rather than a re-alignment, and resulted in a much narrower (but better defined) side gully. Previous excavations across the whole width of Ermin Street further to the north-west between *insulae* V and VI recorded no evidence for a re-alignment of the street, however the final form of the roadside ditch was also much reduced (CE V, fig. 90). The reverse camber apparent at the top of metalling layer 366 (and of subsequent replacements) is unlikely to represent evidence for the north-eastern side of Ermin Street, as elsewhere within the town the street had an overall width in excess of 10m (ibid., 138). However, it is possible that the camber was designed to allow run-off into a central drain such as has been found elsewhere (ibid., 138, fig. 88).

As successive street metalling accumulated, floor levels within the adjacent portico and roadside buildings were correspondingly raised. The limestone slabs of the earliest recorded portico floor surface (310) are paralleled by the large pieces of limestone that formed the first portico floor recorded on the other side of Ermin Street in *insula* VI (CE V, 133, fig. 90). The rebuilding of both portico walls in Period 3 (mid 4th century AD) removed all structural evidence for the early portico in which floor surfaces 310 through to 280 were laid, but the presence of an early portico is apparent from the build-up of silts over surface 310, and the sloping nature of floor surfaces laid above. Reconstruction of the portico in the mid 4th century

AD is paralleled on the same side of Ermin Street at the far end of *insula* V where a stylobate wall survived to a height of seven courses, standing upon the reused foundations of the original wall (ibid., 207–9). In all, ten separate floor surfaces were recorded within the portico.

Five floor surfaces were recorded within Building 1A/1B but there was no evidence to indicate what the building may have been used for. The presence of open areas or courtyards immediately to the rear of a portico is slightly unusual, but there were no recognisably internal surfaces of mortar or *opus signinum* surviving in the small areas excavated.

The date of the abandonment of the street and Building 1B is unclear. The absence of late 4th-century AD coins and pottery from the deposits above the building remains and infilling the side ditch may be significant as these artefacts appear in quantity in equivalent deposits elsewhere in the town. Subsequent truncation had removed any post-Roman deposits over Ermin Street, although the presence of dark earth over the building remains suggests that the uppermost surviving layer of street metalling could represent its final surface. A worked red deer antler recovered from the 'dark earth' deposits is more likely to have been residual rather than representing a post-Roman craft industry within the walls of Corinium.

**The finds** by E.R. McSloy

### Coins

1. Layer 275; Period 2. Worn *As* of Vespasian. AD 69–79.
2. Foundation layer 295; Period 3. Constantius I. GENIO POPULI ROMANI. TR (Trier). AD 293–306.
3. Post-Roman deposit 219; Period 5. AE2. Constantine I. VICTORIAE LAETAE PRINC PERP. AD 318–24.
4. Post-Roman deposit 229; Period 5. AE2. Constantine I. BAETA TRANQUILLITAS. AD 318–24
5. Walkway layer 210; Period 4. AE3 ?copy. As Constantinopolis. Victory on Prow. TRP (?Trier). AD 330–5.
6. Walkway layer 210; Period 4. AE3 copy. As House of Constantine. As Gloria Exercitus (2 std). AD 330–5.
7. Demolition deposit 424; Period 3. AE2. CONSTANTINOPOLIS. Victory on Prow. PLG (Lyons). AD 330–5.
8. Unstratified. AE2. CONSTANTINOPOLIS. Victory on Prow. AD 330–5.
9. Walkway layer 210; Period 4. AE3 copy. As House of Constantine. As Gloria Exercitus (1 std). AD 335–41.
10. Unstratified. AE3. Constans. VICTORIAE DD AUGGQ NN. TRS (Trier). AD 347–8.

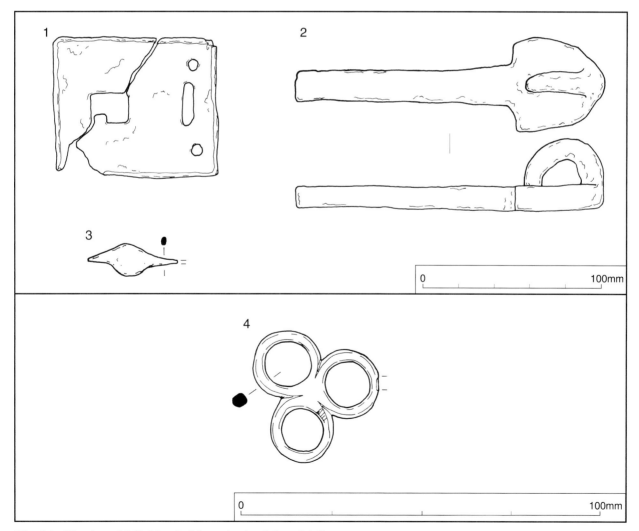

*Fig. 24*  Bingham Hall. Metal objects (scales 2:1 and 1:1)

11. Unstratified. AE3. Gratian. SECURITAS REIPUBLI-CAE. LUGP (Lyons). AD 367–78.

## Metalwork (Fig. 24)

### Iron objects

1. Context 413; Period 3. Two joining fragments from rectangular lock-plate. Rectangular with edges folded over at 90°. X-ray reveals 'L-shaped' aperture, off-set to one side, two rivet/nail holes to the lower corners and a rectangular slot between. Length 91mm; width 76mm; depth of flange 6mm. The form suggests use for simple tumbler lock of the type used throughout the Roman period (Manning 1985, 93), and operated using an L-shaped (lift) key.
2. Road metalling layer 345; Period 2. Linch-pin, Manning form 2b. Length 172mm; width at head 50mm. Its function was to secure the wheel to its axle. Manning's (1985) class 2b linch-pins, defined as 'spatulate headed, with turned-over loop formed from the metal of the head', are the most commonly occurring type from Roman Britain. The class appears to be in use from the late 1st century AD as indicated from finds at Newstead (Curle 1911, 293) and probably continues until the end of the Roman period.
3. Wall 278. Period 3. ?toilet implement with leaf or 'comma'-shaped blade. Length 51mm; width 18mm. The x-ray shows a leaf-shaped 'blade' with distinctive hooked lower edge. This form of blade is seen with toilet/surgical instruments, most often in copper alloy and forming one element of a double-ended implement. A spatula with a similar-shaped blade but in copper alloy was recovered from a ?later 2nd-century AD deposit in Cirencester (CE V, fig. 190, no. 29). Toilet implements of a broader class continue in use throughout the Roman period.

### Copper-alloy object

4. Post-Roman deposit 229; Period 5. Trefoil-form strap union. Cast, with coarse file marks over parts of surfaces. Tapering grooves cut from the junction of each ring to the centre in an effort to accentuate each element. Length 33mm; internal diameter of rings 11.5mm. The trefoil form of this object is comparable to those with military associations from Cirencester (CE I, 108–9, fig. 35, no. 99) and Camerton, Somerset (Jackson 1990, 34, no. 61). These published examples, probably dating to the 1st century AD, are of more elaborate form, the example from Cirencester cast with a naturalistically styled horse's head projecting from the centre. The Cirencester and Camerton examples are identified as harness fittings, with that from Cirencester additionally described as a martingale ring. The martingale in modern usage comprises a 'Y'-shaped arrangement of straps joining the bridle to the girth band, which functions to prevent the raising of the horse's head. There are no indications of a military usage for this object, although there is no reason to doubt a harness-related function.

## THE FORESTERS ARMS, QUEEN STREET, 2003–4
### by Derek Evans

### Introduction

Between December 2003 and September 2004 CA carried out excavation and watching brief at the former Foresters Arms public house in Queen Street during the redevelopment of the site for residential accommodation. The site lies on the extrapolated route of Ermin Street and 100m north-west of the site of the Silchester Gate (see Fig. 17, no. 8 and Fig. 20). As such the excavation represents the most south-easterly archaeological recording of Ermin Street to date within the Roman town.

The fieldwork took place in a series of discrete phases as the project progressed. An initial evaluation of two hand-dug trial pits located the level of surviving Roman deposits within the development area (CA 2004). This was followed by a watching brief during the mechanical sinking of piled foundations and the excavation of foundation trenches and service channels (Fig. 25). The foundation trenches and service channels were mechanically excavated to the top of archaeologically significant deposits. Hand-excavation of these deposits was then undertaken by CA to the formation level required by the development. The remains of Ermin Street were located across the western part of the site. Excavation of the street surfaces was difficult due to their highly compacted nature, and much of this was undertaken by pneumatic drill, making it difficult to identify discrete surfaces. Away from Ermin Street modern intrusions had removed almost all significant remains (at least to the depth of the development formation level) except at the southern end of the site. In the north-eastern corner of the excavation a layer of sand and gravel, possibly representing natural deposits, was exposed in a small area at a height of 105.48m AOD.

### Period 1: Ermin Street, associated ditches and an adjacent structure

### Ermin Street

The remains of Ermin Street comprised up to fifteen layers of highly compact yellow/orange limestone metalling within an exposed depth of approximately 1.2m (Fig. 22b). These metalled layers represent discrete episodes of resurfacing and repair, gradually raising its surface level. The foundation layers of the street lay below the required formation level and were thus unexcavated. The earliest exposed surface was located at *c.* 105.65m AOD. The only layer to produce any dating evidence, layer 121, was at *c.* 105.95m AOD. The street displayed a camber down to its associated drainage ditches to the north-east (see below), which became more pronounced as the metalling layers built up. Metalling layer 048 comprised slightly larger fragments of crushed limestone in a grey matrix, but was still highly compact. The uppermost surviving street surface was at 106.80m AOD.

### Structure 1

Structure 1 lay in the south-eastern corner of the site (Figs 22b and 26). Its north-east wall (029) constituted the earliest visible part and was comprised of large mortar-bonded limestone blocks, irregular in shape but roughly faced on their western side (the eastern side was not exposed). A series of nine compacted sand and ash

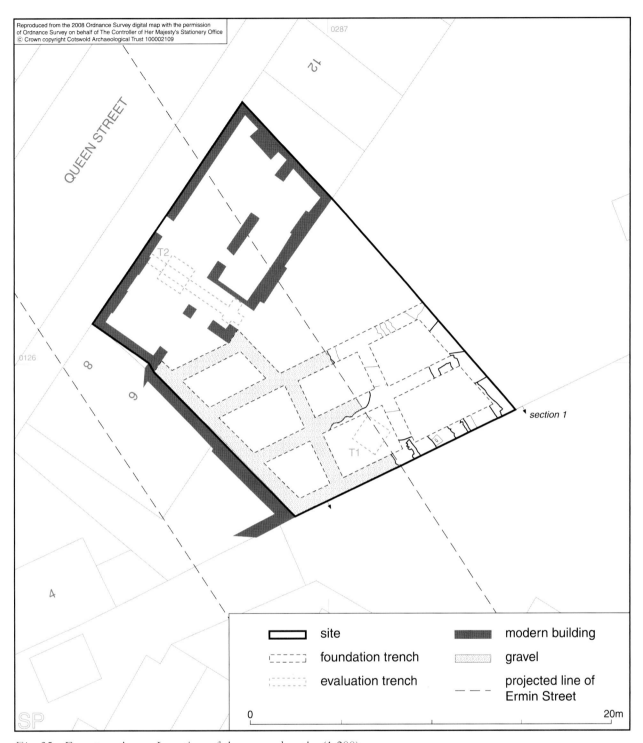

QUEEN STREET

section 1

| | site | | modern building |
| --- | --- | --- | --- |
| | foundation trench | | gravel |
| | evaluation trench | | projected line of Ermin Street |

0                                                                           20m

*Fig. 25*   Foresters Arms. Location of the groundworks (1:200)

layers which built up against this wall (including layers 022 and 025) represented the remnants of successive internal floor levels. The original south-west wall of Structure 1 had been replaced by wall 032 sometime after the construction of the uppermost surviving surface, layer 022. Wall 032 was also composed of large and irregular mortar-bonded limestone blocks, but was of a somewhat more regular construction than wall 029. There is little evidence to indicate the function of Structure 1, although its width of *c.* 2.25m is consistent

with the portico examined at Bingham Hall (see above). The rough sand and ash floor surfaces may have been bedding layers for flagstones that were periodically lifted and reset, or might have acted as simple floors, which would suggest that this was not a high-status building.

### The side ditches

Lying against the external face of wall 032 of Structure 1 was a substantial sandy deposit, 039, which was also

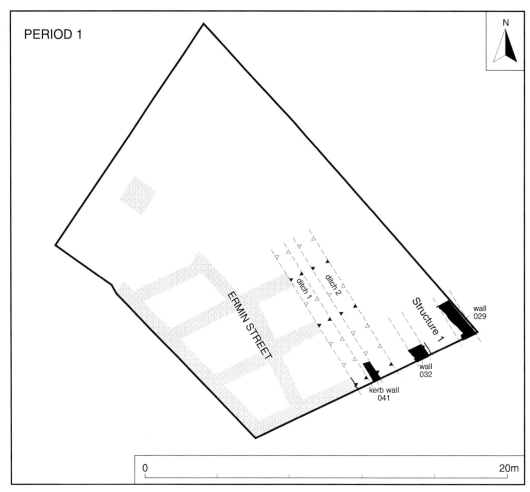

PERIOD 1

*Fig. 26*    Foresters Arms. Plan (1:200)

recorded (as deposit 044) further to the west over-lapping the earliest surfaces of Ermin Street. The exact provenance of this deposit is uncertain, but it appears to represent the final silting with material washed from Ermin Street of a large side ditch. No edges of this ditch were exposed. A single block of dressed limestone present within deposit 039 probably derived from Structure 1.

Two further side ditches were subsequently dug through deposit 039/044. Ditch 1 lay immediately to the north-east of Ermin Street and partly overlay its earlier surfaces. The ditch was *c.* 2.3m wide, 0.44m deep, and ran alongside the street throughout the site. At the southern end of the site, the remains of Ditch 2 were recorded to the north-east of Ditch 1. Ditch 2 was *c.* 1.8m wide, 0.55m deep, and contained the remains of a narrow wall (041) composed of irregular mortar-bonded limestone blocks. This appeared to be a kerb wall at the edge of the street which retained the south-western side of Ditch 2, reducing its width to about 1.2m. Similar kerbs have been found elsewhere in Cirencester, including Bingham Hall to the north (see above) and within *insula* II where it may have also served as a foundation for wooden steps to permit access across the ditch (CE V, 183, fig. 129). Both ditches were presumably cleaned on a regular basis, with their fills representing the final build-up of road

silts before they fell out of use. No evidence was recovered to date this process and no relationship between Ditches 1 and 2 could be ascertained.

### Other Roman deposits

A series of layers recorded in the easternmost section of the site were associated with late 1st to 2nd-century AD pottery sherds. Visible only in a small area between episodes of post-medieval disturbance, interpretation is impossible and no obvious relationship to any of the features described above could be ascertained.

### Dating evidence

Pottery from Period 1 amounts to 44 sherds, with small groups recovered from road construction deposits and a series of make-up, levelling and demolition layers. The small size of the pottery groups render firm dating of deposits impossible. Taken overall, the prominence of white-slipped flagon fabric (TF 9) and Savernake ware (TF 6), including a flat-rimmed bowl in deposit 083 (as CE I, fig. 56, nos 233–4) are suggestive of later 1st or 2nd-century AD dating. An absence of Dorset Black-Burnished ware may also be significant, encouraging a date before *c.* AD 150.

*Ermin Street.* Pottery associated with the surfacings of Ermin Street consists of 21 sherds, in all likelihood from a single vessel (?a beaker) in mica-dusted fabric TF 52, recovered from layer 121. Mica-dusted wares are suggestive of earlier Roman dating, being most prominent in Cirencester in the period *c.* AD 75–160 (CE V, 320–30).

*Structure 1.* A single sherd of samian was associated with Structure 1, from interior surface 025. This is identifiable as a South Gaulish Drag. 27 cup and is almost certainly Flavian (c. AD 70–100) in date.

## Period 2: Post-Roman activity

A number of layers of limestone rubble sealed the remains of the Period 1 structures and ditches, doubtless derived from the demolition of Structure 1. It is possible that the substantial limestone fragments recorded within the fills of Ditches 1 and 2 were deliberately deposited to firm up the softer ground of the infilled ditches. The demolition occurred in at least two phases, with the robber trench of Structure 1 wall 032 cutting rubble layers 021 and 037/038, but being sealed by 015. No evidence was retrieved to date these events.

## Period 3: Post-medieval and modern

The majority of the site to the north-east of Ermin Street was highly disturbed by post-medieval activity associated with the construction of the Foresters Arms in the mid 19th century. This had removed any further evidence for Ditch 2 and Structure 1. The uppermost metalled surfaces of Ermin Street had also been removed to provide a level foundation layer for the modern building, which in part was constructed directly upon the Roman street.

## OTHER MISCELLANEOUS OBSERVATIONS
## by Neil Holbrook

The locations of these observations are shown on Fig. 19.

### Street A (Ermin Street)

A.8 BINGHAM HALL. See above.
A.9 FORESTERS ARMS, QUEEN STREET. See above.
A.10 ST MICHAEL'S FIELD 1999. Geophysical survey in 1999 detected a linear band of resistance, *c.* 15m wide. For further details see p. 83.

### Street B (Fosse Way)

B.4 AKEMAN COURT, LEWIS LANE. Excavation of a test pit, 2.6 × 2.6m square, in 1999 revealed two successive surfaces composed of limestone fragments set in a gravel matrix, separated by a 0.25m thick layer of silt. The surfaces cambered downwards to the north-west. Sealing the uppermost surface was a fragment of a possible sandy mortar floor which might suggest that a late Roman building encroached onto the metalled area. The metalling revealed in the test pit lay *c.* 5m north-

west of the extrapolated edge of the Street B and so these deposits are more likely to be part of an external hardstanding which bordered the street (Havard 1999).

B.5 33 QUERNS LANE. Monitoring of groundworks revealed the south-eastern edge of the street. It was bounded by a ditch which had been recut on two occasions. A wide early ditch had silted up and was recut by a narrower and shallower V-shaped ditch filled with humic silty clay. This ditch was in turn replaced by a broad ditch containing sandy silt which was cut from above the top of the surviving street level. A building fronted onto the street within *insula* III (designated Building III.3). The fill of the primary ditch accumulated against the outside face of a stone wall. Internal deposits within the structure were heavily disturbed, but included a sequence of four successive mortar and limestone surfaces. A second wall which had been reconstructed on one occasion lay 7.5m to the south-east of the first wall. A possible stone-lined well lay within this room and 4th-century AD pottery was recovered from one of the floor levels. A third parallel wall lay 4m south-east of the second wall, beyond which traces of external surfaces were located. A sondage through these layers showed them to overlie 1m of grey-brown silty clay above natural gravel. This is most probably alluvium laid down in a pre-Roman river course (see CE V, fig. 3). Demolition rubble overlying the surfaces within the building yielded late 4th-century AD artefacts (CA 2002)

### Street C

C.6 COTSWOLD MILL. The location of Street C separating *insulae* II and III was identified near Cole's Mill in 1911 by F.W. Taylor (CE V, 27, C.1; location incorrectly marked on fig. 7 there but corrected on Fig. 19 of the present volume). Examination of Taylor's notes (Corinium Museum archives 18/3/16) shows that he recorded the position of the street, which he erroneously believed to be part of the Fosse Way, during the construction of a new pavement on both sides of Watermoor Road in 1911 (see Fig. 42, no. 1). The street was observed personally by Taylor in the north-eastern pavement but only by workmen on the south-western side and as such less weight can be attributed to this sighting. The Roman surface observed by Taylor lay 0.46m below the level of the pavement. Archaeological monitoring of a service trench immediately north-east of Watermoor Road associated with redevelopment at Cotswold Mill in 1998–9 now provides some new information (p. 62). The trench (see Fig. 42, trench 10) was excavated to a maximum depth of 1.8m, but extensive post-medieval disturbance was apparent throughout. However, over a small area measuring 2.2 × 1.3m at the base of the trench, a very hard compact surface composed of fragments of flat and sub-angular stones with some mortar was found. From such a limited exposure it is not possible to be certain whether this was part of Street C. Taylor's plan also shows a Roman well to the south-west of the former waterworks (see Fig. 42, no. 2), which combined with traces of Roman walls discovered in another service trench in 1998–9, suggest that the Street C cannot have lain wholly to the north-east of Watermoor Road as shown in CE V, fig. 7. More plausibly the street lies largely under the modern carriageway hereabouts, which also provides a common alignment with Street I on the other side of the Fosse Way. If this is correct the street does not align precisely with the side ditch and frontage of the buildings excavated at Price's Row 150m further south-east (Fig. 19, C.2; CE V, 228). It is possible that Street C was wider here, or else that a dog-leg lay at the junction with Street F at the southern corner of *insula* II.

## Street D

D.7 FORMER ANGEL CINEMA, LEWIS LANE. Geophysical survey, excavation and watching brief by Oxford Archaeology between 2004 and 2006 revealed further traces of the uppermost street surface. For further details see p. 51.

## Street E

E.3 23 VICTORIA ROAD. Evaluation revealed part of the uppermost surface of Street E in the anticipated location. It was sealed by dark brown silty clay containing later 4th-century AD pottery. To the south-west of the street thick deposits of demolition rubble testify to the presence of structures on the frontage of *insula* XIV/XV. Mortared walls and surfaces were found (CAT 2000a).

## Street G

G.2 52 CHESTER STREET. A test pit excavated as part of a *Time Team* television programme in 1999 revealed the north-west side of the street (see Fig. 20, 1999 trench 2). Part of the flanking ditch was emptied, and a sequence of earlier metalled surfaces was apparent in the side of the cut. The upper fill of the ditch comprised a sandy silt containing late 3rd or 4th-century AD pottery. This fill was partly sealed by a rough layer of compact limestone fragments, 0.12m thick, probably the uppermost street surface spreading over the infilled ditch. The surface was overlain by a further layer of sandy silt beneath a deposit of limestone

rubble (Hirst 2003). This trench now fixes the line of Street G and shows that *insula* VI is about 170m long, almost exactly the same size as *insula* I containing the forum.

G.3 GRAMMAR SCHOOL FIELD. Probing and rudimentary resistivity by Richard Reece in 1960–1 to the north-west of his excavation area indicated that Street G continued to the north-east of Street D for some distance, although it seemed to fade out thereafter. This observation does not match the alignment indicated by observation G.2, which suggests a dog-leg or re-alignment immediately north-east of Street D.

## Street I

I.6 3–7 ASHCROFT ROAD. Evaluation revealed the street close to its extrapolated position separating *insulae* XIX and XXa. The edges of both side ditches were encountered showing that the street was approximately 11m wide in the late Roman period. The uppermost street surface was composed of limestone fragments (CA 2005).

## Street L

L.6 52–4 ASHCROFT ROAD. A watching brief revealed a metalled surface on the projected line of the street on the north-west side of *insula* XXb. Two walls and associated floor surfaces lay to the north-west of the street within *insula* XXI/XXVIII (CAT 2000b).

WOOLMARKET CAR PARK. Evaluation test pits excavated by Oxford Archaeology failed to locate Street L on its projected alignment defining the north-west side of *insula* XVII. Robbed masonry walls were found (Oxford Archaeology 2006a).

## Street K

WATERLOO CAR PARK. An evaluation test pit, 1.5m square, failed to locate Street K in its anticipated location on the south-west side of *insula* XVI, instead finding the robbed wall of a Roman building. The street either lies in a different location to its projected alignment or else did not extend as far as this to the north-west of the Fosse Way (Coleman 1998).

# 3. PUBLIC BUILDINGS

## EXCAVATIONS ON THE SITE OF THE FORUM
### by Andrew Simmonds and Alex Smith

### Introduction

Between September 2004 and September 2006 Oxford Archaeology (OA) conducted a programme of archaeological mitigation during groundworks associated with the redevelopment of the former site of the Angel Cinema in Lewis Lane (NGR: SP 0263 0178) (see Fig. 17, no. 10 and Fig. 27). The site was located near the centre of Cirencester and comprised a rectangular plot measuring 116 × 37m encompassing an area of 0.43 ha, extending between Lewis Lane to the north-west and The Avenue to the south-east. Prior to redevelopment the front of the site was occupied by the former cinema building, which fronted onto Lewis Lane with car parking to the rear. The site sloped gently downwards toward the south-east, with an average current ground level of 110.5m AOD at the north-west end and 109.2m

AOD at the south-east. The site was situated within an area categorised by the Cirencester Urban Assessment as of high archaeological sensitivity (Darvill and Gerrard 1994, 167–9), and its south-eastern half lay within one of the thirty parcels of land that make up the scheduled ancient monument of the Roman town (Gloucestershire 361). Due to the archaeologically sensitive nature of the area in which the site lay, a programme of archaeological monitoring and recording was undertaken in accordance with conditions attached to the planning consent (Ref No. CT3902/P) and a condition of Scheduled Monument Consent (DCMS ref. no. HSD 9/2/4831) for the development provided by the Secretary of State.

### Archaeological background

The earliest recorded activity in the vicinity was the establishment of a cavalry fort in *c*. AD 45–50 a short distance from the site, on the south side of The Avenue (CE I, 60). Excavation on the plot adjacent to

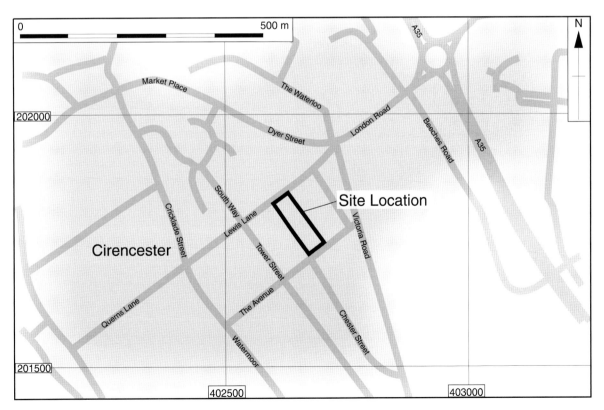

*Fig. 27*   Angel Cinema. Site location

*Fig. 28*   Angel Cinema. Plan of the site, showing locations of all evaluation trenches and test pits, in relation to the conjectured layout of the forum/basilica complex (after CE V, fig. 60)

the south-west side of the present site has uncovered evidence for civilian settlement associated with the fort (ibid.; although cf. Holbrook 2008). The present site encompassed the north-east range of the forum, the adjacent inter-*insulae* street and the south-west frontage of *insula* XIV/XV, where three wings of a large town house had previously been excavated at 17 The Avenue (CE III, 249).

After the end of the Roman period, the site lay outside the limits of the medieval town, forming part of an extensive area of meadow known as the 'Lewes' or 'Leauses' until the mid 19th century, when Chester House was built on the northern part, fronting onto Lewis Lane. The remainder became part of a landscaped garden surrounding the house.

### Evaluation results

The initial evaluation, carried out by CAT in 1997, comprised six small trenches (Fig. 28). This investigation uncovered a mosaic floor within the north-west range of the forum previously discovered in 1937 (trench 1), part of the north-east range of the forum including the outer wall and an adjacent gravel surface (trenches 3 and 4), the surface of the inter-*insulae* street

(trenches 2 and 6), and a sequence of surfaces including a limestone slab floor associated with a town house in *insula* XIV (trench 5) (CAT 1997). Subsequently OA dug a series of 14 test pits, nos 1–7 being part of geotechnical investigations and nos 8–14 intended to clarify specific issues regarding the depth, character and preservation of archaeological deposits. A possible wall or robber trench was recorded in test pit 1 and demolition rubble possibly associated with the destruction of the forum in test pits 5 and 10, but the remainder of the test pits were not deep enough to reach Roman levels and only post-Roman soil layers and modern deposits were encountered (Oxford Archaeology 2002a; 2002b; 2002c).

### Excavation methodology

Following demolition of the superstructure of the former cinema, the remaining wall bases were removed by hand down to the formation level of the development. The basement of Chester House survived beneath the former cinema building, and the backfill of this was removed, along with its internal walls. The outer walls, likely to be retaining archaeological deposits, and the basement floor were left *in situ* and the cavity was

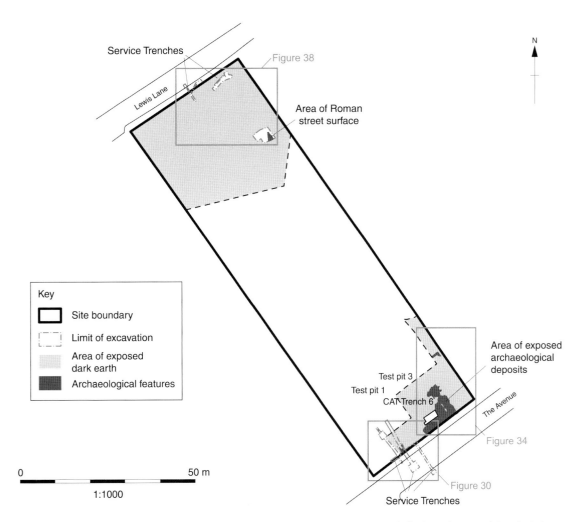

*Fig. 29* Angel Cinema. Plan showing areas where archaeology was exposed during the watching brief

backfilled with crushed concrete and consolidated. These works were subject to archaeological supervision and monitoring but no significant remains were observed.

Ground reduction was carried out across the site, comprising the removal of modern overburden by a mechanical excavator fitted with a toothless bucket down to formation level or to the top of post-Roman soil layers, whichever was encountered first. At the north-east end of the site soil layers were encountered at formation level, but at the south-east end these layers were exposed across an area of *c.* 275 m² at a higher level, and had to be excavated to formation level by hand. It was intended that a layer of undisturbed post-Roman soil would be left as a buffer between the formation level of the development

and the archaeological horizon, thus preserving the archaeological deposits *in situ*, but in the event the archaeological horizon was encountered at a depth of as little as 0.16m below ground level – higher than had been predicted from the information from trench 6 of the CAT evaluation, and above the proposed formation level. As a consequence, the excavation of the post-Roman soil layers resulted in the exposure of an area of *in situ* archaeological deposits measuring *c.* 28 × 14m (Fig. 29). Trench 6 was consequently re-excavated and re-recorded to clarify the position of the archaeological horizon. As the archaeological horizon was higher than expected, it was decided to avoid disturbing *in situ* archaeological deposits by laying new services and storm drains in this part of the site within pre-existing service and drain trenches. Foundation

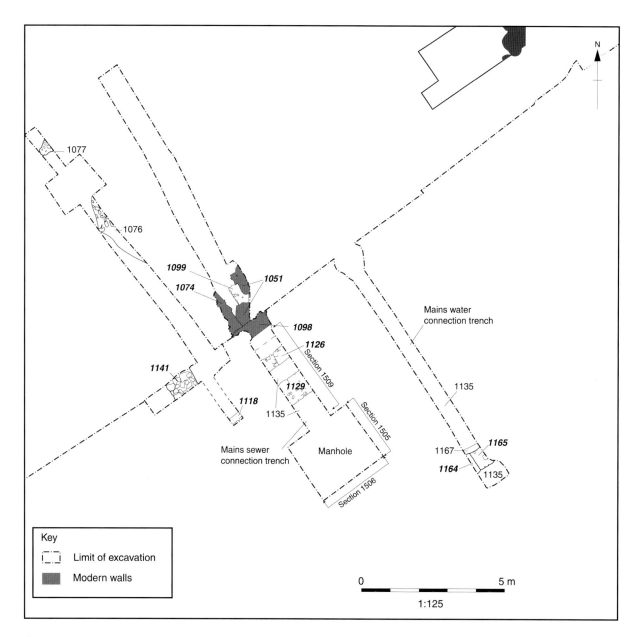

*Fig. 30*   Angel Cinema. Plan of features revealed in service trenches in the south-eastern end of the excavation

trenches were also dug to accommodate a new boundary wall on The Avenue frontage and along the south-eastern end of the boundary with the adjacent property to the north-east, and new service trenches were excavated across The Avenue. Archaeological remains were also exposed during the re-excavation of two existing service trenches along the Lewis Lane frontage of the site, and a small area of Roman street surface was exposed during ground reduction to the east of the footprint of the former cinema (Fig. 28).

All archaeological deposits exposed during the works were drawn in plan and recorded in accordance with standard OA practice (Wilkinson 1992), and the sections of the reopened service trenches were recorded prior to the new services being inserted into them. All spoil from the hand excavation of the post-Roman soil layers was scanned with a metal detector to enhance artefact recovery. No intrusive excavation of archaeological features was carried out.

## The archaeological sequence

### *Deposits exposed at the south-east end of the site*

#### *Mains sewer connection trench*

The deepest stratigraphic sequence recorded during the investigation was located in a manhole and associated service trench excavated in The Avenue for a mains sewer connection (Figs 30–31). The earliest deposits encountered here were a gravel and mortar surface 0.06m thick (1131) set on a bedding layer of gravelly clay (1130; n.i.) at the base of the manhole at 106.9m AOD, 2.2m below the current ground level. A sequence of thin layers of dark silty clay (1156–9) recorded in the southern part of the manhole appear to represent a build-up of occupation material associated with the surface. These layers were overlain by up to 1m of levelling deposits consisting of mixed gravel with bands of limestone rubble and lenses of clay and mortar (1137), with an upper layer of sandy clay

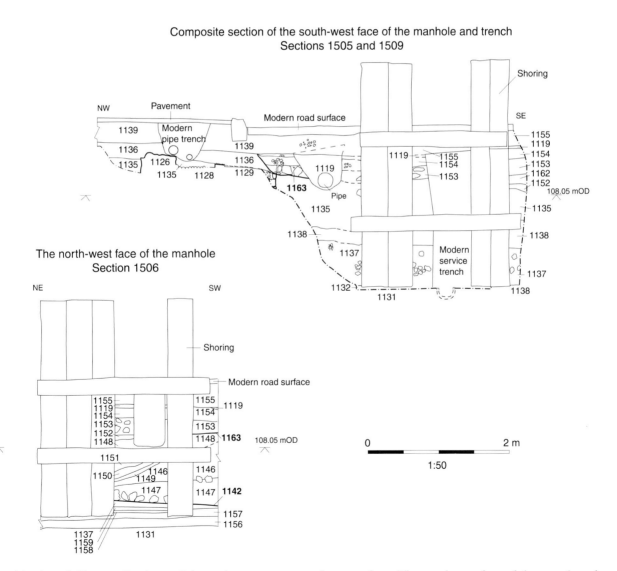

*Fig. 31*  Angel Cinema. Sections of the mains sewer connection trench. a. The north-east face of the trench and manhole. b. The south-west face of the manhole

*Fig. 32*   Angel Cinema. Wall 1126 seen from the north-west, showing the opening and the adjacent rebate. Wall 1129 can be seen in the background (scale 0.3m)

(1138). A thin band of compacted and possibly scorched, reddish brown clay (1160; n.i.) seen in the southern and western faces of the manhole at 107.9m AOD may have been the remnant of a surface overlying the levelling layers.

Two walls situated on parallel NE–SW orientations were recorded in the service trench associated with the manhole (1126, 1129; Fig. 32). Wall 1126 was 0.5m wide, constructed from limestone blocks bonded with gravelly brownish orange mortar, and was exposed to a height of two courses of stonework, or *c*. 0.25m. There was a step *c*. 0.2m high in the profile of the wall, the inner face of which was lined with a light pinkish grey mortar or plaster, and which is likely to be one side of an opening, perhaps for a door or window. An irregularly shaped rebate in the wall adjacent to this step may have been associated with the opening, but could equally represent damage caused during the demolition of the basilica. Located 0.55m to the south-east was a more substantial wall (1129), which measured 0.9m wide and comprised a core of limestone and mortar with dressed stones forming both faces. The north-west face of this wall (1118) was also exposed in a

small trench excavated 1.5m south-west of the mains sewer connection. A layer of limestone cobbles (1128) was exposed in plan between the two walls, and may be a deliberately constructed surface associated with one or both of these walls.

A block of limestone measuring at least 0.83 × 0.54m (1099) partly exposed a short distance north-west of wall 1126 may also represent the remains of a wall, although it was not certain whether the stone was *in situ* as it was partly obscured by the overlying post-Roman soil layer (1046) and by modern walls (1051, 1075, 1098).

All archaeological remains recorded in the mains sewer connection trench were sealed by post-Roman soil layers 1135/1136, which were 0.2m thick where overlying walls 1126 and 1129 and the possible surface 1128, but increased in thickness to as much as 0.65m to the south-east of wall 1129, where they overlay possible surface 1160 (n.i.) and the associated levelling layers. A substantial post-medieval pit (1142) was recorded cutting through the soil layers and truncating much of the stratigraphic sequence on the south side of the manhole, and was itself sealed by deposits associated with successive surfaces of The Avenue (1153–4, 1119, 1139, 1155).

*Mains water connection trench*

A wall was recorded extending on a parallel NE–SW orientation to 1126 and 1129, *c*. 6m further south-east than 1129, in a mains water connection trench that ran parallel to the mains sewer connection trench. The wall comprised masonry constructed from faced limestone blocks bonded with a lime mortar (1165), with the edge of a single large slab of limestone *c*. 0.7 m wide and at least 0.30 m high (1164) exposed at the south-west edge of the trench (Fig. 33). The latter may be part of an architectural element such as a pillar or column base, arch or doorframe. A deposit of demolition rubble (1167) butted the north sides of both 1164 and 1165, and was overlain by the post-Roman soil layer (1135), which was the only deposit exposed in the rest of the trench.

*Fig. 33*   Angel Cinema. Impost 1164 exposed in the south-west face of the mains water connection trench (scale 2m)

*Other deposits related to the forum/basilica*

Part of a wall (1141) lying on a NW–SE orientation was exposed during the digging of a foundation trench for a new boundary wall along The Avenue frontage of the site (Fig. 30). The wall measured 1.0m in width and is likely to be part of the north-east range of the forum. Two areas of limestone rubble and mortar (1076, 1077), interpreted as demolition material associated with the destruction of the forum, were exposed in a reopened service trench running along the south-western edge of the area where archaeological deposits were exposed.

*The inter-*insulae *street and other deposits exposed during ground reduction*

The inter-*insulae* street was exposed by ground reduction near the north-eastern end of The Avenue frontage, where it was recorded as being *c.* 4m wide

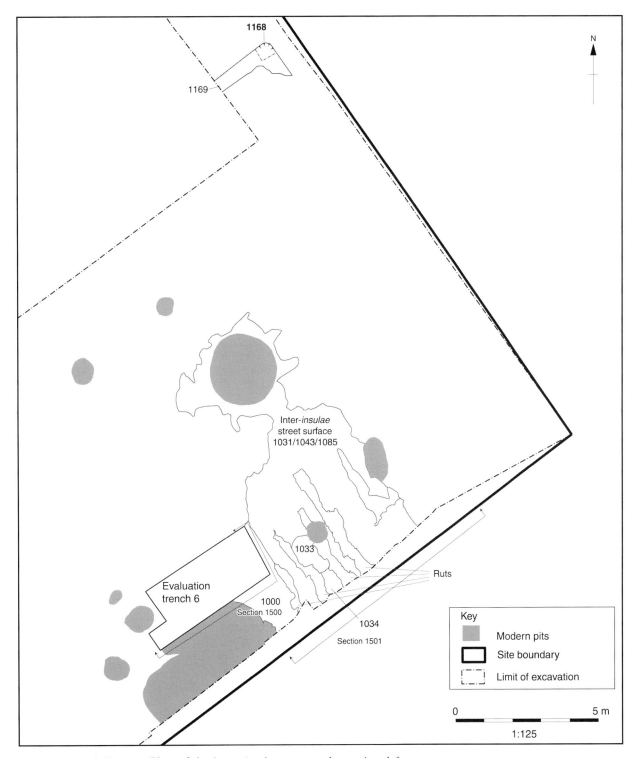

*Fig. 34* Angel Cinema. Plan of the inter-*insulae* street and associated features

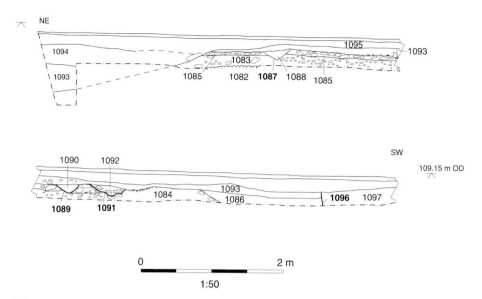

*Fig. 35*   Angel Cinema. Section through the inter-*insulae* street at the south-east end of the site

*Fig. 36*   Angel Cinema. The rutted surface of the inter-*insulae* street exposed at the south-eastern end of the excavation (scale 2m)

(Figs 34–36). Groundworks disturbed the agger to a depth of 0.25m, exposing a small area of compact limestone cobbling (1082) that is likely to have been a surface (Fig. 35), stained to a mottled orange colour by the effects of iron panning. This surface was sealed by a make-up layer of sand and gravel *c.* 0.2m thick (1083), on which was bedded the upper, final surface of the street (1031/1043/1085; Fig. 34), constructed from limestone cobbles up to 0.15m across. Pottery dating from the 4th century AD was recovered from this final surface. The surface was considerably rutted (Fig. 36), although there was some evidence for repairs in the form of a patch of limestone cobbles that may have been filling a pothole (1033), and at least one rut had been deliberately in-filled with a yellow sandy mortar (1034). However, most of the ruts were filled by a natural accumulation of brown clay silt (1088, 1090, 1092). Layers of silty sand (1081; n.i., 1084, 1086) were recorded on either side of the agger, most likely representing a build-up of material washed off the street surface, but without further excavation it was not possible to establish whether they lay within street-side

ditches or whether they were layers accumulating against the slope of the camber. These layers and the street surface were sealed by a thin accumulation of grey silty clay (1093) that increased in thickness to 0.36m to the north-east of the street.

CAT evaluation trench 6, which was situated a short distance to the south-west of the exposed street surface, was re-excavated and extended a short distance to the south west, and the section thus exposed was recorded (Fig. 37). A layer of hard, reddish brown sandy gravel (1078) was encountered at the base of the north-eastern end of the re-excavated trench 6, but only a small area of this deposit was exposed and it was uncertain whether it was the natural gravel or a metalled surface. The remainder of the stratigraphic sequence recorded in this trench comprised deposits (1m deep) of silty sand with varying, though not substantial, proportions of gravel (1000–4, 1008–1010, 1012–1014, 1023–4, 1027–8). As these layers were only seen in section, and had been partly dug away during the evaluation, it was not possible to establish their form or extent, and no artefactual material was recovered from them save a few sherds of pottery and small pieces of animal bone from layers 1023 and 1027. They had also been substantially disturbed by the digging of pits during the 19th–20th centuries (1005, 1017), and cannot easily be understood, although they clearly represent a build-up of material during the Roman period, the pottery from the uppermost deposits (1023, 1027) dating from no earlier than the mid 3rd century AD. The areas of cobbles at the north-east edge of the trench (1011, 1015) may represent the edge of the adjacent inter-*insulae* street, or may have been material displaced from the agger.

*Robber trench 1168*

An L-shaped feature (1168) interpreted as part of a robber trench was recorded during excavation of the foundation for a new boundary wall along the north-eastern edge of the site (Fig. 34). The trench cut the post-Roman soil layer (1170; n.i.) and was exposed

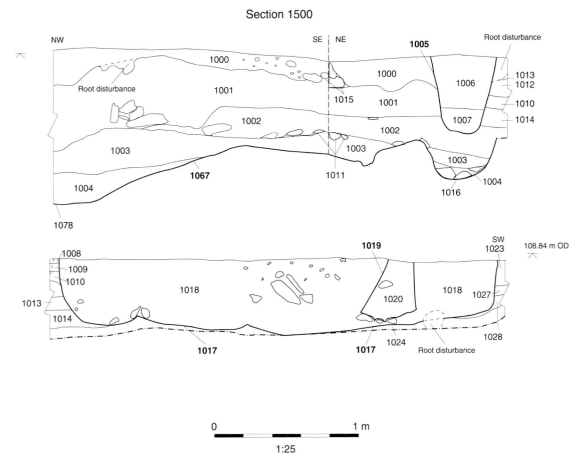

Section 1500

*Fig. 37* Angel Cinema. Section of re-excavated CAT trench 6

within the foundation trench for a length of 1.75m SW–NE, turning a right-angle to extend at least 0.95m towards the south-east. It is likely to have continued further towards the south-east, but was masked by modern garden soil (1171; n.i.). It measured 0.50m wide and at least 0.50m deep, and was filled by a deposit of limestone rubble and mortar (1169) from which a piece of painted wall plaster (sf 3262) was recovered.

*Modern pits*

At the south-east end of the site (Fig. 34) the post-Roman soil layer was cut by a number of pits containing material dating from the 19th–20th centuries, which also penetrated into the *in situ* archaeological layers. Pits 1005, 1017 and 1019 were exposed in section in the re-excavated CAT evaluation trench and were 0.50–0.85m deep, but the depth to which the other pits may have disturbed archaeological deposits is unknown as they were only recorded in plan.

**Remains exposed in service trenches at the north-west end of the site**

At the north-west end of the site archaeological deposits were exposed in two service trenches that were reopened for the insertion of new service connections (Fig. 38). A substantial wall and two

areas of metalling were exposed in plan at the base of the western trench, which extended into Lewis Lane. The wall (1113), probably the outer wall of the north-west range of the forum, was aligned NE–SW and measured 1.6m in width. It was constructed from roughly hewn limestone pieces up to 0.3m across and was neatly faced on at least its south-east side, and had been reused during the 19th century as a footing for the boundary wall of Chester House. The two areas of metalled surface (1114, 1115) were exposed in separate parts of the trench, and it was not possible to establish conclusively whether these were part of the same surface due to an intervening area of unexcavated ground, although both areas were to the north-west of wall 1113. The stratigraphic relationship between the wall and the metalled surfaces could not be established as this was masked by the lower part of the post-Roman soil layer. A layer of demolition rubble (1116) 0.25m thick overlay gravel surface 1115 and wall 1113.

The eastern trench was not re-excavated to the full depth of the original trench, but archaeological deposits including the south-western edge of the inter-*insulae* street were exposed in section (Fig. 39). The trench was *c.* 2.50m deep, excavated to 107.87m AOD, at which level a layer of silty sand (1108), likely to be part of the agger of the street, was exposed in the base of the trench. Above this, the lower half of the face of the trench was not exposed, and only the upper part of the agger could be recorded. This consisted of two layers of sandy make-up (1106, 1107), the lower containing a high proportion of limestone, and the final surface of the street (1105), which consisted of a layer of compacted limestone cobbles 0.15m thick. Material washed off the street surface subsequently built up against the edge of the camber, forming a layer of silty sand at least 0.35m thick (1104), partly overlain by a deposit of calcareous sand *c.* 0.85m wide (1111) that may represent the repair of a rut or pothole (1112) at the edge of the street. Both the repair and the layer of street wash were overlain by a metalled surface formed by a layer of gravelly sand 0.10m thick (1110) with limestone gravel set into its upper surface (1109), extending westward for at least 2m from the edge of the street surface and continuing beyond the edge of the trench.

The surface of the inter-*insulae* street was also exposed near the eastern edge of the site, where an approximately triangular area of compact gravel (1069) measuring 2.3 × 1.6m was uncovered, directly underlying the post-Roman soil layer (Fig. 38).

## The finds

### *Pottery* by Edward Biddulph

A total of 195 sherds of pottery, weighing 3157g, was recovered from the site. Of this, some 1650g, or 52% by weight, belonged to the Roman period. The remainder was largely post-medieval – probably 19th-century or later – with a smaller proportion of medieval pottery also represented. The Roman-period pottery was largely residual in post-medieval deposits and with this in mind the assemblage was quantified only to a basic level.

### *Assemblage composition*

Sixteen Roman fabrics were identified in total (Tables 1–2). Continental wares were represented by amphorae and samian. Sherds of the former were exclusively south Spanish (Baetican) (A11) and are likely to have belonged to the late Roman olive oil form Dressel 23, arriving after AD 250. Samian reached the site during the later 1st century AD from La Graufesenque (S20), and in the 2nd century AD from Lezoux (S30). Forms recognised in the latter included a Drag. 33 cup and possibly a Drag. 15/31 bowl. A base sherd, probably from a Drag. 18/31 dish, was also recorded.

Most British finewares came from Oxford sources (Young 1977). The red colour-coated ware (F51) was recorded as undiagnostic body sherds, and North Wiltshire colour-coated ware (F67) was recorded to a lesser extent. The Oxford industry was also the source of the mortaria present in the assemblage. These included a white-slipped oxidised ware mortarium (M31), and wall-sided (Young C97) and bead-and-

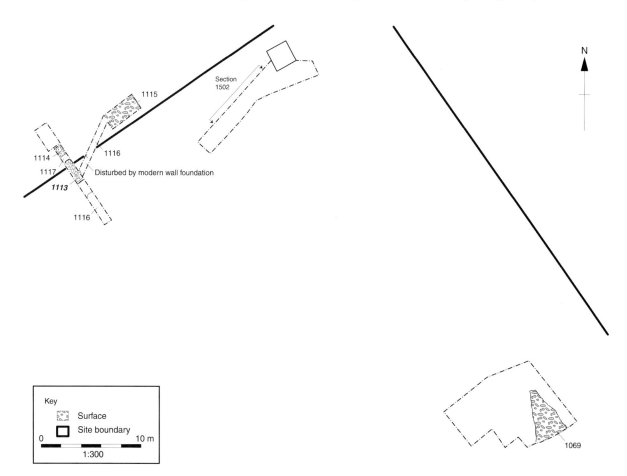

*Fig. 38*    Angel Cinema. Plan of the north-western end of the excavation

## Section 1502

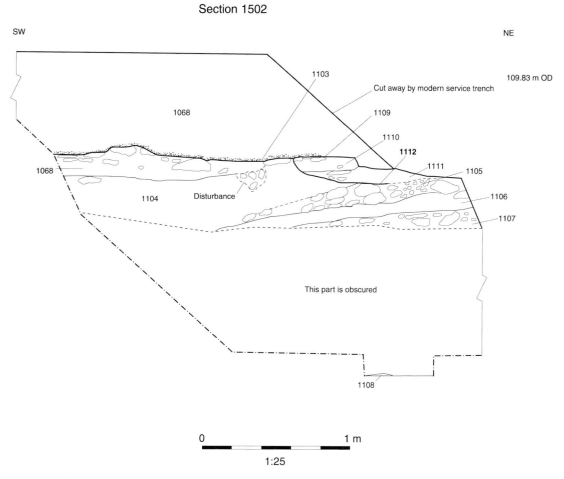

*Fig. 39* Angel Cinema. Section through the inter-*insulae* street exposed in the face of the re-excavated service trench at the north-western end of the excavation

**Table 1:** Pottery fabrics represented at the Angel Cinema

National Roman Fabric Reference Codes in parentheses after description (Tomber and Dore 1998)

| Ware | Description | Sherds | Weight (g) |
|------|-------------|--------|------------|
| A11 | South Spanish amphora fabric (*BAT AM 2*) | 3 | 423 |
| B10 | General handmade black-burnished wares | 19 | 190 |
| B30 | General wheel-made imitation black-burnished wares | 1 | 18 |
| C11 | Late Roman shelly ware (*HAR SH*) | 2 | 19 |
| F51 | Oxford red colour-coated ware (*OXF RS*) | 9 | 112 |
| F67 | North Wiltshire red/brown colour-coated ware | 4 | 19 |
| M31 | Oxford white-slipped ware mortaria (*OXF WS*) | 1 | 13 |
| M41 | Oxford red colour-coated ware mortaria (*OXF RS*) | 6 | 72 |
| O30 | Wiltshire oxidised wares | 1 | 7 |
| Q22 | South-west white-slipped ware (*SOW WS*) | 2 | 24 |
| R10 | General fine grey wares | 2 | 18 |
| R20 | General coarse sandy grey wares | 1 | 18 |
| R30 | General medium sandy grey wares | 47 | 620 |
| R85 | Medium sandy grey wares with abundant mica | 5 | 40 |
| S20 | South Gaulish samian ware (*LGF SA*) | 3 | 6 |
| S30 | Central Gaulish samian ware (*LEZ SA 2*) | 4 | 52 |
| Z20 | Medieval wares | 17 | 158 |
| Z30 | Post-medieval wares | 68 | 1348 |
| **Total** | | **195** | **3157** |

**Table 2:** Summary of vessel forms by ware at the Angel Cinema. Quantification by vessel count based on rims

| | B10 | B30 | C11 | M41 | O30 | R30 | R85 | S30 | Total |
|---|---|---|---|---|---|---|---|---|---|
| Flagon | – | – | – | – | 1 | – | – | – | 1 |
| Jar | – | – | – | – | – | 4 | – | – | 4 |
| Narrow-necked jar | – | – | – | – | – | 1 | – | – | 1 |
| Oval-bodied necked jar | – | – | 1 | – | – | 1 | – | – | 2 |
| 'Cooking-pot' jar | 4 | – | – | – | – | 3 | 1 | – | 8 |
| Conical cup | – | – | – | – | – | – | – | 1 | 1 |
| Carinated bowl | – | – | – | – | – | 1 | – | – | 1 |
| Straight-sided dish | – | 1 | – | – | – | 1 | – | 1 | 3 |
| Curving-sided dish | – | – | – | – | – | 1 | – | – | 1 |
| Mortarium | – | – | – | 1 | – | – | – | – | 1 |
| Wall-sided mortarium | – | – | – | 2 | – | – | – | – | 2 |
| Bead-and-flanged mortarium | – | – | – | 2 | – | – | – | – | 2 |
| **Total** | **4** | **1** | **1** | **5** | **1** | **12** | **1** | **2** | **27** |

flanged mortaria (Young C100) in red colour-coated ware (M41); the latter was among the latest of Oxford products, dating to the 4th century AD.

A small amount of white-slipped oxidised ware was present, and included sherds from south-east Gloucestershire or north Wiltshire (Q22), possibly from the Wanborough area (Tomber and Dore 1998, 192). Wiltshire potters are likely to have been responsible for the unslipped oxidised ware (O30) also present. A similar origin can be given to the reduced coarse wares (R10, R20 and R30), though a small amount may have arrived from Gloucestershire or the Oxford region.

No fine or coarse grey ware vessels were recognised, but forms in medium sandy grey wares comprised jars, including cooking-pot type jars and oval-bodied necked jars, and plain-rimmed (curving-sided) and bead-and-flanged (straight-sided) dishes. These forms date from the 2nd century AD onwards, with the bead-and-flanged dish characteristic of the period after AD 250. A very micaceous sandy grey ware (R85) was present to a lesser extent. The abundant mica gives the ware a south-western Britain source (P. Booth, pers. comm.), and the form recorded, a cooking-pot type jar, places its use from the mid 2nd century AD. Handmade Black-Burnished wares (B10) was second only to fabric R30 in quantity and arrived from Dorset or possibly from south-west Britain after *c.* AD 125. Cooking-pot type jars were recorded. These were complemented by locally made wheel-thrown imitation Black-Burnished wares (B30); a bead-and-flanged dish was recorded. A shelly ware (C11) oval-bodied, necked jar (cf. Going 1987, type G27) and a bead-and-flanged dish identified from a body sherd arrived from the Harrold kilns in Bedfordshire during the 4th century.

A small amount of medieval wares was recovered, including one sherd of a sandy ware complete with tooling marks on its external surface and probably of late Saxon date (J. Cotter, pers. comm.).

### Chronology

The assemblage spans the entire Roman period, although the early Roman material is negligible, and there is a strong late Roman emphasis, with some pieces likely to have been used well into the 4th century AD. It

had an average sherd weight of 15g (11g excluding amphorae) and included some large, relatively unabraded, pieces. Based on these factors, the possibility that post-medieval activity disturbed the latest Roman deposits and that the Roman pottery had been redeposited to some degree is a strong one.

### Coins by Paul Booth

Some 193 Roman coins and coin fragments were recovered during the fieldwork. This material is overwhelmingly of 4th-century AD date, with very late coins well represented. The fragments, however (some of which are very small), include pieces which are not closely dated and one or two which may not be Roman.

The coins are generally in good condition in terms of surface encrustation and corrosion, but many are very small and worn. They were initially scanned rapidly and then re-examined after selected pieces had been cleaned. Detailed identification has not been possible in all cases, particularly because of the issues of size and wear already mentioned. In most cases the mintmark, the key to identification of 4th century AD coinage, either did not survive or the flan was so small that it never accommodated the mintmark in the first place.

### Context

The coins were recovered from an area at the south-east end of the site. This was excavated in spits, usually down to the top of surviving archaeological deposits, as described above. The area concerned overlay parts of the north-eastern end of the basilica and of the adjacent north-west to south-east road to the east. The coins therefore include material derived from the very latest part of the Roman sequence on the forum site. Consequently the collection exhibits a number of distinct chronological biases (see further below).

### The assemblage

The assemblage is summarised in terms of chronological units in Table 3. These are defined with varying degrees of precision. No 'pre-radiate' (mid–late 3rd

**Table 3:** Chronological breakdown of the coin
assemblage at the Angel Cinema

| Approximate date range (AD) | Certain | Probable | Possible | Total |
|---|---|---|---|---|
| 250/260–295 | 8 | 2 | – | 10 |
| 330–335 | 26 | – | 1 | 27 |
| 335–341 | 22 | 5 | – | 27 |
| 330–341 | 3 | – | – | 3 |
| 341–348 | 5 | 2 | – | 7 |
| 330–350 | 1 | 1 | – | 2 |
| 348–353 | 3 | – | – | 3 |
| 350–365 | 32 | 16 | 2 | 50 |
| 330–365 | 1 | 1 | – | 2 |
| 364–378 | 9 | – | – | 9 |
| 378–388 | 1 | – | – | 1 |
| 388–402 | 21 | 6 | 1 | 28 |
| 350+ | 1 | 1 | – | 2 |
| 320+ / 4C | 10 | 5 | 1 | 16 |
| 250–400 | 1 | – | – | 1 |
| uncertain | 5 | – | – | 5 |
| **Total** | **149** | **39** | **5** | **193** |

century AD) coins were identified. Later 3rd-century
AD pieces formed only a small part of the assemblage
(10 coins), with a single further coin which might have
been of this period or later (assigned to a date range of
AD 250–400). The 3rd-century AD material included
two CONSECRATIO issues of Claudius II (*c.* AD 270)
and a probable coin of Tetricus I (AD 270–3); none of
the other coins of this date was assigned to a specific
emperor and most were probably irregular issues,
including the coin of Tetricus and perhaps one of the
CONSECRATIO pieces. Early 4th-century AD coinage was absent: only two coins, both fragmentary and
worn, could possibly have dated to the period before
AD 330.

The great majority of the coins were therefore of the
period from AD 330 onwards. The Constantinian peak
was well represented, by issues of URBS ROMA,
CONSTANTINOPOLIS and GLORIA EXERCI-
TUS (2 standards) in the period AD 330–5 and
almost exclusively by GLORIA EXERCITUS (1
standard) issues in the period 335–41. The 330–5
group included a 'mule' (SF3200) with an obverse of
URBS ROMA and a reverse of GLORIA EXERCI-
TUS (2 standards). Otherwise, only two irregular issues
of this period were definitely identified, but this is
almost certainly an underestimate. There were few later
Constantinian issues, and only two regular coins of the
period AD 348–53, including one of Decentius.
Irregular issues of this and the subsequent period
(together broadly *c.* 350–65) were particularly common,
however. Thirty-five coins were assigned to this period
with varying degrees of confidence, and further coins of
this period may be included in the categories dated 'AD
350+' (2 coins) and '4th century' (16 coins). The
former group is assigned to this date range largely on
the basis of size, and these coins are likely to have been
of one of two periods, 350–65 or 388–402, when coins
of small module were particularly common. Coins
dated 350–65, where identifiable, were mostly copies of

the FEL TEMP REPARATIO Fallen Horseman type,
but included four or five pieces which appeared to
imitate the VICTORIAE DD NN AUG ET CAE(S)
(two victories holding shield) type of Magnentius and
Decentius. Three coins (SF3001, 3067 and 3202) were
clearly of this type, while the identification was much
less certain in the case of SF3068 and 3209.

A relative absence of issues of the House of
Valentinian (mainly AD 364–78) is notable and not
readily explained: only nine coins were so dated, of
GLORIA ROMANORUM, GLORIA NOVI SAE-
CULI and SECURITAS REIPUBLICAE types (4, 3
and 2 examples respectively). A single coin of Magnus
Maximus (a SPES ROMANORUM issue of *c.* 387–8)
was identified. Thereafter the final period of significant
coin loss in Roman Britain (AD 388–402) was well
represented, with 28 coins, but as with the period AD
350–65 the degree of confidence in identification was
variable. These coins are typically small and poorly
struck. In many cases, therefore, although coins could
be assigned to the general period on the basis of the
victory reverse types, further precision of identification
was not possible (cf. CE V, 293).

Some 44 4th-century AD coins were assigned to mints
with varying degrees of confidence. The list of these
contains no surprises and is dominated by Trier (22)
followed by Lyons (10) and Arles (8), with a single issue
of Amiens, 2 of Aquileia and one possibly of Rome.

*Discussion*

The assemblage forms a useful addition to recently
reported material from Cirencester (CE V, 247–93)
providing in particular some insight into the character
of the latest deposits in the area of the forum. The use of
a metal detector to assist recovery means that the
present assemblage should be reasonably representative
of the material present in these deposits, although it
does not clarify the issue of which coins were in
circulation at the end of the Roman period and which
occurred in these deposits only as residual material. In
view of the nature of the excavation the strong
emphasis on the very latest coins, of the period AD
388–402, and the complete absence of coins earlier than
the second half of the 3rd century AD is unsurprising.
However the apparent emphasis on the latest coins is
put in perspective by comparison with the latest
components of the assemblage from nearby St
Michael's Field (*insula* VI), noted as producing a very
substantial proportion of all the coins of this period
from Cirencester (ibid., 264, 268, 280–1).

The comparison (Table 4) shows that at the Cinema
site the proportion of early and mid 4th-century AD
coins is significantly higher than at St Michael's Field,
despite work being confined to post-Roman levels. At
the latter site, however, all periods from the House of
Valentinian onwards are better represented, and
Theodosian coins are three times as prevalent as at
the Cinema. While activity involving coin loss at the
end of the 4th century AD and beyond was clearly
significant at the Cinema site, it was not on the same
scale as that seen nearby in *insula* VI. The Cinema coins
came from an area of *c.* 275m² at the south-east end of

**Table 4:** Comparison of mid to late 4th-century AD groups at the Angel Cinema with St Michael's Field

| Approximate date range (AD) | Cinema | | St Michael's Field | |
|---|---|---|---|---|
| | No. | % | No. | % |
| 330–348 | 76 | 45.0 | 138 | 22.0 |
| 348–365 | 55 | 32.5 | 113 | 18.0 |
| 364–378 | 9 | 5.3 | 54 | 8.6 |
| 378–388 | 1 | 0.6 | 8 | 1.3 |
| 388–402 | 28 | 16.6 | 315 | 50.2 |
| **Total** | **169** | | **628** | |

the site, giving an incidence of approximately one House of Theodosius coin per 10 m². This figure is in fact closely comparable to that inferred on the basis of the material noted from the late demolition deposits within the corridor of the *insula* VI courtyard building south of the forum (CE V, 134–5), but the significance of this, if any, is uncertain; as the 'dark earth' deposits, referred to in relation to the coins, were not discussed in the narrative of that excavation.

In relation to the duration of the final Roman phase at the Cinema site, it may be noted that 19 of the 28 coins of the period AD 388–402 were recorded as very worn or extremely worn. Allowing for some caution in assessing these data, they still suggest a relatively extended period of use after their date of minting and therefore imply activity in the forum area at least into the early decades of the 5th century AD, assuming that the soils in which the coins were found formed *in situ* rather than being imported from elsewhere in the town.

***Metal finds*** by Ian Scott

There are 77 metal objects from the site, excluding coins. These comprise 52 copper-alloy finds, 13 lead and 12 iron. The majority of the metal finds come from post-Roman soil layers, the only items from stratified contexts being two iron nails recovered from make-up layers for the inter-*insulae* street (1083 and 1106).

The copper-alloy finds were the most numerous, but all the dateable objects, with the exception of two fragments of Romano-British armlets (see below), were post-medieval in date. The lead objects comprise five medieval or post-medieval seals, four possible tokens or weights, three pieces of melted lead waste and a fragment of window leading. The iron finds comprise nine nails and three hobnails.

*Copper-alloy armlets* (Fig. 40)

1. Armlet fragment of thin D-section decorated with close-set transverse grooves. The fragment tapers to a narrow terminal apparently in the form of a head, possibly that of a snake. L 42mm. 1068, SF 3245.
2. Armlet fragment from a narrow band, decorated with crenellations with teeth between. Both terminals of the band are missing. L 40mm. 1068, SF 3270.

*Discussion*

There are several examples of armlets of D-section with transverse grooves from Colchester (Crummy 1983, 40, fig. 42, nos 1676, 1683 and 1684). One example from Butt Road (no. 1676) has a D cross-section and continuous transverse grooving, while the other examples from Balkerne Lane (nos 1683–1684) are of D cross-section with discontinuous blocks of transverse

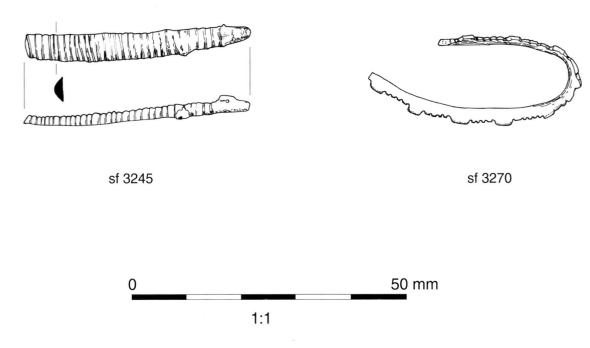

sf 3245                                        sf 3270

0                                        50 mm

1:1

*Fig. 40*   Angel Cinema. Copper-alloy armlets (scale 1:1)

grooving. The terminals on the Colchester examples lack the zoomorphic head terminal of the Cirencester example. Two of the Colchester armlets are from 4th-century AD or later contexts, and the third is unstratified. A similar, though not precisely similar, example of an armlet with transverse grooves and terminals identified as snakes' heads comes from Cirencester (Cool 1979, 168 and fig. 2B). It is a reasonable assumption that the head on the armlet under discussion was that of a snake. Snakes in the ancient world did not have the negative associations which tend to be applied in the modern world, but were associated with the paterfamilias and the household gods, the *Lares*, and had positive associations. They were also a symbol of death and rebirth. Snake jewellery and the associations of snakes are discussed more fully in Cool 2001.

Crenellated armlets like sf 3270 are quite common from late Roman contexts. Examples can be cited from Uley (Woodward and Leach 1993, 164–66, fig. 128, nos 1–2, 8 and 16) from late 4th-century AD or later contexts. An example from Colchester was found in a 4th- to 5th-century AD context in the Butt Road excavations (Crummy 1983, 40, fig. 43, no. 1659).

### *Worked stone* by Ruth Shaffrey

Little worked stone was recovered. A single whetstone of Old Red Sandstone was recovered from post-medieval pit 1005. It utilised what was probably a floor stone but which was unworked. Of more interest are five almost certainly Roman tesserae recovered from post-Roman soil layers 1046 and 1068. All five are roughly square or rectangular in plan and two have a single smoothed surface. All are made from the same hard limestone.

### *Building material* by Cynthia Poole

Ceramic, stone and miscellaneous building materials were recovered amounting to 86 fragments weighing 9694g. Sixty-three pieces (5815g) were of fabrics used during the Roman period (Table 5) and the remainder was of modern origin. The Roman material was recovered almost exclusively from the post-Roman soil layer and from post-Roman features, and no complete objects were recovered.

### *Roofing materials*

Roofing materials included both ceramic tile and roof stone, indicating that a variety of roofing materials were in use. Only one tegula flange survived complete, whilst others appeared to be deliberately removed, presumably to enable reuse in walls or floors. Imbrices exhibited no unusual characteristics, though one appeared rather thicker and may have been a piece of ridge tile. Some of the plain tile is likely to derive from tegulae.

Stone roofing material was equally sparse, only two fragments of pennant sandstone and limestone slabs being found, and as these were not from secure Roman contexts their date is uncertain. Only the limestone slab retained evidence of shaping with a trimmed curving edge.

### *Other building materials*

Three fragments of box flue tile were found, all of which had evidence of combing, in straight bands 35–45mm wide using combs of eight and nine teeth. On one with two diagonal bands forming an X, one of the spaces had been filled with a tightly curved horseshoe-shaped band of combing. One small fragment of cream sandy plaster (type M1) with a dark red painted surface was recovered from the backfill of robber trench 1168 and a fragment of mortar (type M3) characterised by its tile grit component was probably used in floor construction or wall render, but was recovered from the fill of a modern service trench.

### *Discussion*

The assemblage is typical of what might be expected from a Roman site in Cirencester, consisting primarily of roofing and walling. The different roofing materials may reflect alterations over time, variety for decorative effect or different roofing materials utilised in different buildings. The painted wall plaster recovered from the robber trench in *insula* XIV/XV indicates that the feature represents the remains of a building of some status. The presence of box flues indicates the presence of a heating system, but as this material was not recovered *in situ* it is not possible to establish whether it was associated with the forum/basilica complex or with a building in the adjacent *insula*. There is evidence that

**Table 5:** Quantification of Roman building material at the Angel Cinema by form

| Form | No. | Weight (g) | Thickness (mm) | Comments |
|---|---|---|---|---|
| Roof stone | 2 | 800 | 13–18 | Pennant sandstone, limestone |
| Tegula | 4 | 1485 | 20–24 | – |
| Imbrex | 19 | 339 | 14–21 | may include a ridge tile |
| Box flue | 3 | 873 | 15–20 | – |
| Brick | 3 | 600 | >40->50 | – |
| Plain tile | 11 | 1498 | 18–38 | – |
| Unidentified | 19 | 153 | – | – |
| Mortar | 1 | 60 | – | – |
| Plaster | 1 | 7 | – | surface painted red |
| **Total** | **63** | **5815** | | |

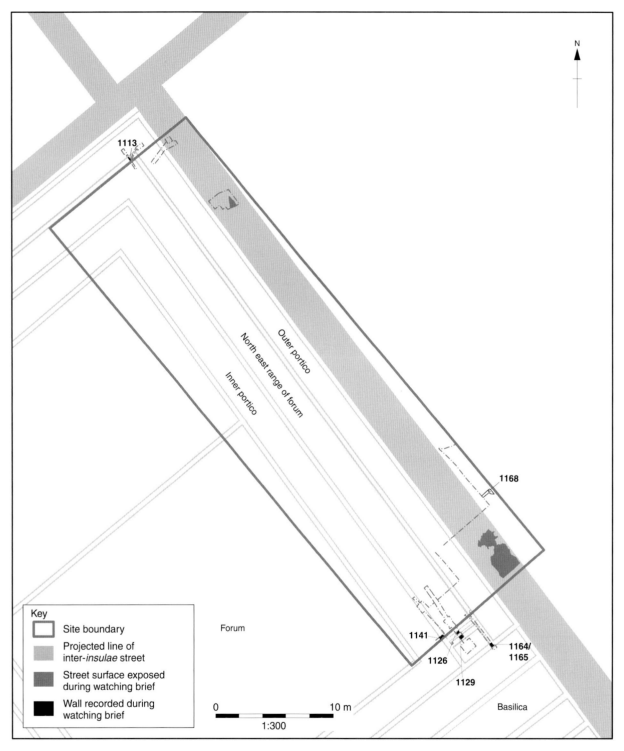

*Fig. 41*   Plan of the structures recorded during the watching brief at the Angel Cinema in relation to the forum/basilica complex

some of the building materials were reused, indicative of alterations to or rebuilding of structures in the area.

### Discussion

The programme of archaeological mitigation recorded walls that formed parts of the forum/basilica complex, as well as part of the surface of the adjacent inter-*insulae*

street and associated deposits and a robber trench associated with a building in the adjacent *insula* XIV (Fig. 41). Due to the nature of the fieldwork, which was intended to minimise disturbance to archaeological deposits, most of these remains were only recorded in plan, or in section in the case of layers exposed in the sides of service trenches, and consequently only features dating from the latest phases of Roman occupation were exposed. In the case of the walls of the forum/basilica complex, this means that generally only the upper surface of the masonry was seen. Previous excavations have demonstrated that walls within the complex can survive to a considerable height (CE V, fig. 67) and it is likely that the masonry recorded at the Cinema site was upstanding parts of the walls, which projected into the overlying post-Roman soil layers. As only the tops of the walls were exposed it was not possible to identify different phases of construction of the complex, or to establish the relative chronology of those walls that were recorded. No intrusive excavation of archaeological deposits took place, and consequently only a very small artefactual assemblage was recovered, most of which came from the post-Roman soil layers. These layers contained a mixture of Roman and modern artefacts and may be 'dark earth' layers that have been reworked as garden soils since the development of the area during the 19th century. As no evidence was uncovered for large-scale landscaping, it is assumed that modern cultivation has not displaced the artefacts within these layers any great distance from their original place of deposition, and that they can still be of assistance in interpreting the use of this area in the late Roman period.

The structural remains recorded during the investigation are consistent with the layout of the forum/basilica complex conjectured from previous excavations, and have added fresh details, particularly in relation to the area around the junction of the basilica with the north-east range of the forum. This is a part of the complex that had not previously been investigated, since earlier excavations had mostly been concentrated on the south-west end of the basilica, the north-west range of the forum and the adjacent part of the courtyard (CE V, 99 and fig. 60). Wall 1141 was part of the inner wall of the north-east range of the forum, and walls 1126 and 1129 appear to be partition walls within the range, which is likely to have been divided into a series of rooms, as is known to have been the case at other *fora* such as Caerwent and Silchester (Wacher 1995, figs 8 and 9). Walls 1126 and 1129 are *c.* 6 m from the north-west wall of the basilica, represented by wall 1164/1165, a distance that is consistent with the range of dimensions recorded for the rooms on the south-west side of the basilica. One or other of these walls is therefore likely to be the north-west wall of the room at the end of the north-east range of the forum, adjacent to the basilica. Due to the limited nature of the excavation it was not possible to establish conclusively how these two walls related to each other. Only a small part of each wall was exposed within the limited confines of the trench, and excavation did not extend deep enough to examine their foundations and establish whether they were associated with the same ground surface. As only the top of the surviving parts of the walls were exposed it is also not known how high above the contemporary ground surface the exposed parts are. If the walls are contemporary their proximity makes little sense, as they are only 0.55m apart: too close even for the walls of a narrow corridor, and the opening in wall 1126 would have opened onto the blank face of wall 1129. It is possible that one of the walls was demolished down to

the level of cobbled surface 1128 and the other built to replace it, perhaps in order to alter the sizes of the two rooms on either side, in the same way as the partition wall between rooms 2 and 3 on the south west side of the basilica was moved 1m to the north-east during alterations dated to the second half of the 4th century, enlarging room 2 at the expense of its neighbour (CE V, 108). This would certainly explain the opening in wall 1126, which would then be at the right level to be a doorway. However it is not certain that 1128 is a surface, and it would be difficult to reconcile this arrangement with the lower ground level recorded on the south-east side of wall 1129. On current evidence it is not possible to resolve this issue.

If walls 1126 and/or 1129 form one side of the final room at the end of the north-east range of the forum, gravel and mortar surface 1131, recorded at the base of the mains sewer connection manhole, may be the original floor surface within it, although this could not be confirmed as its stratigraphic relationships with the walls were obscured by unexcavated parts of the post-Roman soil layers. The sequence of deposits overlying this surface comprised a series of thin occupation layers overlain by demolition rubble. The final clay surface (1160) of this part of the forum is similar to a sequence recorded in the range of rooms behind the basilica in a trench dug at the rear of 12 The Avenue in 1994, where a mortar surface was overlain by a charcoal-rich occupation deposit, demolition rubble and a crude rubble surface (CE V, 112). The occupation deposit in the 1994 trench was dated to the later part of the Roman period by the presence of a coin of Victorinus (AD 268–70). The heights of the final surfaces in these sequences are strikingly similar, surface 1160 being found at a height of 107.88m AOD and that in the 1994 trench at 107.92m AOD, and also correspond with a gravel surface within the nave of the basilica recorded at 107.82m AOD. It is possible that the raising of the ground level with demolition material and establishment of new floor surfaces recorded in these two parts of the complex are part of a more widespread programme of refurbishment, perhaps associated with the modifications recorded elsewhere by Wacher and dating from the 4th century AD (CE V, 108–10 and 116–19).

The large slab of limestone (1164) partly exposed in the mains water connection trench, which formed part of the north-west wall of the basilica, may be part of a monumental frame for a doorway between the basilica and the portico along the north-east side of the forum, or an impost for a column or pillar if this opening was arcaded. Although only the north-east edge of the slab was exposed within the confines of the trench it appears to be similar to the imposts that supported the arcade dividing the rooms behind the basilica from the portico fronting onto the street to the south-east (CE V, 106).

No evidence was found for a portico along the outer side of the north-east range of the forum, fronting onto the adjacent inter-*insulae* street. In the final phase of Roman occupation the area between the forum and the street seems to have been occupied by the gravel surface (1110) exposed in section in a re-excavated service trench at the north-west end of the site, and which is presumably the same surface that was recorded further south-west in evaluation trench 4. There is also a parallel for this surface on the south-west side of the basilica, where a rough surface of mixed material including cobbles was laid down following the demolition of the portico (CE V, 109). The stylobate of that portico was buried 0.3m beneath the surface that replaced it, and it is possible that the portico along the north-east side of the forum was similarly demolished, and that the stylobate lies buried at a greater depth than that reached by the current groundworks.

The structural remains exposed at the north-west end of the site comprise part of the outer wall of the north-west range of the forum (1113) and two areas of gravel surface within the area of the adjacent outer portico, which may be either a surface associated with the portico or a later surface like those that replaced the north-east and south-east porticoes.

The robber trench recorded near the eastern edge of the site is the result of robbing of one of the walls of a town house that stood across the road from the forum/basilica complex in *insula* XIV. The painted wall plaster recovered from the backfill of the trench is consistent with the highly decorated nature of this house, which possessed at least five mosaics and presumably belonged to an individual of some wealth and importance (CE III, 249).

The assemblage of metal artefacts from the site was dominated by coins, and as a metal detector was used to assist recovery this is likely to be an accurate representation of the material present on the site rather than the result of any bias in collection. The apparently greater incidence of coin loss is presumably associated with the particular activities taking place in and around the forum/basilica, and is perhaps evidence for the continued role of the forum as the site of a market during the final phase of the Roman period. The assemblage includes coins dating from the very latest phase of Roman coinage in Britain (AD 388–402) and the worn condition of some of these latest coins suggests a relatively extended period of use after their date of minting and therefore implies activity at least into the early decades of the 5th century. This apparent continuation of commercial activity is significant evidence for the continued use of the forum as a civic building that contrasts with evidence for disuse and demolition of such complexes during the later 4th century AD at some other towns, such as Caerwent and Exeter (Wacher 1995, 418). The evidence from the exposed parts of the inter-*insulae* street between the forum/basilica complex and the adjacent *insula* XIV may also support the argument for the continuity of activity into the 5th century AD. The final surface of this road was constructed at some point during the 4th century AD, and its rutted condition suggests use continuing for some considerable length of time thereafter.

## EXCAVATIONS IN *INSULA* II AT COTSWOLD MILL, 1998–9
### by Neil Holbrook and Alan Thomas

### Introduction

CA undertook an excavation and watching brief between August 1998 and April 1999 on a site on the corner of Lewis Lane and Watermoor Road during the conversion of Cotswold Mill (formerly Cole's Mill) into residential accommodation (Thomas 1999) (see Fig. 17, no.6 and Fig. 42). An area 5.2 × 4.8m in size was examined within a grain silo inside the mill prior to the insertion of a new floor and a lift-shaft pit. After the removal by contractors of a concrete floor, three trial holes were excavated in order to evaluate the survival of archaeological deposits. In the event all three trial holes demonstrated that significant remains including stone walls survived just below the modern make-up. The lift pit, 2.7 × 2m in area, was sited so as to avoid extant Roman walls and was archaeologically excavated to a depth of 1.5m (trench 9; Fig. 42). Thereafter the trench was shored and half of it further excavated to the natural gravel (a change in the design of the lift shaft rendered the excavation of the remaining half of the pit unnecessary). The lift pit was excavated under artificial light and in cramped conditions, especially after the insertion of the shoring. The remainder of the area in the former grain silo was lowered to the top of archaeological levels which were planned before being covered with a protective layer of terram fibre and polythene. A further 13 trenches for foundations or services, within or in the grounds of the mill buildings, were excavated by contractors under archaeological supervision. In two cases (trenches 10 and 14) archaeological deposits were identified and excavation was continued by CA staff to the depth required by the builders. The other trenches were either too shallow to encounter archaeological deposits or had been subject to post-medieval disturbance resulting in the loss of earlier levels.

The pre-Roman ground level was identified in Trench 9 at a depth of 3.06m below the current street level of Lewis Lane. The succeeding Roman deposits in the excavations clearly relate to structures within the western corner of *insula* II, and to Street C separating *insulae* II and III. The evidence for the street is described under observation C.6 elsewhere in this report (p. 43). Despite the extensive post-medieval and modern use of the area, archaeological deposits generally survived in an excellent state of preservation and it is probable that over much of the site Roman levels survive in excess of 3m thick.

### Results

*Trench 9* (Figs 42 and 43 sections 1 and 2)

Natural gravel 967 was covered by 0.1m-thick reddish-brown clay subsoil 966 and 0.2m-thick greyish-brown silty clay 957, which mark the pre-Roman ground surface. This surface was cut by the foundation trench 980 of a stone wall aligned north-west to south-east

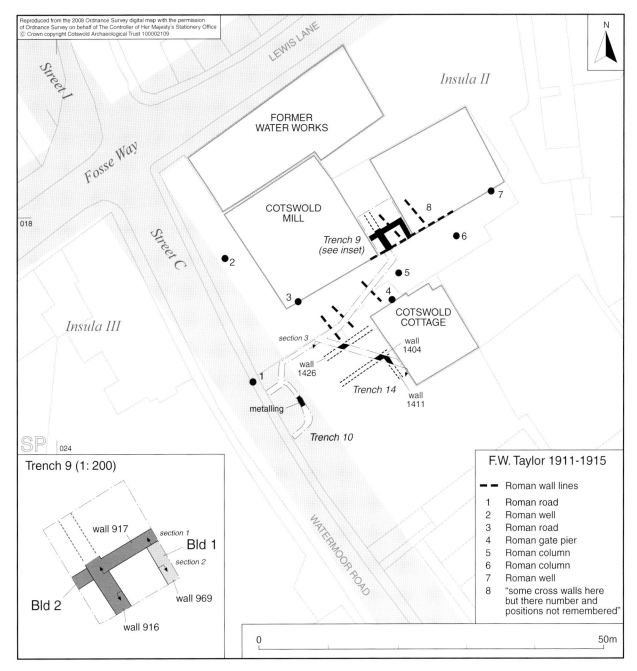

*Fig. 42* Cotswold Mill. General plan of 1998–9 investigations with details added from F.W. Taylor's sketch plan of 1915 (1:500)

(Building 1). The wall was built from trench-laid rubble and gravel foundations 972 supporting a 0.49m-high plinth 971 composed of four courses of mortar-bonded dressed limestone facing stones. Above the plinth there was an offset of 140mm and further courses of stonework bonded with an identical pale brown mortar which survived to a height of 0.59m (969). Neither the width of this wall nor the full depth to which the foundations cut into the natural gravel were established.

To the south-west of the wall the turf line was covered by layers of gravel make-up (956, 955) for a 60mm-thick yellow gravel surface 981 which lay just below the top of the plinth. The surface was cut by a shallow pit 965 which had been dug directly up against the plinth. The pit was covered by stony make-up 962 beneath a thin trodden surface 961, and a pale brown mortar and gravel surface 960, which was level with the top of the plinth. Cutting this surface was a series of pits, the first of which (952) was not fully investigated. It was excavated to a depth of 1.37m and augered for a further 0.9m before reaching the natural gravel. The pit fills (958, 954, 953, 937) produced 30 animal bone fragments and 28 sherds of pottery. The pit was recut (982) and had accumulated fills 951 and 935 before an oven was cut into the top of it. Oven 940 was of two phases, the later of which comprised a cracked stone base with fired clay and slab surround 944. A sample

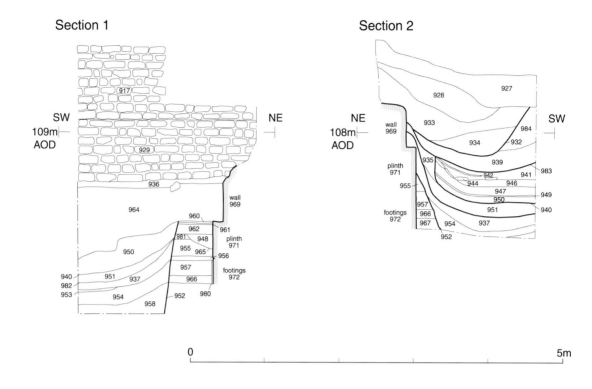

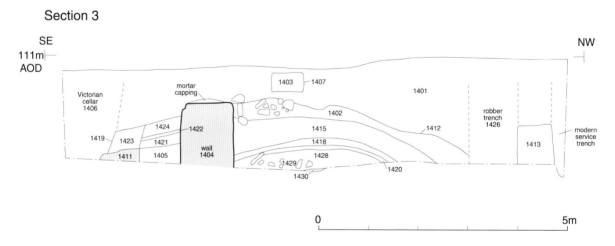

*Fig. 43*   Cotswold Mill. Section 1 (trench 9), Section 2 (trench 9) (both 1:50); and Section 3 (trench 14) (1:75)

from the oven produced large pieces of charcoal and a small amount of charred plant remains. The oven subsided into the pit over time and was sealed by further fills (939, 984) which were cut by pit 932 containing fills 934 and 933.

After the final infilling of the pits the surrounding ground level was raised by 1m by the dumping of spreads of gravelly clays heavily mixed with red clay and numerous tile fragments, possibly a product of the demolition of Building 1 (928). The demolition debris of Building 1 was cut by the walls of a new structure (Building 2), however the foundation trenches for these walls were difficult to identify with certainty due to the conditions in which the excavation was carried

out. The foundations consisted of undressed rubble footings 964 set in a gravel matrix, their upper surface covered by a thin layer of mortar and gravel 936, probably a working surface associated with the construction of the mortared upper courses. The sequence in which the two walls were constructed was readily apparent. The south-west wall was constructed to a height of seven courses, the north-west wall 929 butting directly against this work. Above this level both walls (916 and 917) were bonded together for the further surviving nine courses. Only the top four courses of wall 916 were mortared flush to the face suggesting that it had been rebuilt or repointed above this level.

Very little evidence survived for the activities carried out within this part of Building 2. A 0.6m-deep pit 920 (n.i.), which cut the dumps associated with the demolition of Building 1, was found on the south-eastern edge of the trench. This pit was sealed by dumps of gravel mixed with silty clay 918 (n.i.) and a pale brown gravel 915 (n.i.), the surface of which roughly coincided with the base of the flush-pointing on wall 916. Surface 915 was covered by a stony make-up for a second gravel surface 913 (n.i.). Outside of the area of the lift shaft further levels were identified which can be assigned to this period. The north-western continuation of wall 916 was traced for a short distance before it was cut away by a medieval pit. Another wall butted onto and formed a south-western continuation of wall 917. This latter wall had been robbed in the medieval period thereby destroying its stratigraphic relationships, but it was probably associated with an *opus signinum* floor to the south-east, which was sealed by subsequent floors of cracked stone slabs and rounded cobbles respectively.

The uppermost Roman levels within and outside the lift shaft were sealed by a black loam 901 (n.i.), up to 0.36m thick, which contained a large quantity of stone rubble and tile demolition debris. Two medieval pits and a stone wall were found in the area immediately to the north-west of wall 917. The wall 908 (n.i.) lay at right-angles to the line of Lewis Lane and consisted of thin stone slabs. It had been reused in the mill building as a foundation for an internal wall. Butting onto this wall was a stone-lined pit 902 (n.i.), *c.* 1m square. Its fill was partially excavated to a depth of 0.7m and produced pottery of 12th to 15th-century date along with residual Roman sherds. The south-eastern corner of this pit had been cut by a further pit which had been dug up to the face of Roman wall 917. This pit was only partially excavated and it produced no artefacts.

### Trench 14 (Figs 42 and 43 section 3)

Trench 14 was excavated to a maximum depth of 2m. Two parallel walls aligned north-east to south-west were found (Building 3). They probably defined a corridor 3.5–4m wide. One of these walls was represented only by robber trench 1426 but the other (1404) survived in excess of 11 mortar-bonded courses (1.26m) high. It was approximately 0.6–0.9m wide and bonded at right-angles with another wall 1411 which had been heavily robbed. Within the corridor silty clay 1430 was the earliest deposit exposed at the base of the trench. It was covered by stone and gravel make-up 1429.The make-up was sealed by a patchy yellowish-brown mortar floor 1428 which was covered by a probable occupation layer of charcoal-flecked silty clay with patches of gravel 1420, and a second yellow-brown mortar floor 1418. All of these layers had slumped sharply to the north-west and south-east, suggesting the presence below the base of the trench of cut features containing loose uncompacted fills.

Floor 1418 was sealed by a 0.35m-thick make-up 1415 containing frequent stone rubble and spreads of mortar and gravel. This may mark demolition or rebuilding of the structure. Only the top two courses of

wall 1404 were flush-pointed suggesting that the wall was either rebuilt or heightened from above this level. The top of the wall was capped by a cambered layer of mortar, indicating (in the latest phase at least) that this was its full height. It probably served as a stylobate supporting a colonnade (it does not appear to be high enough above the level of floor 1418 to have served as a wall supporting a colonnade of dwarf columns).

In the angle between walls 1404 and 1411 a sequence of layers was revealed which, within the limited confines of the trench, could not be clearly understood. The earliest of these was silty clay 1405 which was covered by gravelly mortar 1421 and a thin deposit of heavily charcoal-stained black silty clay 1422. As with the deposits inside the corridor these layers had also clearly slumped to the south-east. To the north-west of the corridor a yellow-brown gravelly mortar 1431 at least 0.76m thick was found. Its interpretation is uncertain.

The demolition of Building 3 is represented by a dump 1402/1424 of pale brown mortar packed with rubble and tile. The Roman levels were covered by a thick layer of black loam 1401 which incorporated a stone-lined drain 1407 which produced a medieval potsherd. No differentiation could be made between 1401 and the fills of robber trenches 1426 or 1419.

### Trench 10 (Fig. 42)

Trench 10 was excavated to a maximum depth of 1.8m, but extensive post-medieval disturbance was apparent throughout. A fragment of external surfacing, possibly part of Street C, was found. This is discussed elsewhere (p. 43).

### Dating evidence

*Trench 9*

Pit 952: *Pottery* (28sh.): early Wiltshire oxidised and reduced sandy wares, a grog-tempered sandy ware, Dressel 20 amphora, South Gaulish samian, wheelmade black-burnished ware, and Dorset Black-Burnished ware. A later 1st or early 2nd-century AD date is likely for this small group.

Pits 982 and 932: *Pottery* (30sh.): pottery of generally later 1st to early 2nd-century AD date.

Levelling 928 etc. *Pottery* (142sh.): Dorset Black-Burnished ware, Wiltshire finer wheelmade grey wares, a decorated samian sherd with a cursive mould-makers signature below the decoration, other samian wares, south Spanish Dressel 20 olive oil amphora and North Gaulish mortaria. Overall this assemblage is consistent with an early to mid 2nd-century AD date with a residual 1st-century AD component.

Pit 920. *Pottery* (10 sh.): Oxfordshire red-slipped ware mortarium and triangular-rimmed jar in late Roman shell-tempered ware suggesting a date after *c.* AD 360 for its filling.

Dark earth 901: *Pottery* (40 sh.): 4th-century AD Oxford-shire bowls and mortaria, along with some medieval sherds.

*Trench 14*

Make-up 1429: *Pottery* (4 sh.): red-slipped mortarium, probably from Caerleon, Dorset Black-Burnished ware and Wiltshire reduced wares consistent with a date in the 2nd century AD.

Silt 1405: *Pottery* (1 sh.): Oxfordshire mortarium of later 3rd or 4th-century AD date.

Demolition dump 1402: *Coin*: *follis,* early decades of the 4th century AD.

## Artefacts

### The coins by Peter Guest

1. *Follis,* early decades of the 4th century AD. 1402.
2. Local copy overstruck on top of an earlier official coin. The copy is of the common Falling Horseman type that dates to the period AD 350–64, while the coin flan was originally struck in AD 347–8 as a two victories type. Such overstrikes are relatively common from Roman Britain and it is thought that production of these copies dates either to the years immediately after the demonetisation of the two victories type between AD 348 and 352, or to the years AD 360–4 when the supply of official coins to Britain did not meet demand. 1406, unstratified.

### The pottery by Jane Timby

Approximately 418 stratified sherds of Roman to post-medieval date were recovered from the site, the vast majority from trenches 9 and 14. Some 87% are of Roman date, 7% medieval and the remainder post-medieval. Most of the fabrics have been well documented from other excavations in Cirencester and so tell us little about the status and function of the buildings. Full details are contained in the archive. One unusual vessel of note is a mortarium in a hard creamish-orange fabric with a darker orange, slightly streaky core. The paste is very fine with a sparse scatter of dark brown iron, orange argillaceous inclusions (grog) and sub-angular white ?calcareous inclusions. The trituration grits appear to be the same as the argillaceous inclusions in the paste, with fragments up to 2–3mm in size. It is possibly equivalent to TF 33 (CE I, 157) dated to the pre-Flavian or Flavian period, and is probably a Rhenish import from near the Eifel region where mortaria with red grog trituration grits were made and imported into Britain in the 1st century AD (Davies *et al.* 1994, 71).

**Table 6:** Quantities of animal bone from selected deposits at Cotswold Mill

**KEY:** *Bos* = cow; *Equus* = horse; *ovid/caprid* = sheep/goat; *Sus* = pig; *Gallus* = chicken (bantam); LAR = large artiodactyl (horse, cow, deer); SAR = small artiodactyl (sheep, goat, pig, small deer); small = small mammal (cat, dog, etc.); v. small = rodent; unid. = unidentified

| Context | Feature | No. | Species |
|---|---|---|---|
| 901 | n/a | 49 | *Bos* (16); LAR (12); unid. (12); *ovid/caprid* (5); *Equus* (2); *Sus* (1); *Gallus* (1) |
| 921 | 920 | 31 | unid. (12); LAR (8); *ovid/caprid* (5); *Bos* (4); SAR (1); feline (1) |
| 923 | 920 | 12 | *Bos* (3); LAR (2); small (2); unid. (2); *ovid/caprid* (1); SAR (1); *Sus* (1) |
| 937 | 952 | 22 | LAR (8); *Bos* (5); *ovid/caprid* (4); small (3); v. small (2) |
| 954 | 952 | 6 | *Bos* (3); *ovid/caprid* (2); unid. (1) |
| 958 | 952 | 2 | *Bos* (1); LAR (1) |

## Biological remains

### The animal bone by Tracey Stickler

Thirty-four contexts produced 281 animal bones. Full details are contained in the archive. Of the bone identifiable to species in Roman deposits, cattle were the best represented (46 bones) followed by sheep/goat (26), pig (4), horse (2), bantam (2), feline (1) and dog (1). This accords with the species representation found in other faunal assemblages in Cirencester (CE V, 369). The majority of the bone came from the fills of pits 952 and 920, and late/post-Roman loam 901 (Table 6). Some 62% of the specimens had been fragmented, and 30% display butchery marks. Weathering evidence is scarce (8%) with 39% of specimens being in a normal condition.

### The environmental evidence

A sample of 10 litres was taken from the fill of oven 940, and floated using a 250 micron sieve to catch the flot. The sample was sorted and the extracted plant material identified under a low-powered binocular microscope. The sample contained several large fragments of oak charcoal, *Quercus* sp. Few other plant remains were recovered. These consisted of one wheat grain, *Triticum* sp., which could not be identified further, two seeds of possible ribbed meliot, *Melilotus officinalis,* a seed tentatively identified as prickly poppy, *Papaver argemone* L., and a seed of knapweed, probably cornflower *Centaurea cyanus* L. although given the similarity of seeds of *Centaurea* sp. no certain identification could be made.

Prickly poppy and cornflower both prefer drier, light sandy or loamy soils, while ribbed meliot is common on such soils (Hanf 1983). All three are also common within cultivated or arable fields, with ribbed meliot also being a fodder plant. This species too has some interest as it possibly a Roman introduction.

Unfortunately the lack of plant remains in the sample does not aid in any interpretation of the function of the oven discussed above.

## Discussion

No pottery was recovered from the earliest levels associated with Building 1 and little can be deduced of its plan or function. The pits to the south-west of wall 969 may relate to either occupation or disuse of the structure. Given the late 1st to early 2nd-century AD date of the reasonably sized pottery group from pit 952, and the fact that this is later than two successive mortar surfaces associated with the use of the building, it is likely that Building 1 was constructed in the late 1st century AD. Pottery associated with the demolition of Building 1 dates to the early–mid 2nd century.

Building 1 was replaced by a new structure laid out to a different plan. The absence of a substantial build-up in stratigraphy within the angle formed by the walls suggests that this area was outside the building. The area to the south-west of wall 916 on the other hand clearly lay inside the structure as a poorly preserved *opus signinum* floor was found here. A late 4th-century AD pit was dug in the external area, sealed beneath further make-ups and a possible surface suggesting the continued use of the building until at least this date. In seeking to interpret the findings we can also make use of a sketch plan produced by F.W. Taylor during the replacement of the pavement of Watermoor Road in 1911 and construction work inside the mill in 1915 (Corinium Museum archives 18/3/16). Taylor marks the approximate position of some walls in the vicinity in trench 9 (Fig. 42). It is likely that one of these is the slightly misplotted alignment of wall 917 of Building 2, and that there were at least two north-west to south-east aligned walls defining rooms to the north-west of wall 917. One of these walls may be the same as the north-westerly continuation of 916. Parallel with wall 917, and lying *c.* 6m to the south-east, Taylor records two Roman columns beneath a wall of the mill building (Fig. 42, nos 5 and 6)

As wall 1404 in Trench 14 appears to have been a stylobate supporting a colonnade it is probable that a courtyard lay to the south-east of it. To the north-west of the corridor Taylor records three walls suggesting that rooms lay here. Beyond these he shows an area of metalling that he interpreted as a street surface (Fig. 42, no. 3), although it is more likely to be part of an external yard judging from the probable alignment of Street C (p. 43). The walls survived several feet higher than the top of the metalling. Adjacent to the most north-easterly of the cross walls Taylor records a pier protruding from beneath the foundations of Cotswold Cottage (Fig. 42, no. 4). His sketch shows a base with two half-round mouldings supporting a square block 0.6m thick. On top of this was a second block 0.33m thick with two rebates cut from the front corners and two further shallow rebates on the one visible side. It is likely that these blocks formed an impost supporting an arch of a gateway or arcade.

The top four courses of wall 916 of Building 2 and the top two courses of wall 1404 of Building 3 were much better pointed than the lower work, suggesting that these sections of wall were a later rebuild. Certain similarities can be drawn with the treatment of the public building (probably a range of shops) on the south-east side of *insula* II. Here the external portico was rebuilt in Period 3 (early–mid 2nd century AD) with well-pointed masonry, and the top of the stylobate wall was rendered with a flat mortar surface (CE V, 181). Little dating evidence was associated with Building 3, although it may have been in existence by the 2nd century AD if weight can be attributed to the four sherds of this date from make-up 1429. The building evidently continued in use into the 4th century to judge from material associated with its occupation and demolition.

Little can be said of the plan of the structures in this corner of the *insula*, although the traces that we have suggest a public building which originated in the late 1st century AD. *Insula* II contained the public baths of Corinium, and it is plausible that the Fosse Way frontage might have been occupied by a similar range of shops to those examined on the south-eastern frontage of the *insula* (CE V, 188). Indeed the buildings within the *insula* might have been planned and constructed as a unified programme of works. The slender dating

recovered here, and that associated with the construction of the Period 2 shops on the south-east side of the *insula*, suggests a date for the event at either the very end of the 1st century or early decades of the 2nd century AD.

Lewis Lane was an important thoroughfare in the medieval period, and the medieval features in trench 9 are probably associated with a structure fronting the south-eastern side of that street. The only stratified pottery was of 12th to 15th-century date.

## THE PROBABLE THEATRE AND SURROUNDING AREA: OBSERVATIONS IN 1969
### by Peter Grace and Neil Holbrook

Observations within various small trenches in 1962 and 1966–8 have combined to make it likely that a Roman public building, very probably a theatre, lay within *insula* XXX just inside the Gloucester Gate (CE V, 142–5). Further information on archaeological deposits in this area was recovered by Peter Grace in 1969.

### Observations during the Dollar Street, Thomas Street and Coxwell Street 'Triangle' Development 1969 by Peter Grace

Observation and recording occurred during site clearance and the excavation of trench foundations for the third phase of the Triangle development. A number of builders' trenches were observed to the east of the theatre, adjacent to trenches BWI and BWII where fragmentary traces of successive timber and stone buildings had been found in 1962 (Fig. 44). Three walls were found during construction in this area, all 0.76m wide of dressed mortared stonework. Walls A and B survived 0.6m high. A robber trench (D) abutted wall C and the area contained within these walls was covered with a mortar and stone surface. Some 4.8m to the south-east of the robber trench the line of a second robbed wall (E) was detected. The space between the two walls was occupied by a mortar floor. To the south-east of the second robber trench a deposit of clay containing fragments of charcoal and oyster shell was found. Artefacts were scarce in this area, but fragments of a glass goblet (identified by Mr J. Real as a Syrian product dateable to the 3rd century AD) lay on the surface of the mortar floor and numerous pieces of roof tile upon the cobbled surface.

Builders' trenches further to the west uncovered traces of the probable theatre. The observations lay very close to trench BWVI excavated in 1962 and, indeed, given the difficulties in surveying in both 1962 and 1969 it is conceivable that the remains examined in 1962 may have been at least partially re-exposed in 1969. At the very edge of the builders' trench the face of a wall standing at least six courses high was exposed (Wall 1). This was abutted by a second wall at a very oblique angle (Wall 2). Both walls had pitched stone footings. Just to the south of the intersection a robber trench abutted Wall 1 at right angles, and at the extremity of

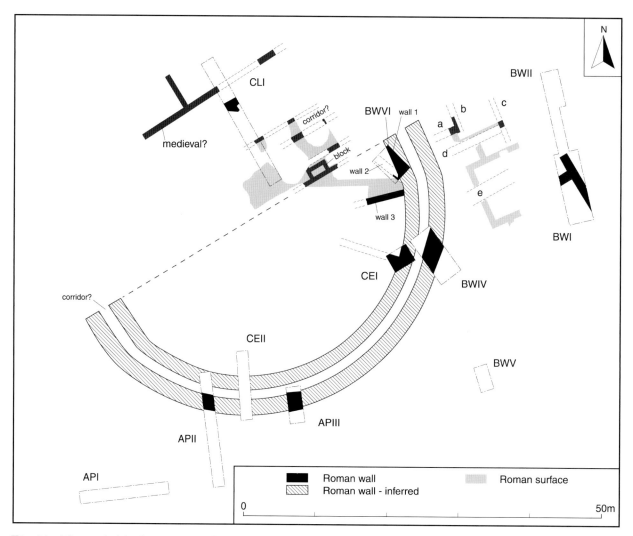

*Fig. 44*   The probable theatre in *insula* XXX and surrounding area. Plan of all observations (1:500)

the builders' trench a short section of this 1m-wide wall (Wall 3) survived intact. The area between Walls 2 and 3 was covered with a mortar and stone surface at least 0.3m thick. Not enough of Wall 1 was exposed to ascertain whether it displayed any curvature. It is conceivable that Wall 2 was the same radial wall encountered in 1962, although the latter was thought to lie at right-angles to the main curving wall. Two post-medieval pits were also discovered in this area. The cobbled surface was exposed over a distance of almost 15m to where further structures were found, although in some cases it was not clear whether these were Roman, medieval or post-medieval in date. One masonry wall appeared to be overlain by a second phase of walls forming three sides of a small rectangular space. One of the walls was composed from a single monolithic stone block 1m long, 0.6m wide and 0.6m deep. The block overlay a substantial mortar floor. To the north-east of this feature three further parallel walls were found, two of them defining a cobbled corridor 1.8m wide. Further walls were found to the north-east, although whether these are Roman or medieval is not readily apparent. One at least was abutted by a mortar floor upon which medieval pottery was found. In one

area to the south-east of the corridor a deep section was observed. This showed that natural gravels were overlaid by 1m of greyish silty clay, most probably alluvial deposits such as have been found previously on this site. The clay was sealed by a deposit of stone rubble, presumably consolidation and make-up, beneath a layer of mortar. A number of medieval and later pits, and other intrusions, were also found.

*Discussion* by Neil Holbrook

The observations made by Mr Grace are welcome, although they pose difficulties of interpretation. It is probable that Wall 1 can be equated with the inner wall of the corridor surrounding the theatre found in 1962, which was 1.83m wide and survived to a maximum height of ten courses. How Wall 2 relates to the radial wall which is recorded as springing at right-angles from the corridor wall in trench BWVI is somewhat less clear. On balance it is likely that they are one and the same, the alignment of the radial wall having been misplotted in 1962. In this case it is conceivable that Wall 2 may have been part of a polygonal or semi-circular internal buttress such as occur in similar locations in the theatre at Canterbury and sites in Gaul such as Augst and Thénac (Frere 1970, 89–90; Sear 2006, 205, 215–16). In the Gaulish examples the buttresses served to retain the weight of the solid mass of the seating bank. At Canterbury, however, the area in front of the buttress was not filled with soil and so the walls must have served as a substructure to support tiers of seating. This is also likely at Cirencester as no trace of an earthen bank has been found, and a metalled surface was found in the angle between Walls 2 and 3. It is most likely that the theatre was equipped with wooden terraced seating, with a void below, and that the rear of the timber decking was supported by the buttress and the inner corridor wall (cf. Sear 2006, 80 for other examples of part-timber theatres). Surprisingly no trace of a masonry wall defining the base of the terracing and the start of the orchestra has been observed, and so this was presumably also of timber. The width of Wall 3 (1m) is similar to that of the radial wall encountered in trench CE1 (1.1m). While these might have defined the sides of adjacent entrance passages or staircases through the *cavea*, another possibility is that they were also part of the substructure beneath the timber *cavea*. The other walls found by Mr Grace might have been part of the stage building, perhaps with a corridor to the rear. The monolithic block suggests a construction of some magnitude, although it may have been reused in the location where it was found. Mr Grace recalls that a second similar block was discovered somewhere on the site by the builders.

The other walls and surfaces recorded by Mr Grace lay just outside of the reconstructed line of the outer corridor wall, perhaps uncomfortably so if the reconstructed line is correct. Little can be said of the type of structure represented or its relationship with the walls in trench BWI. Overall the difficulties of reconstructing the fragmentary remains as the components of a theatre should be recognised, and it is possible that future work will show this interpretation to be entirely erroneous. On current evidence, however, no other interpretation readily suggests itself.

# 4. HOUSES AND SHOPS

The numbering system for individual buildings within each *insula* of the Roman town was created by John Wacher in 1963, and has been added to subsequently as new discoveries have been made (Wacher 1963, fig. 1). Structures reported in this chapter which appear to be part of previously unknown buildings have therefore also been numbered according to this system.

## EXCAVATIONS AT
## STEPSTAIRS LANE, 2002–3
### by Mark Brett and Martin Watts

### Introduction

Between December 2002 and January 2003 CA carried out an excavation prior to the construction of a three-storey residential development at the junction of Stepstairs Lane and School Lane. The development lies within *insula* IV/VII close to the projected alignment of Street C (see Fig. 17, no. 16 and Fig. 45). An archaeological evaluation of the site undertaken in 2000 identified evidence of Roman activity including pits, ditches and a well dating from the 1st and 2nd centuries AD, sealed by a layer interpreted as a post-Roman dark earth deposit (CAT 2000c). The apparent discovery of dark earth deposits during the evaluation demanded that they should be sampled for environmental analysis, which necessitated a two-stage approach to the excavation. Initially, the entire footprint of the development, covering an area of approximately 170m$^2$, was cleared by machine of modern overburden to the top of the dark earth horizon. The dark earth deposits were found to be significantly less extensive than had been expected, surviving only within the southern part of the site, having been truncated by modern activity further north. Five 1m$^2$ test pits were excavated through the dark earth for environmental sampling and the recovery of dating evidence. Two monolith samples were taken from the dark earth, but subsequent excavation showed that Monolith 1 had sampled a sequence of make-up deposits for the construction of a Roman building, and that the layers of dark earth sampled by Monolith 2 yielded modern finds and had clearly been recently reworked. As both monoliths had sampled re-deposited and/or contaminated layers no further analysis was undertaken. The remainder of the dark earth was then mechanically removed to expose the surviving archaeological deposits and features

beneath, which were excavated by hand. Modern activity had truncated the northern part of the site to the level of the natural clay, so only features cut into natural survived in that area. At the southern end of the site up to 0.5m of archaeological deposits survived above natural.

The majority of the deposits and features dated to the Roman period. However, three pits, a well and a layer of clay were dated to the medieval or post-medieval periods.

### Period 1: Ground consolidation and levelling (late 1st century AD)

The natural clay substrate was reached in almost all areas of the excavation, lying at approximately 106.2m AOD except for the north-eastern corner of the site, where it sloped down to approximately 105.3m AOD (Fig. 46). Remnants of a subsoil overlying the natural substrate survived in places, including layers 378 (n.i.) and 458 (Fig. 47).

The earliest constructional activity identified was concerned with consolidation and levelling of the site prior to more extensive development. Within the south-eastern part of the site, the remains of a limestone surface (362, n.i.) survived. This was relatively insubstantial, being only one or two stones thick, and overlay dumped deposits of clay and gravel, including levelling layers 332 (n.i.) and 363 (n.i.), both of which produced significant quantities of pottery and other finds. A spread of limestone rubble (316, n.i.) was found further to the west, possibly representing material left over from the laying of surface 362.

### *Dating evidence*

The pottery consists of a mix of 1st and 2nd-century AD material that may have been subject to some disturbance. Included are small quantities of mid 1st-century AD date consisting of native-type grog and shell-tempered and 'silty' wares including a girth-beaker related to southern British 'Belgic' forms. A Nauheim derivative brooch dateable to the period *c*. AD 40–60 and a sherd of typically 1st-century AD deep blue coloured glass were also recovered from subsoil deposit 378.

The pottery groups from Period 1 are comparable in most respects to Ceramic Phases 2 and 3 (Early). Samian occurs in all key groups. It is all South Gaulish and comprises mainly Flavian forms with only a small, residual, pre-Flavian component. Plain forms (principally Drag. 27 and Drag. 35 cups and Drag. 18 platters) dominate, with occasional decorated (Drag. 29) bowls. Further continental imports

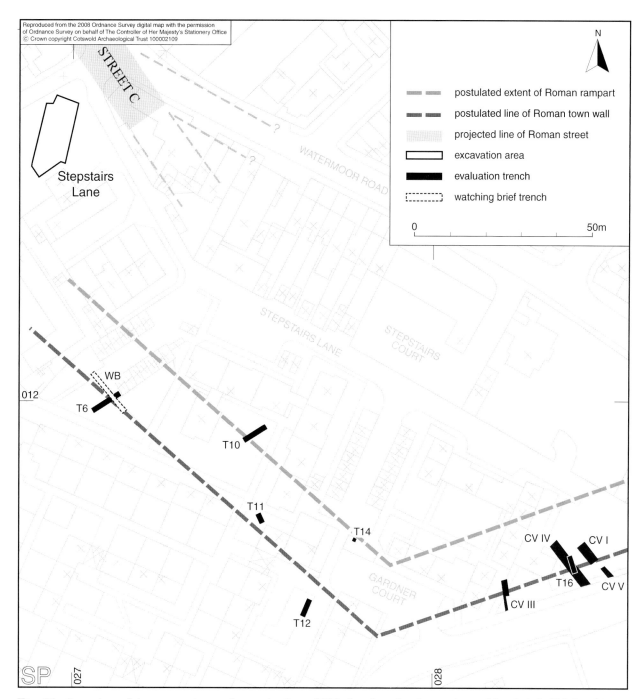

*Fig. 45* Location of the excavation at Stepstairs Lane 2002–3 and evaluation and watching brief off School Lane 2003–5 (1:1000)

occur in the form of small quantities of Spanish Camulodunum 186 (TF 34) and Dressel 20 (TF 40) amphora and Southern Gaulish Gauloise 4 (TF 35) amphora. The Camulodunum 186 'salazon' type amphora sherds are most significant here in terms of dating, their manufacture ceasing in the first quarter of the 2nd century AD. Non-sigillata finewares are dominated by local (North Wiltshire) types. The assemblage from levelling layer 332 represents a large and discrete group which is described in more detail below. Overall a Flavian or possibly Trajanic date is indicated.

Levelling layer 332: *Pottery* (458sh./5858g). *Samian*: SG. Drag. 18 (× 3), 29, all pre-Flavian; Drag. 35, 27 (× 6), 18 (× 3), all Flavian. *Coarsewares*: TF 5, 6, 10, 17, 9, 52, 34, 35, 40, fine greyware, Wiltshire red-slipped.

Levelling layer 363: *Pottery* (67sh./721g). *Samian*: SG. Drag. 27, Flavian. *Coarsewares*: TF 5, 6, 17, 18, 35, 95/98, grog, coarse black-sandy.

Rubble layer 316: *Pottery* (60sh./3898g). *Samian*: SG. Drag. 18, pre-Flavian; Drag 27, Claudio/Neronian; Drag. 27, Neronian. *Coarsewares*: TF 5, 6, 9, 17, 40, 74, 95, 95/98, 106.

## Period 2: Construction and occupation of Building A (late 1st/early 2nd to late 2nd century AD)

The consolidation deposits were overlain by a masonry structure which is now classified as Building VII.2. Two phases of construction have been identified within

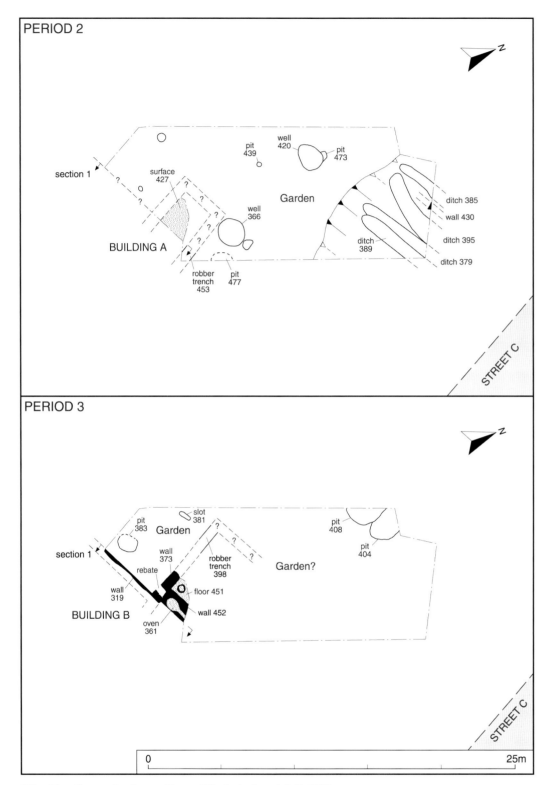

*Fig. 46*    Stepstairs Lane. Plan of Periods 2 and 3 (1:250)

this structure and these are termed Buildings A and B. It is not certain whether the consolidation event should be viewed as the first stage in the construction of the building, or whether there was an interval between the two events. On general grounds it seems hard to understand why effort would be expended on site preparation if construction was not anticipated. It is possible, however, that the original building lay outside the excavation area, and that Building A was a subsequent addition. It is clear that during the life of Building A sustained efforts were made to keep the site well drained.

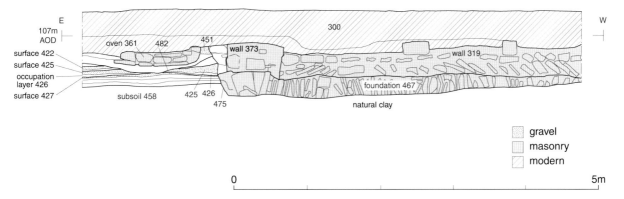

*Fig. 47*    Stepstairs Lane. Section 1 (1:50)

## Building A

Although no walls survived, the remains of a room from a Roman building dating from this period were apparent from levelling deposits, clay floors and associated layers of occupation-derived material identified along the southern edge of the site (Figs 46–7). Construction of the floor to this room commenced with the deposition of clay levelling layers above subsoil 458, over which the first surface (427) was laid. Surface 427 comprised compacted yellow clay up to 70mm thick. This was overlain by a thin layer of organic material (426) derived from occupation of the building which contained abundant artefactual material. This construction and occupation sequence was repeated twice more during this period (surfaces 422 and 425), presumably as the surfaces became worn, resulting in the floor level eventually being raised by approximately 0.15m.

The floor layers and occupation deposits extended beyond the southern limit of excavation and were truncated to the west by Period 3 wall 373, almost certainly a rebuild of the original western wall to this part of Building A. To the north and east, the walls of the room had been completely truncated by later activity; however, robber trench 453 (seen only in section) may mark the line of the eastern wall of the room. If so, the internal width of the room would have been about 2.5m. While there was no indication as to its northern extent, if the room served as a porch or small antechamber to larger building to the south it may not have extended much further to the north than the surviving extent of its floor (Fig. 46). Wall 319, running along the southern limit of excavation may have replaced an earlier wall associated with Building A, as Period 3 wall 373 also seems to have done.

## Garden area

During this period the area to the north of Building A was used as a garden. Deposits interpreted as garden soils were found to either side of the remains of Building A, surviving at their deepest (up to 0.35m; layer 303, n.i.) to the west (i.e. furthest away from Street C). The abundance of artefactual material within this deposit suggests that domestic waste may have been disposed of simply by throwing it out into the garden, although artefactually rich pit 477 (which was recorded only in section) may represent a refuse pit cut through the garden soil to the east of the room. Another pit, 439, lying to the north of the room and beyond the extent of surviving garden soil, contained concentrations of burnt material and bones from at least two young sheep, the majority of which were from a single individual. Numerous butchery marks on these bones indicate that the contents of this pit also represent domestic refuse.

Two wells dating to this period were found. Well 420, to the north of Building A, was roughly circular with vertical sides and a diameter of 1.5m. Due to waterlogging, excavation of this feature ceased at a depth of 0.75m, however, hand-augering established an overall depth of 1.45m. It was filled by a deposit containing abundant limestone rubble, suggesting that it had been deliberately backfilled. Immediately to the east of Building A was well 366 which had a diameter of 1.85m. Although it was not possible to excavate this feature below the water table its bottom was located at a depth of 2m using an auger. Its homogeneous fill appears to represent gradual silting up, although the abundant and mixed nature of artefactual material recovered also suggests occasional episodes of dumping. Both wells are likely to be associated with Building A; whether they were contemporary or sequential is uncertain.

A small number of other discrete features were found, including three small pits and two postholes, but their purpose is unclear. While the majority were unexceptional, pit 473 (truncated by well 420) contained scorched red clay indicative of *in situ* burning.

## Drainage ditches and possible boundary wall

A series of ditches was revealed at the northern end of the site, running eastwards from the base of the natural slope towards the projected alignment of Street C. Although all contained similar dating evidence, a basic chronological sequence was established. The earliest ditches, 379, 389 and 392 (n.i.), all contained fills that suggested each silted up gradually, to be replaced by a new ditch in a slightly different location. The earliest ditch (379) was also the deepest, surviving to a depth of 0.7m. All three ditches were sealed by silty accumulations, up to 0.3m thick (including layer 345), suggesting a brief hiatus in efforts to keep the site well drained. Ditches 385 and 395 were dug through these silts, but unlike the earlier ditches, they were deliberately back-filled with occupation waste and demolition debris.

Lying between ditches 385 and 395 was a masonry wall, 430, of which two foundation courses survived. The wall was constructed following the accumulation of the silts in this area, and was therefore broadly contemporary with the ditches. Little survived of this wall but it appeared to be aligned perpendicular to the projected line of Street C and may have been a property boundary with drainage ditches to either side.

### Dating evidence

Only a few broadly dateable sherds of pottery are associated with Building A. Larger quantities of material were however recovered from drainage ditches, a well and occupation layers associated with the use of this building. The pottery includes some large and diagnostic groups with significant quantities of samian. In many instances the samian is dominated by South Gaulish material with only a few Central Gaulish sherds of Hadrianic and Antonine date. Non-sigillata continental imports are also present, including small rough-cast decorated beakers in Central Gaulish 'Argonne' type colour-coated ware (TF57). Other continental wares present include Spanish amphora TF35, and TF40 and Rhone Valley mortaria TF67. The overall scarcity of Antonine samian and absence of black-slipped Gaulish or Rhenish fabrics probably indicate that the bulk of the Period 2 contexts date to before *c.* AD 150/60.

In most respects the range of coarseware fabrics from Period 2 groups is ostensibly similar to that from the preceding phase. However, the representation of certain fabrics is different, most significantly with lesser quantities of reduced fabrics TF5 and TF6 and North Wiltshire oxidised TF 95/98 increasing in quantity. Other differences are evident in the forms present, with new flagon and beaker forms occurring. Well group 318 produced a number of oxidised flagons, some substantially complete and probably representing accidental losses. Ring-necked flagons would appear still to be most common, although these differ from earlier examples in having a pronounced upper rim and only vestigial lower rings.

Also significant is the relative abundance of Dorset Black-Burnished ware, which occurs mainly as everted-rim jars and flat-rimmed dishes/bowls. The influence of Black-Burnished wares is elsewhere evident in the form repertoire of local reduced wares with jars and open forms imitating its rim forms and decoration.

Material from the garden soils cannot be used as dating evidence for Period 2 as the deposits were not sealed and continued to collect material into at least the late 4th century AD to judge from coin nos 4, 9, 14, 15, 19, 21 and 22.

Occupation layer 426: *Pottery* (20sh./469g). *Samian*: SG, Drag. 35 and 18, Flavian. CG, Drag. 18, Antonine. *Coarsewares*: TF 5, 35, 9, 40, 74, 17/98.

Fill 333 (Ditch 379): *Pottery* (87sh./1222g). *Samian*: SG, Drag. 37, *c.* 70–85, Drag. 18, Flavian, Drag. 27. *Coarsewares*: TF 5, 6, 17, 10, 74, 95, 95/98.

Silt layer 345: *Pottery* (90 sh./1190g). *Samian*: SG, Drag. 37 and 18, Flavian. CG, Drag. 37, AD 145–65 (Cinnamus ii). *Coarsewares*: TF 5, 6, 9, 10, 17/98, 32, 40, 52, fine greyware.

Fill 318 (well 366): *Pottery* (135 sh./3640g). *Samian*: SG, Drag. 37, Flavian. CG, Drag. 27, Hadrianic/Antonine, Drag. 18/31r, Antonine, *Coarsewares*: TF 5, 6, 10, 17/98, 74, 85, 95, 98, 40.

Fill 421 (well 420): *Pottery* (65 sh./553g). *Samian*: SG, Drag. 18 and 18r, Flavian. CG, Drag. 31, Antonine. *Coarsewares*: TF 5, 6, 10, 17/98, 74, 90, 95/98, 35,40, 106.

Garden soil 303: *Coin*: Trajan AD 103–11 (no. 2); illegible 4th century (no. 4); H. of Theodosius AD 388–402 (no. 22). *Pottery* (332 sh./6265g). *Samian*: SG, Drag. 37 and 35, Flavian, Drag. 18, 1st century. CG, Drag. 37, Hadrianic, Drag. 33, 35, 27 and 18/31r, all Hadrianic/Antonine. *Coarsewares*: TF 5, 6, 40, 67, 74, 90, 95, 95/98, 17/98, misc. whiteware.

Garden soil 412: *Pottery* (193 sh./3152g). *Samian*: SG, Drag. 27 and 18, Flavian. CG, Drag. 37, Hadrianic. *Coarsewares*: TF 5, 6, 34, 40, 67, 74, 95, 95/98, 17/98.

Garden soil 479: *Pottery* (216 sh./4343g). *Samian*: SG, Drag. 27, 18 and 18r, all Flavian. *Coarsewares*: TF 5, 6, 9, 17, 17/98, 32, 40, 52, 67, 74, 90, coarse black sandy.

## Period 3: Construction and occupation of Building B (late 2nd to 3rd century AD)

Activity within this period primarily involved the remodelling of Building A into Building B, the main part of which once again lay beyond the southern limit of excavation.

### Building B

Perpendicular walls 319 and 373 were the main structural elements of Building B revealed in the excavation. Wall 319 was aligned approximately east/west along the southern limit of excavation. Keyed into this and extending a short distance (2.1m) to the north was wall 373, the alignment of which continued further northwards where it was represented by robber trench 398. Wall 373 was undoubtedly a direct replacement for an earlier wall associated with Building A, although it may well have extended further northwards. Wall 319 truncated garden soil 303 associated with Building A, but could also have replaced a pre-existing Building A wall. Walls 319 and 373 were of a similar construction, comprising foundations of pitched limestone, with the construct-

*Fig. 48*   Stepstairs Lane. Oven 361. View to the south-west (scales 0.2m and 1m)

ion trenches backfilled with clay. The foundations were approximately 0.3m deep and were directly overlain by two surviving courses of mortared limestone blocks, each up to 0.35m in length. The mortared parts of the walls survived to a height of up to 0.45m. Wall 373 contained a 0.4m-wide niche or rebate, the purpose of which was not clear.

Within the remodelled room oven 361 was constructed and floor 451 was then laid. The construction of oven 361 truncated all earlier occupation layers and surfaces associated with Building A. The oven, which survived to a height of three courses, was built with limestone blocks set directly into clay scorched red through use. The oven was oval, approximately 0.8m in length and its southern side lay just beyond the southern limit of excavation (Fig. 48). The stokehole did not survive. The back of the oven was aligned directly with the rebate within wall 373. Much of its stonework was scorched grey and red, some stones reduced to a powdery, crumbling state. Once the oven was built, floor 451 was laid to either side. The floor comprised limestone blocks set in mortar, a much more durable surface than those associated with Building A. A single course of limestone blocks (452) along the northern side of oven 361 was laid directly upon floor 451. It may represent the remains of an internal wall. A scorched red ring revealed on the surface of the floor in the corner formed by wall 373 and possible wall 452 may have been made by a brazier.

From wall 452 to the excavated end of robber trench 398, the remodelled room measured at least 5m north/south, longer than its predecessor. Although there was no evidence to help define its eastern extent, the presence of oven 361 indicates that it was also probably broader than Building A. As with Building A, the majority of Building B lay beyond the southern limit of excavation.

### Other activity

The limited evidence for the use of the remainder of the site during this period suggests that it continued in use as a garden. To the west of Building B, pit 383 and slot 381 were recorded, although their purpose was not clear. A series of intercutting pits in the northern corner of the site may also be associated with this period and reflect its continued use as a garden. The earliest of these pits (404) silted up slightly and was then backfilled with demolition debris. Pit 408, slightly later in the sequence, was used for the disposal of domestic refuse.

### Dating evidence

A reasonably large assemblage of pottery was recovered from features associated with the construction of Building B. The pottery from 372/380/411/476/481 would appear to be indistinguishable in terms of its composition from Period 2 groups and presumably contains much derived material. An enamelled plate brooch from backfill 476 of a construction trench is broadly dateable to the 2nd century AD.

Walls 372/380/411/476/481: *Pottery* (76 sh./656g). *Samian*: SG, Drag. 37, Flavian. *Coarsewares*: TF 5, 6, 17/98, 40, 74, 95/98. *Other*: enamelled plate brooch (2nd century AD).

## Period 4: Disuse of Building B (later 3rd or 4th century AD)

Dating evidence recovered from the demolition layers (including 376, n.i.) overlying the remains of Building B suggest that it went out of use in the later 3rd or 4th century AD. Demolition of Building B was accompanied by the collapse of the oven 361 which was also sealed by demolition deposits. This may reflect the fate of the whole of Building B or it could represent the demolition of a single room.

Overlying a thin layer of clay in the base of the oven was a layer of fine charcoal, 358 (n.i.), possibly derived from its final firing. Analysis of the charred plant remains showed the deposit to be dominated by bread-type wheat and other indeterminate wheat and cereal grain, with the fragments of charcoal suggesting that the fuel used was probably whatever came to hand rather than being specifically chosen (see below). Unusually for a Roman assemblage, there were no confirmed occurrences of hulled wheats, and cultivated vetch seeds appeared to be present. While this is more typical of medieval assemblages, it certainly does not necessarily preclude the Roman date for the oven indicated by the stratigraphic evidence (see below).

### Dating evidence

Small quantities of pottery and other dateable artefacts were associated with this period. Material from deposit 358 within oven 361 produced good evidence for a late 3rd to 4th-century AD date in the form of a substantially complete funnel-necked beaker in Oxfordshire red colour-coated ware (TF83), a Dorset Black-Burnished ware flanged bowl (sherd) and fragments from a bone armlet of late Roman type.

Much of the remaining pottery, particularly from layers sealing Building B, consists of derived material similar in composition to groups from Period 2 deposits. Layer 376, overlying Building B, contains a mix of 2nd and early to mid 3rd-century AD pottery, including Black-Burnished ware bead and flanged bowls and plain-rimmed dishes. Demolition deposit 356 contained no pottery but did produce a coin of AD 367–75 (no. 16).

Evidence for Roman activity continuing into the late 4th century AD at least is also apparent from the coins recovered from the garden soils, including issues of the House of Theodosius, and from sherds of late Roman shell-tempered ware (TF115), dateable to after *c*. AD 360.

Oven fill 358: *Pottery* (30 sh./67g). *Coarsewares*: TF 74, 83. *Other*: bone armlet late 3rd or 4th century AD

Demolition layer 376: *Pottery* (115 sh./2418g). *Samian*: SG, Drag. 27, 33, 18, all Flavian. CG, Drag. 37 Hadrianic/Antonine, Drag. 37, Antonine. *Coarsewares*: TF 5, 6, 17/98, 34, 35, 40, 74, 90, 95/98 misc. whiteware.

Demolition layer 356. *Coin*: H. of Valentinian, AD 367–75 (no. 16).

## Period 5: Medieval and later activity (n.i.)

A single pit and a well were found which dated to the 11th to 13th centuries. Pit 401, containing demolition debris, was located in the vicinity of the earlier Roman pits in the north-eastern part of the site. The construction of well 443 slightly truncated Roman well 420 and the upper part of the feature was cut wide enough to allow access for excavation of the main shaft and the construction of the stone lining. Due to the feature extending below the modern water table, excavation ceased at a depth of 0.7m, however hand-augering established the true depth of the feature as 2.5m. Well 443 was infilled mainly with limestone rubble. During the period between the 13th and 15th centuries wall 373 of Building B was robbed of its stone and subsequently the backfilled robber trench was cut through by a quarry pit. The northernmost extent of wall 373 had been completely robbed of stone and survived only as a shallow trench filled with clay. This was cut by a vertically sided quarry pit (366) which had a diameter of 1.85m. The base of the feature was not reached during excavation, due to the section becoming waterlogged, however with the use of an auger, its overall depth was established as approximately 2m. It was filled by a series of at least six dumped deposits comprising alternating waste limestone fragments and domestic waste. Pit 322 was identified in the southern section of the trench, cutting the earlier Roman garden soil. It was used primarily to dispose of charcoal-rich waste, on top of which further waste material containing abundant 13th to 14th-century pottery was dumped. Although devoid of dating evidence a layer of redeposited natural clay (331) which sealed the majority of the Roman features in the eastern part of the site and a small pit (366) are also likely to date to the medieval or post-medieval periods.

### Dating evidence

Small quantities of medieval and post-medieval pottery were recovered from Period 5 contexts. In most instances medieval sherds are present amongst larger quantities of residual (mostly late) Roman pottery. Typically for Cirencester and the southern Cotswolds the range of pottery fabrics types present is restricted and the dating necessarily broad. Two types dominate, 'Cotswold oolitic' TF202, dateable to the 11th to 13th centuries and splash-glazed Minety ware TF200, which dates from the late 12th/early 13th to the early 16th centuries. Single sherds of (12th to 13th-century) Bristol Ham Green ware TF206 and a miscellaneous quartz-tempered ware are the only other medieval types present. Few pottery forms are identifiable and of those which are, only the Minety ware tripod ?pitcher from 324 is helpful in terms of establishing chronology, suggesting a 13th-century date. Non-ceramic medieval items are restricted to a single worked bone ?comb fragment from 423. A 12th or 13th-century date is most likely for this item.

Quarry pit fill 324: *Pottery* (83 sh./1961g). *Coarsewares* (RB): TF 83, 88, 98,115, 17/98; (medieval): TF 200, 202, 206, misc. sandy.

Pit fill 423: *Pottery* (48 sh./346g). *Coarsewares* (RB): TF 83, 88, 98,115, 17/98; (medieval): TF 200, 202, 206, misc. sandy.

### The finds by E.R. McSloy

### Roman pottery

The group of pottery from Period 1 levelling dump 332 has been selected for a higher level of recording and quantification, including minimum vessel count (sherd families) and Estimated Vessel Equivalence (EVEs) (Table 7, Fig. 49). Attributes such as decoration, use wear evidence, visible residues and any cross-context matches are also recorded for each sherd family. The significance of Group 332 derives from its Flavian date and the location of the site on the south-eastern fringe

**Table 7:** Quantification of Pottery Group 332 from Stepstairs Lane

**KEY:** Count = sherd count; Min. vess. = minimum number of vessels; EVEs = estimated vessel equivalents

| Description | Fabric | Count | Min. vess. | Weight (g) | EVEs | %EVEs |
|---|---|---|---|---|---|---|
| *Imported finewares* | | | | | | |
| La Graufesenque samian (LGF SA) | 154a | 17 | 12 | 123 | 1.18 | 8.9 |
| *Amphorae* | | | | | | |
| Baetican (BAT AM2) | 40 | 3 | 3 | 140 | – | – |
| Cadiz (CAD AM) | 34 | 1 | 1 | 226 | .18 | 1.5 |
| Gaulish (GAL AM1) | 35 | 1 | 1 | 9 | – | – |
| *Sub-total* | | *5* | *5* | *375* | *.18* | *1.5* |
| *Mortaria* | | | | | | |
| Verulamium region (VER WH) | 32 | 1 | 1 | 15 | – | – |
| *Local wares* | | | | | | |
| Early Severn Valley Ware (SVW OX2) | 4 | 16 | 11 | 180 | – | – |
| Early wheel-thrown black sandy | 5/15 | 77 | 69 | 750 | 3.0 | 25.0 |
| Savernake type (SAV GT) | 6/13 | 133 | 97 | 2430 | 3.0 | 25.0 |
| Early Wiltshire oxidised | 9 | 39 | 8 | 320 | 1.31 | 10.9 |
| ?Kingsholm flagon fabric | 11 | 21 | 6 | 147 | 1.0 | 8.3 |
| Early Wiltshire grey | 17 | 166 | 159 | 1283 | 2.96 | 25.0 |
| Mica-dusted | 52 | 6 | 5 | 44 | .17 | 1.4 |
| Grog tempered | – | 4 | 3 | 40 | .05 | 0.4 |
| ?local red-slipped | – | 2 | 1 | 25 | .17 | 1.4 |
| ?London-ware type fine grey | – | 1 | 1 | 21 | .07 | 0.6 |
| miscellaneous reduced | – | 22 | 8 | 219 | .1 | – |
| *Sub-total* | | *487* | *368* | *5459* | *11.83* | *98* |
| **Total** | | **510** | **386** | **5972** | **13.19** | |

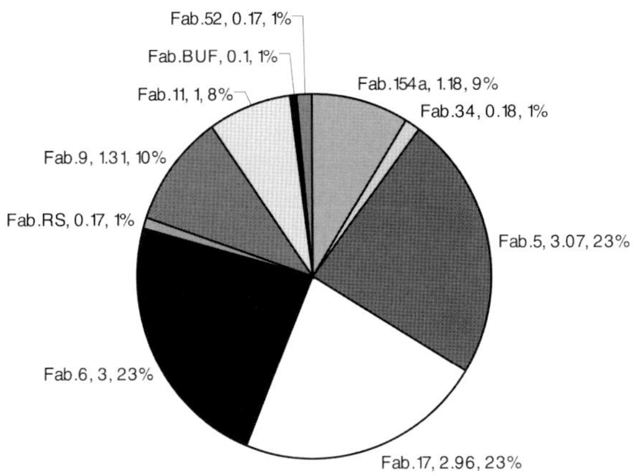

POTTERY GROUP 332 COMPOSITION

*Fig. 49* Quantification by EVEs of the composition by fabric of Pottery Group 332 from Stepstairs Lane

of the town. Groups of comparable date derive mainly from the area of the Leaholme fort to the north-west, which increases the risk of a large residual component from the underlying military occupation. The single quantified group from this area is almost exactly comparable in terms of size and date (CE V, table 19, Ceramic Phase 2; *c*. AD 75–100/120).

The samian from Group 332 is exclusively South Gaulish (La Graufesenque). Four of the twelve vessels represented are pre-Flavian, while the remainder are Flavian (see listing in dating evidence section above). Non-sigillata finewares are predominantly of North Wiltshire manufacture. White-slipped fabric TF9 includes a 'collared' flagon probably derived from pre-Flavian 'Hofheim' types and similar to forms known from Gloucester (Rawes 1972, no. 111). Also present in this fabric are examples of honey pots and a beaker with 'ledge' rim which can be directly paralleled among 1st-century AD groups from St Michael's Field (CE I, fig. 55, no. 187 and fig. 50, no. 32). Mica-dusted ware (TF 52) occurs as curved-sided platters and a thin-walled beaker similar to an example from a Flavian-dated context (CE I, fig. 63, no. 425). A ring-necked flagon in probable Kingsholm fabric (TF 11) is likely to be residual.

Coarsewares are dominated by three types: reduced North Wiltshire fabrics (TF 5 and TF 17) and grog-tempered Savernake type grey wares (TF 6 and TF 13). Of this material, black-sandy fabrics TF 5/TF 15 demonstrate the greatest variety of forms and include platters, bowls and lids which are closely comparable to previously published (Flavian) groups (CE I, fig. 55, nos 193–7; fig. 56, no. 232). Grey ware TF 17 and grog-tempered grey wares includes a number of sherds with clay slip rustication, a feature of Flavian to Hadrianic groups elsewhere in Cirencester. Conspicuous by their absence are sherds of Dorset Black-Burnished ware (TF 74). Correspondingly, vessel forms in black-firing fabrics TF 5 and TF 15 which imitate Black-Burnished ware, are also absent. Importation of Dorset Black-Burnished ware into Cirencester prior to *c*. AD 120 is

thought to be little more than a 'trickle' (CE I, 168). Its appearance after this date in rapidly increasing quantities is also, it seems, marked by efforts to copy the common jar and bowl forms in the locally made wares (CE II, MF 1, C13). All indications are that the assemblage dates to the Flavian or possibly Trajanic period (*c*. AD 70–110), with only a very few residual pre-Flavian vessels present.

The composition of Group 332 compares in most respects to that from St Michael's Field (CE V, table 19). The range of fabrics represented (Table 7) is similar with local material, particularly reduced types, heavily dominant in both groups. Samian is slightly more common in the St Michael's Field group, which may be residual from the underlying military occupation there. The samian clearly dominates the non-flagon fineware component of both groups, with only small amounts of mica-dusted wares and fine grey wares. Group 332 also includes single instances of a presumably local (north Wiltshire) red-slipped platter and a fine grey ware bowl, possibly in the 'London-ware' style. The balance of certain coarseware fabrics is in some respects divergent in Group 332 compared to the St Michael's Field material. North Wiltshire oxidised TF 9 is significantly more abundant at St Michael's Field, whereas reduced fabrics TF5 and Savernake type TF 6/TF 13 occur in greater quantities here. It is unclear whether such differences are an effect of the chronology, although the presence of Central Gaulish samian and sherds of Dorset Black-Burnished ware at St Michael's Field indicate that the group was collecting material until *c*. AD 100/120, somewhat later than Group 332.

## Coins

All coins were of copper alloy. Condition is mixed and not all were fully identifiable. Early Roman coins include issues of Vespasian (AD 69–79) and Trajan (AD 103–11). Most coins are late, the majority of identifiable types dating to the second half of the 4th century AD. The dearth of issues of the House of Constantine is surprising.

1. Cultivation layer 304. Period 5. Vespasian, *Dupondius*, reverse illegible. AD 69–79.
2. Cultivation layer 303. Period 2. Trajan, *Dupondius*, AD 103–11. RIC 505.
3. Cultivation layer 302. Period 5. AE1, Corroded and illegible. Late 1st/early 2nd.
4. Cultivation layer 303. Period 2. AE4 ?copy, corroded and illegible. 4th century.
5. Quarry pit fill 423. Period 5. AE4, corroded and illegible. 4th century.
6. Quarry pit fill 417. Period 5. AE4, corroded and illegible. 4th century.
7. Quarry pit fill 423. Period 5. AE4, corroded and illegible. 4th century.
8. Pit fill 409. Period 4. AE4 ?copy, corroded and illegible. 4th century.
9. Cultivation layer 302. Period 5. AE4 copy. Corroded and illegible. 4th century.
10. Layer 358. Period 4. AE4 minim copy. Corroded and illegible. 4th century.
11. Cultivation layer 302. Period 5. Theodora AE3. PIETAS ROMANA, Trier. 337–41. HK 120.

12. Well 443. Period 5. Theodora AE3. PIETAS ROMANA. Mintmark illegible. AD 337–41.
13. Cultivation layer 302. Period 5. Valentinian I/Valens/ Gratian AE3. SECURITAS REIPUBLICAE. Mintmark illegible. AD 364–78.
14. Cultivation layer 320. Period 2. Valentinian I/Valens/ Gratian AE4 ?copy. SECURITAS REIPUBLICAE. Mintmark illegible. AD 364–78.
15. Cultivation layer 320. Period 2. Valentinian I/Valens/ Gratian AE3. SECURITAS REIPUBLICAE. Mintmark illegible. AD 364–78.
16. Demolition layer 356. Period 4. Valentinian I/Valens/ Gratian AE3. SECURITAS REIPUBLICAE, Lyons. AD 367–75. CK 317–26.
17. Cultivation layer 302. Period 5. Gratian AE3 ?copy. Mintmark illegible. Obverse shows wreath. AD 378–87.
18. Quarry pit fill 419. Period 5. Gratian AE3. Mintmark illegible. Obverse shows wreath. AD 378–87.
19. Garden/cultivation soil 320. Period 2. AE4. SALUS REIPUBLICAE. Mintmark illegible. AD 388–402.
20. Garden/cultivation soil 321. Period 5. AE4. SALUS REIPUBLICAE ?copy. Mintmark illegible. AD 388–402.
21. Well fill 367. Period 2. AE4. SALUS REIPUBLICAE ?copy. Mintmark illegible. AD 388–402.

22. Cultivation layer 303. Period 2. AE3. VICTORIA AUG. Mintmark illegible. AD 388–402.

### *Brooches* (Fig. 50)

1. Subsoil 378. Period 1. Nauheim derivative brooch. Copper alloy. Four coil spring with internal chord. Flat, strip-like bow, with two parallel rows of square punched decoration down each side. The catchplate is plain. Length 54mm. Simple, one-piece brooches such as this are known from the 1st century BC. This particular form, characterised by broad flat bow decorated with parallel lines of punched decoration, can be readily paralleled from various sites, mainly in central-southern England. A number of examples of the type, which almost certainly dates from the mid 1st century AD, were recovered from Wanborough, Wiltshire (Butcher 2001, nos 5–14).
2. Wall construction backfill 476. Period 3. Copper alloy with iron pin. Complete moulded plate brooch with four enamelled lugs. The central plate and umbonate projection are plain. The enamel in the lugs appears yellow-green. The hinge is a simple perforated lug type and the catchplate is simple and sturdy. Length 34mm. A brooch of identical form is known from Nor'nour, Isles of Scilly (Hull 1968, no. 201). This form of brooch together with the similar but composite construction 'Tutulus' forms is broadly dateable to the 2nd century AD.

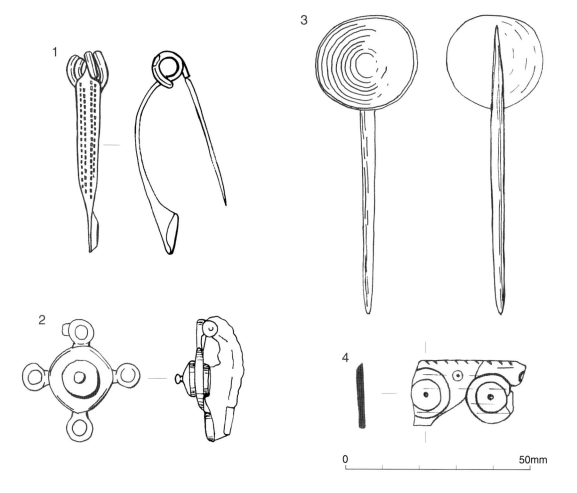

*Fig. 50*    Stepstairs Lane. Objects of copper alloy (nos 1–2) and worked bone (nos 3–4) (scale 1:1)

### Worked bone (Fig. 50)

3. Occupation layer 426. Period 2. Complete round-bowled spoon. Handle and underside of bowl are highly polished. Length 78mm. Width of bowl 25mm. Similar spoons are known from most larger Roman towns in Britain and a workshop producing these items is known from Winchester (Crummy 1983, 69). Comparable examples are widely known, although predominantly from major towns and most probably date to the second half of the 1st or 2nd century AD (Crummy 1983). The narrowing extension of the handle to the underside of the bowl serves no practical function, but mimics the form of similar spoons in metal.

4. Quarry pit fill 423. Period 5. Two joining fragments from the side plate of a comb. Decorated with large roundels and small rings and dots, with diagonal slashes to the single surviving edge. Portion of one rounded rivet hole survives. Surviving length 30mm. Thickness 1.3mm. The deep, flat and straight-sided plate is consistent with it deriving from a double-sided composite comb. Combs of this type have a long period of currency, extending from the Anglo-Saxon period to the 11th–13th century. Even with more complete examples there is little to distinguish early from late examples (MacGregor 1985, 93–4). The decoration on this example is characteristic of the type, and a very similar scheme alternating paired small rings and dots with larger twin-ringed roundels occurs on an early Anglo-Saxon (Anglian) comb from Settle, North Yorkshire (ibid., fig. 51f).

### Worked stone (Fig. 51) by Fiona Roe

5. Layer 336. Period 2. Quern fragment of Niedermendig lava. The fragment is probably from a rotary quern. The surviving rim area is too small for accurate measurement of its diameter. It is an upper stone with a raised rim around the circumference, and has a wedge-shaped slot for a handle cut into the upper surface and a thickening of the edge at this point. Neidermendig querns, originating from the Mayen quarries of Germany, were used throughout the Roman period. Querns of this type are highly susceptible to decay

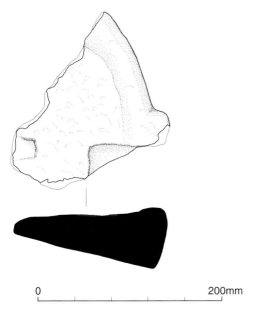

0                                200mm

*Fig. 51*  Stepstairs Lane. Niedermendig lava quern (scale 1:4)

and this fragment is unusual in preserving its handle fixing and other features.

### Stamped tile

One unstratified fragment of ceramic tile possessed an incomplete stamp T.[, almost certainly of the TPF/TPFA series (RIB II.5, 2489.44–9).

## The biological remains

A single 25-litre soil sample was taken for the recovery of environmental remains from charcoal-rich layer 358 in the bottom of oven 361. It probably represents waste from the last use of the oven. The sample was processed using standard methods of flotation.

### Charred plant remains by Wendy Carruthers

A total of 242 charred plant fragments was recovered from the sample (Table 8). The remains were not particularly well preserved, with many of the cereal grains being vacuolated and fragmented. The assemblage was dominated by bread-type wheat (*Triticum aestivum*-type), indeterminate wheat grains (*Triticum* sp.) and indeterminate cereal grains. Also present were hulled barley (*Hordeum vulgare*) and large vetch seeds (*Vicia/Lathyrus* sp.) and a variety of other fragments of seeds in very low quantities.

Unusually for the Roman period, no confirmed occurrences of hulled wheats (emmer and spelt) were recorded, either as grain or chaff fragments. While a few Roman sites have produced large deposits of bread-type wheat, such as the granary at South Shields (Van der Veen 1988), hulled wheats are usually also present. It is not until the Anglo-Saxon period that naked bread-type wheats are the only type of wheat recovered from charred plant assemblages. It is possible that the deposit represents an exclusively bread-wheat crop being dried in the oven. However, some chaff fragments of hulled wheats might be expected in a Roman deposit, as chaff was frequently used as tinder and is readily preserved by charring (Van der Veen 1989).

A further unusual factor of the deposit was the presence of cultivated vetch seeds (*Vicia sativa* ssp. *sativa*). Although only two seeds retained hilums enabling identifications to be made, ten other vetch seeds were recorded of a size (3–4mm diameter, average = 3.5mm) which is much larger than most weedy vetch/tare seeds. *Vicia sativa* was recorded in a charred assemblage from the Roman port at Caerleon (Helbaek 1964), but that assemblage is thought to have been imported. Confirmed cultivated vetch (V. *sativa* ssp. *sativa*) is usually found in medieval assemblages, for instance 12th-century deposits at Raunds, Northamptonshire (Campbell 1994). The remaining weed taxa provide no further clues as to the date of the deposit, as they are commonly recovered from charred plant assemblages dating from the Iron Age onwards. They included field madder (*Sherardia arvensis*) and docks (*Rumex* sp.).

The nature of the charred plant assemblage from the oven is therefore unusual for the late Roman period. Remarkably few archaeobotanical assemblages

**Table 8:** The charred plant remains from oven 361 (context 358) at Stepstairs Lane

**KEY:** Habitats: * = cultivated plant; A = arable; C = cultivated land; D = disturbed soils; G = grassland; H = hedgerows; S = scrub; W = woods

| Taxa | Common name | Habitat | No. |
|---|---|---|---|
| *Triticum aestivum*-type | Free-threshing bread-type wheat grain | * | 63 |
| *T. aestivum/spelta* | Bread-type/spelt wheat grain | * | 3 |
| *Triticum* sp. | Indeterminate wheat grain | * | 65 |
| *Hordeum vulgare* L. | Twisted lateral six-row barley grain | * | 4 |
| *Hordeum vulgare* L. | Hulled barley grain | * | 5 |
| *Avena* sp. | Wild/cultivated oat grain | A* | 4 |
| Indeterminate cereal grains | – | * | 76 |
| Cereal-sized culm node | – | * | 1 |
| *Bromus* sect. *Bromus* | Chess caryopsis | A | 1 |
| *Rumex* sp. | Dock achene | CDG | 2 |
| *Sherardia arvensis* L. | Field madder nutlet | CD | 5 |
| *Sambucus nigra* L. | Elderberry seed | DHSW | 1 |
| *Vicia sativa* ssp. *sativa* | Cultivated vetch seed (3.5mm) | * | 2 |
| *Vicia/Lathyrus* sp. | Large vetch seeds (3–4mm) | *CH | 10 |
| **Total** | | | **242** |

have been examined from Cirencester and it is therefore difficult to place this assemblage in context. Evidence for large-scale processing of spelt wheat during the later Roman period has been recovered from a number of sites in southern and central England, as for instance at Ilchester (Murphy 1976). The fact that there was no evidence of this in oven 361 could be due to the chance nature of preservation by charring. In conclusion, the charred bread wheat, barley and cultivated vetch could represent imported crops being dried in the oven in its last period of use. Although the pottery dates the oven to the late 3rd or 4th century AD, radiocarbon dating needs to be carried out on the charred plant remains before they can be considered to be an early record of cultivated vetch.

### *Charcoal* by Phil Austin

The sample submitted for assessment was composed of two separate sub-samples, one each from the flot and residue, containing an approximate total of 600 fragments. As only one sample was being assessed, 25 fragments from each of the sub-samples were identified; a total of 50 fragments for the sample. Preservation varied from good to poor.

A total of five taxa, all indigenous to the UK, was identified (Table 9). *Quercus* sp. (oak) was the most abundant of these, followed by *Prunus* sp. (blackthorn, cherries) and *Corylus avellana* (hazel). However, given the low quantity of material studied it is unlikely that this is an accurate reflection of actual relative taxon abundance. The genera *Salix* (willows) and *Populus* (poplars) are difficult to distinguish anatomically and, though some fragments of this taxon are believed to be *Salix* sp., this determination lacks certainty. Differentiation between species of *Prunus* was similarly inconclusive. A few fragments were tentatively identified as *P. spinosa* (blackthorn). The virtually indistinguishable wood anatomy of the Maloideae prevents differentiation between members of this sub-family of the Rosaceae; which includes the genera *Sorbus* (rowan, whitebeams, wild service tree), *Pyrus* (pear), *Malus* (apple) and *Crataegus* sp. (hawthorn). Hawthorn is the most likely representative of the Maloideae on this site. The majority of fragments of all taxa derived from round-wood. In many instances this appeared to be from small diameter round-wood and a number of fragments were further identified as twig-wood. Only fragments of oak consistently appeared to derive from larger round-wood. Evidence of woodworking was noted in a single fragment of hazel.

**Table 9:** Assessment of the wood charcoal from oven 361 (context 358) at Stepstairs Lane

**KEY:** RW = roundwood; SW = stemwood; SP = sapwood; TW = twig/twigwood; ID = insect damage (boreholes); FH = fungal hyphae; A = angiosperm (hardwood); Ty = tyloses.

| Taxa | Count | Weight (g) | Comments |
|---|---|---|---|
| *Corylus avellana* | 8 | 0.787 | Most: small RW; Some: ?RW/TW, ID, FH. Includes 1 fragment with probable worked end |
| Maloideae | 5 | 0.380 | All: RW |
| *Prunus* sp. | 11 | 0.959 | Most: RW; Some: ?TW, FH. Includes *cf. P. spinosa* |
| *Quercus* sp. | 17 | 1.156 | Most: RW/SW. No Ty; Some: SP |
| *Salix/Populus* sp. | 5 | 0.716 | Most: RW, TW; Some: ID, FH |
| Indeterminate | 4 | 0.195 | All: A. Includes 2 ?bark fragments |
| **Total** | **50** | **4.193** | |

The range of wood identified provides some insight into the woods locally available in the later Roman period. The sample contains both woodland-forming trees, notably oak, and taxa that prefer more open conditions, such as *Prunus*. Willow/poplar is associated with damp conditions and is typically present in wet woodland and in association with ponds, streams and rivers. It is likely that woodland stands were present locally within a predominantly open landscape. It is not possible to establish from the samples if some form of woodland management or silviculture was practised locally, although it is highly probable that such techniques were in use.

The fragment of hazel retaining evidence of woodworking is of particular interest. It appeared to be the remnants of the tip from a cut end of a round-wood pole, apparently cut or shaped with a single oblique stroke. While this indicates that some form of woodworking was carried out on or near the site, equally significant is that it demonstrates that the charcoal recovered from the oven included material that had previously functioned in another capacity and had not been purposely gathered as fuel-wood.

The charcoal represents wood burned on the last occasion that the oven was used. However, it is unclear how representative this sample is of typical day-to-day fuel-wood use. Though all taxa are good to excellent as fuel, the degraded condition of many fragments prior to burning and the presence of worked wood, small branches, and twigs, suggest opportunistic use of whatever was to hand, rather than a well-organised activity. Possible explanations include a decline or halt in the availability of fresh wood supplies or that the sample reflects an episode in which woody debris was disposed of by burning in the oven, independent of its usual function.

### *Animal bone* by Ellen Hambleton

#### *Sample size and preservation*

A total of 1325 fragments of animal bone was recovered by hand excavation from the site, 1275 of them from

**Table 10:** Animal bone fragment counts from deposits at Stepstairs Lane (hand recovered only)

**KEY:** NISP = number of specimens identified to species

| | Period 2 | | Total | |
|---|---|---|---|---|
| | **NISP** | **%** | **NISP** | **%** |
| Cow | 204 | 44.9 | 320 | 44.2 |
| Sheep/Goat | 181 | 39.9 | 302 | 41.7 |
| Pig | 58 | 12.8 | 85 | 11.7 |
| Dog | 6 | 1.3 | 9 | 1.2 |
| Horse | 4 | 0.9 | 7 | 1.0 |
| Deer | 1 | 0.2 | 1 | 0.1 |
| *Sub-total (identified)* | *454* | | *724* | |
| Bird | 6 | | 12 | |
| Unidentified mammal | 342 | | 589 | |
| **Total** | **802** | | **1325** | |

stratified contexts. It was possible to identify 55% of this assemblage (724 fragments) to species level (Table 10). A full assessment report is contained in the site archive. It did not recommend any further work on this assemblage, and this report therefore provides a summary of the principal conclusions of the study. By far the majority of the faunal material (1052 fragments) came from Roman contexts. Most bone-yielding contexts produced only relatively small hand-recovered assemblages, although several stratigraphic groups did produce assemblages of greater than a hundred fragments. The largest collection of faunal material (335 fragments) came from the garden soils/refuse deposits. The state of preservation of the faunal remains for each context was assigned to one of five categories from good to poor. Most contexts (52) produced moderately preserved assemblages with some evidence of fragmentation, gnawing and occasional surface erosion. Only a very small number of contexts produced assemblages that could be described as quite good or good. A small number of burnt fragments were recovered from several different contexts but there is no evidence for extensive burning of faunal material. Overall the assemblage can be described as moderately well preserved at best.

#### *Species representation and assemblage composition*

Among the 724 identified hand-recovered fragments, the assemblage is dominated by domestic species, in particular cattle (44%), sheep/goat (42%) and to a lesser extent pig (12%). Dog (1%) and horse (1%) are also present in small numbers. There is a distinct lack of wild species, represented only by a single fragment of antler (possibly that of red deer). Bird remains are only present in low numbers. Several of these fragments were identified as domestic fowl (chicken), while duck (mallard/domestic duck) and raven are also present. There is variation apparent in the relative abundance of species between different periods, but the sample sizes for most periods are too small to provide any reliable indication of relative species importance. Only the Period 2 sample is large enough to warrant any detailed consideration of species representation. From a total of 802 fragments recovered, 454 were identified to mammal species, with cattle (45%) and sheep/goat (40%) fairly equally represented in the fragment counts. Pig is the third most abundant species (13%), while dog (1%), horse (1%) and deer (0.2%) are present in only small numbers. Variation in the relative abundance of cattle and sheep/goat is apparent within different features assigned to this period. Within the garden deposits consisting of cultivation layers and pits, probably dug for the disposal of domestic refuse, cattle (52%) are substantially more abundant than sheep/goat (28%) in the assemblage of 208 identified fragments. The relative abundance of pig (17%) is high in this group compared to other major Romano-British groups across the site. This pattern of species abundance is a reflection of the assemblages that derived from two of the cultivation soils (303 and 412). However, a third large group from the fill of pit 477 produced hand-recovered cattle and sheep/goat fragments in equal numbers (although sheep/goat was more abundant than cattle in the sieved sample from this context). The sheep bones from pit 477 were mostly metapodials and some cranial fragments (including one hornless specimen) could represent a deposit of primary butchery waste from the processing of sheep carcasses. The majority of cattle remains from the pit have chop marks which also suggests butchery waste, although a broader suite of skeletal elements is represented than for sheep.

A number of other contexts also produced assemblages worthy of note. A collection of 27 sheep fragments from levelling deposit 455 associated with the construction of Building A could represent primary butchery waste from the processing of a sheep carcass. Most areas of the body are represented and the bones could all belong to the same old adult individual. There are knife cuts indicative of skinning on the right metacarpal and other evidence of butchery on the pelvis, skull and vertebrae. Another of these levelling dumps (428) produced 24 fragments of sheep/goat, including several complete bones and associated groups of articulating and butchered vertebrae from the cervical, thoracic and lumbar regions, as well as a matching pair of complete femur and part of the pelvis, which also bore butchery marks. The assemblage from dump 428 therefore appears also to represent the butchery waste from the processing of at least one sheep carcass. By contrast the fill of well 366 was dominated by cattle (65%). Sheep/goat was the only species identified in the bulk sieved sample from the fill of pit 439. At least two individuals are represented in this assemblage but the majority belong to the skeleton of a single young sheep, aged 1–2 years at death. Butchery marks on the femur, tibia, ribs and lumbar vertebrae indicate that the carcass had been processed.

### Ageing and metrical data

The ageing data are very limited. Fusion data were available for cattle, sheep/goat, pig, horse and dog but the sample sizes are too small to provide a reliable indication of mortality patterns. General observations made during the assessment scan noted the presence of both adults and juveniles in the cattle and sheep/goat assemblages, including the presence of some very porous bones belonging to very young infant/neonatal or possibly even foetal individuals. As with the ageing data, the number of fragments with the potential of providing metrical data is small and no single period assemblage contains sufficient numbers of measurable fragments to warrant any detailed analysis.

### Butchery data

Butchery marks were not quantified as part of the assessment scan, but general observations were made and occasional specific comments noted. Both chop marks and knife cuts were observed on all three species, although the knife cuts most commonly noted relate to probable skinning marks on proximal sheep metapodials and cattle 1st phalanges. There were examples of cleaver butchery marks on some sheep/goat fragments

as well as knife butchery. The cattle butchery in the assemblage is characterised by heavy chop marks from a cleaver or similar heavy-bladed tool. Observations included horizontal and oblique chops through many long bone epiphyses, probably associated with disarticulation, and also some examples of saggital chops on the distal humerus and tibia probably indicative of marrow extraction. Also apparent on numerous cattle long bone shafts are surface axial scrapes from a heavy blade made during meat removal (filleting). The type of butchery marks evident on the cattle, sheep/goat and pig remains from Stepstairs Lane are typical of those observed and discussed in other contemporary deposits at Cirencester and indeed at several other Romano-British urban sites (see the discussion of the animal bones from Trinity Road; p. 103).

### Summary and discussion

The overall composition of the assemblage from the Period 2 deposits from Stepstairs Lane shares similarities with many other urban Romano-British sites in that domestic species predominate and cattle and sheep/goat are well represented. Cattle, although only slightly more abundant than sheep/goat in terms of fragment count, clearly provided the main meat component of the diet, which is typical of other Romano-British urban sites (King 1978; 1999: CE V, 352–70). However, cattle fragments do not significantly outnumber sheep/goat in the assemblage, nor is the overall percentage of pig particularly high, which according to King could be considered an assemblage profile more typical of a native rural site. It should be noted, however, that such broad patterns fail to take into account the considerable intra-site variability often seen on urban sites, and already demonstrated within Cirencester (CE V, 352–70). The assemblage from Stepstairs Lane represents only part of the picture of animal consumption and deposition in Roman Cirencester.

Comparisons with other assemblages from Cirencester are clearly relevant when considering the composition of the Period 2 assemblage at Stepstairs Lane. Maltby (CE V, 354) noted considerable variation in the relative abundance of cattle, sheep/goat and pig among the different assemblages from Cirencester, a feature that is also borne out by the assemblages from this excavation and that at Trinity Road (see below). In reporting on a series of assemblages analysed in the early 1990s, he categorised the material into three main groups based on species representation. The Stepstairs Lane assemblage appears most similar to those from Sheep Street and Querns Road, which fall into his Type 3 category. At these sites cattle and sheep/goat fragments are fairly equally represented at around 40% each and there are slightly fewer pigs (c. 15–20%). Overall there is a slightly lower prevalence of pig in the Period 2 Stepstairs Lane assemblage (13%) than at Sheep Street and Querns Road but the pattern is nevertheless broadly similar. The Type 3 sites are also typified by the absence of any large-scale dumping of cattle bones and the presence of a reasonably high proportion of domestic refuse. The Stepstairs Lane material is mainly derived from garden deposits and pits and the evidence for small-scale processing of sheep and mixed deposits of cattle and sheep bones appears to be representative of domestic waste. Certainly the assemblages from this site contain no large deposits of cattle like those found at other sites in Cirencester, Winchester and Dorchester which are associated with a meat market and large-scale specialist butchery (ibid.; Maltby 1994). Although no quantitative analysis of the butchery was carried out as part of the assessment, the butchery marks observed here clearly followed similar patterns of butchery in the cattle and sheep/goat assemblages to those discussed by Maltby (CE V, 354; Maltby 1989) from Cirencester and other Romano-British towns.

## Discussion

The excavations at Stepstairs Lane revealed evidence for Roman activity dating from the late 1st century to the 3rd or 4th century AD. If the Period 1 consolidation can be viewed as the preparation of the site for the construction of Building A, then that event can be dated to the Flavian–Trajanic period. Occupation material 426 resting on the first floor of Building A included a sherd of Antonine samian and Black-Burnished ware. The floor was replaced on another two occasions before the building was demolished, which is therefore unlikely to have occurred before the late 2nd century. There is little useful dating evidence for the construction of Building B, and only a broad late 2nd or 3rd-century date can be ascribed for this event. Building B appears to have fallen into disrepair sometime after the later 3rd century AD.

Although the hydrology of the town during the Roman period is not fully understood, it would appear that in pre-Roman times a river channel flowed through Watermoor and rejoined the main course of the Churn to the south-east of the site adopted for the Silchester Gate (CE V, 8–11). Any such channel would have lain to the north of the excavation area, at the base of the north-east facing slope encountered during the excavation, and it is quite probable that this site was susceptible to flooding. This would explain the presence of the series of short-lived drainage ditches that went out of use some time in the 2nd century AD at the eastern end of the site and also the requirement for consolidation of the site prior to development. The ditches were aligned perpendicularly to the line of Street C and it is likely that they would have drained directly into a ditch running alongside it.

As the main parts of both Buildings A and B appear to have been situated outside the excavation area, interpretation of their function is very difficult. It is possible that Building B represents the rear of a building fronting on to Street C. This would mean that the building would have extended at least 27m back from the street frontage. The presence of an oven in Building B suggests a non-domestic use for this room. A similar horseshoe-shaped oven is known from Shop V.3 in *insula* V (CE V, 206–9), and an interpretation of Building B as the rear part of a shop is possible.

The evidence for the robbing of stone and digging of pits and wells in the medieval period is of some note as the main focus of medieval Cirencester lay to the north of Lewis Lane/Querns Lane. Throughout the medieval period, the site is believed to have lain within a large meadow known as the Lewes (Slater 1976a, fig. 6.7).

In recent times, as part of an initiative to establish a 'new town' in Watermoor by a property speculator, the 'New Town Hall' was built on the site in 1922. This building was demolished in 1971 and replaced with modern garage blocks. It is evident that the extensive truncation observed across the site is attributable to this modern development.

# INVESTIGATIONS BY THE TIME TEAM IN INSULA IX, 1999
## by Neil Holbrook and Katie Hirst

Trial excavation was undertaken at four locations within *insula* IX as part of a *Time Team* television programme in 1999 (Hirst 2003). The excavations were supplemented by geophysical surveys in St Michael's Park and the gardens of 50–56 Chester Street, Stonewalls House and One Plus One Nursery (see Fig. 20).

## The geophysical survey

Seven areas totalling approximately 1.2ha were surveyed by GSB Prospection Ltd using the resistance technique, and two of these were additionally subjected to gradiometry totalling 0.4ha (Figs 52–53). A full report has been prepared on the survey (GSB 1999) and the following account summarises only the most archaeologically significant results. Within St Michael's Park a linear band of high resistance clearly equates with the projected line of Ermin Street. To the north-east of Ermin Street a broad area of high resistance parallel to the street is likely to reflect rubble derived from a range of buildings, and within this zone a number of linear and rectilinear high resistance responses which probably represent wall lines are visible in the filtered data. Overall it is difficult to make much of their plan although there appears to have been a substantial range of shops or other buildings *c.* 25m deep. The gap between the buildings and the street might have been occupied by a portico similar to those found flanking Ermin Street to both the north-west and south-east of this point. The data in the western half of the park are dominated by a large area of low resistance. It is most likely that this response is due to an increased depth of topsoil resulting from the levelling and landscaping of the park in the recent past. A number of high resistance anomalies in the south-western part of the survey area have some elements of rectilinearity, and might be of archaeological significance, although they could also reflect debris associated with landscaping. The broad area of high resistance to the south-east of the tennis courts is also more likely to reflect landscaping than the alignment of Street G of the Roman town. It is likely that the resistance anomalies within the garden of Stonewalls House also relate to Roman archaeology, although some might also be a product of more recent activity.

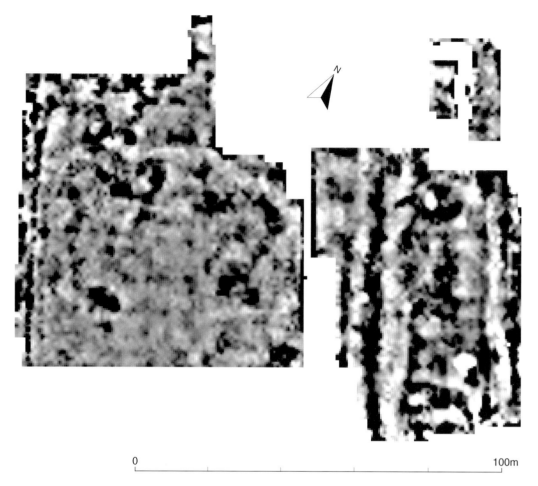

0                                                                                                           100m

*Fig. 52*   St Michael's Park. High pass filtered data from resistivity survey by GSB Prospection (1:1000)

The gradiometry data within the park are dominated by a large area of ferrous disturbance, a product of adjacent boundaries and buildings, which has masked any archaeological responses present. A broad linear band that is magnetically relatively quiet adjacent to a positive linear anomaly can be correlated with the line of Ermin Street. The positive anomaly is likely to reflect a roadside ditch. Further anomalies to the north-east of Ermin Street may also be associated with Roman structures, although they do not have any clearly recognisable pattern. Positive anomalies within the garden of Stonewalls House are likely to have an archaeological origin and testify to the presence of burnt or fired material. The areas of resistance survey within the gardens of 50, 52, 54 and 56 Chester Street and the One Plus One nursery were of too small an extent for reliable interpretations of the data to be obtained.

### The excavations

### *56 Chester Street*

A trench 3 × 3m square (see Fig. 20, 1999 Trench 1) was opened in the back garden of 56 Chester Street in order to investigate the area around the site of a tessellated pavement discovered *c*. 1864 while building an out-

house to Claremont Place, Chester Street (Beecham 1887, 271; Haverfield 1920, pl. XI, no. 34). It was quickly established that no previous investigation of Roman levels had taken place within the bounds of the trench, although a Victorian intrusion on the edge of the trench may relate to the discovery of the pavement just outside the area examined. Excavation did not continue below late Roman levels associated with a masonry building, and natural was not reached in any place.

The masonry building was represented by a mortared limestone wall, 0.38–0.5m wide, which survived to a height of 0.7m (106) (Fig. 54). This defined the inside corner of a probable corridor which turned through a right-angle. The width of the corridor was not established although, based on the design of the mosaic and assuming that the borders were of equal width, it would have been about 2.30m. A mosaic pavement had been laid over the foundation trench 125 for the wall. Within the south-western corridor the scheme was a running pelta pattern, the peltae outlined in dark blue-grey and infilled red and white with dark blue-grey centres; the central point of each terminated in a T-shape (Figs 55–6). The panel in the north-west corridor was based on a scheme of alternate squares and poised squares creating triangles at the margins where the latter were truncated by the frame of simple

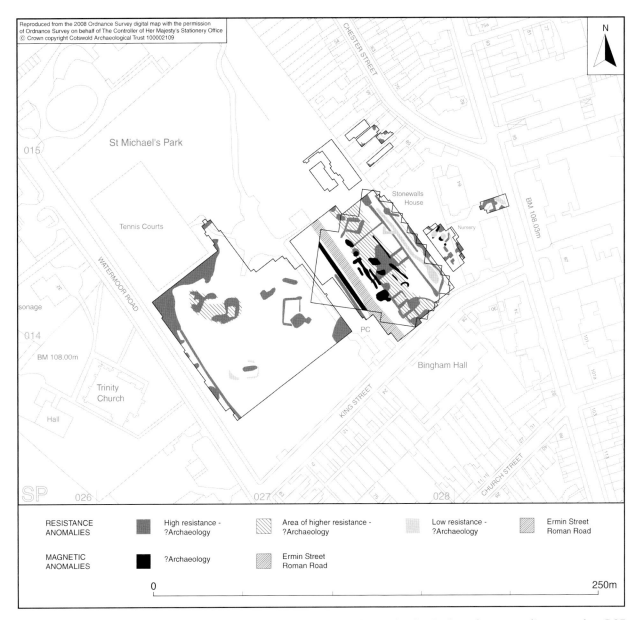

RESISTANCE ANOMALIES — High resistance - ?Archaeology — Area of higher resistance - ?Archaeology — Low resistance - ?Archaeology — Ermin Street Roman Road

MAGNETIC ANOMALIES — ?Archaeology — Ermin Street Roman Road

0     250m

*Fig. 53*  Summary interpretation of geophysical surveys in St Michael's Park and surrounding area by GSB Prospection (1:2000)

guilloche. The mosaics probably date to the 4th century AD. The junction of the two panels was patched in antiquity with blue lias slate, tile and loose tesserae in a rough attempt to continue the original pattern. Overlying the repair was a ragged-edged spread of white mortar which was presumably left over from that event.

The mosaic in the north-west corridor was cut through by a stone-lined drain 119, 0.42m wide. The drain passed though the wall beneath a lintel stone which had been inserted into the original fabric. The drain was filled with deposits of silt (127, 118, 116), one of which spread beyond its walls and covered part of the mosaic. The fills of the drain contained four coins (AD 330–45, 337–40 and two uncertain 4th-century AD issues; nos 9, 10, 95, 96) and a small amount of pottery including two sherds of late shell-tempered ware suggesting a date after *c.* AD 360 for the final filling.

The mosaic floor was covered in one area with light grey sandy silt, possibly street wash, which was in turn sealed by a spread of mortar, possibly the remnants of a much disturbed surface. Overlying deposits of demolition rubble contained tile, painted plaster, coins, pottery, bone and iron nails. The latest artefacts from these layers comprised coins of AD 388–402, 388–92 and 364–78 (nos 73, 57, 42) and late shell-tempered pottery. Elsewhere the mosaic floor was directly overlain by a dark earth which contained 12th to 15th-century pottery along with residual Roman wares. The dark earth was cut by a Victorian intrusion which is likely to relate to the discovery of the tessellated pavement recorded by Beecham. The intrusion had been backfilled with a series of deposits which contained numerous fragments of tile, plaster, oyster shell, slag, pottery, bone, iron and copper-alloy objects.

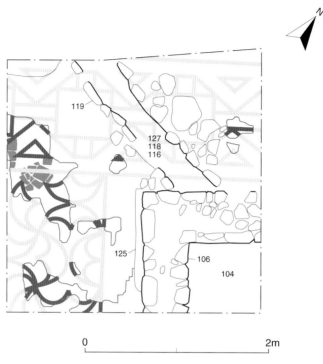

*Fig. 54*    56 Chester Street. Plan of Time Team trench 1 (1:40)

Most of the pottery is residual, dating from the late Roman period with some post-medieval sherds.

It is difficult to reconstruct the layout of the building from this very limited investigation. It was presumably a town house, and one possibility is that the corridor ran around two sides of an open courtyard 104, into which the drain emptied. In this case the main range of rooms would have lain to the north-west and south-west. There would be sufficient room to the north-west for a corridor *c*. 3m wide and a range *c*. 8m wide in the available space to the extrapolated frontage of the *insula* with Street G (if we assume that the street was *c*. 7–8m wide as has been found elsewhere in Cirencester). The south-west range of the town house presumably lay behind the buildings detected in the geophysical survey flanking Ermin Street. This building has be termed

*Fig. 55*    56 Chester Street. Time Team trench 1 showing mosaic with drain cut through it (scales both 2m)

IX.1 as it is probably part of the same structure marked in this general location by Wacher (1963, fig. 1)

### *Discussion of the mosaics* by S. Cosh and D.S. Neal

A running pelta pattern is fairly common in Britain and, where it is possible to ascertain date, has been found in a 4th-century AD context. Only one other example of this design has been found within the walled area of Cirencester, however, a narrow panel on a mosaic from Ashcroft House. This has been attributed by D. J. Smith to his Corinian Saltire School (CE III, 209–18, figs 130, 134) which operated in the mid 4th century AD. Another narrow panel of running pelta pattern occurs on an Orpheus pavement from Barton Farm just outside the town, which sealed a coin of Allectus (AD 293–6) and has been dated to the first half of the 4th century AD. Neither matches the form or colour of the Chester Street mosaic. A closer parallel is the mosaic paving the *porticus* of Box villa, near Bath (Cosh and Neal 2005, no. 233.1). Although a 2nd-century AD date is possible there, it could have been laid during the late 3rd or 4th-century AD rebuild ('the mosaic and character of the make-up inclines towards the later [date]'; Hurst *et al.* 1987, 27). Pavements in town houses of the 2nd century AD tend to be composed of coarse tesserae, normally simple patterns in red and grey. Running pelta patterns are employed in corridors at Lydney (Bathurst 1879, pl. XIV), Whittington Court (O'Neil 1952, 39–40, pl. IV), Castle Copse, Wiltshire (Cosh and Neal 2005, no. 238.3), Wellow, Somerset (ibid., no. 219.3) and on another extremely rare example in Britain of fine mosaic paving two arms of the *porticus* at Somerleigh Court, Dorchester (ibid., no. 165.34). All are dateable to the 4th century AD.

*Fig. 56*    56 Chester Street. Painting of mosaic by D.S. Neal (1:25) (© D.S. Neal)

The scheme of alternating squares in the other panel is more normally associated with 2nd-century AD pavements. The only (fragmentary) example from Cirencester is probably from the former grounds of Ashcroft House and has several stylistic characteristics of the 2nd century AD (Cosh 2007, 12–13, figs 3–4), and the scheme occurs in a probable passage of a house in Bath dated archaeologically to the same century (Cosh and Neal 2005, no. 188.2). However, the Chester Street example differs in important respects to the others, particularly in its lack of double fillets parallel to the guilloche and, as it is clearly contemporary with the adjacent running pelta pattern, a 4th-century AD date is likely. The quality of the mosaic suggests that the rooms of the ranges were also well appointed and that the building was of high status.

### Stonewalls House

A trench, 2.9 × 1.9m, was excavated within the grounds of Stonewalls House to examine the area around the site of a tessellated pavement marked on the 1875 Ordnance Survey map and Beecham's (1887) map of the Roman town (see Fig. 20, 1999 Trench 4). It was presumably this discovery which led Wacher (1963, fig. 1) to designate this area as building IX.2 on his town

plan. In the event little investigation occurred here due to lack of time, although part of a Roman building was discovered. A wall aligned north-west to south-east constructed from roughly faced limestone blocks at least four courses high was found. It was 0.45m wide and was probably an internal partition. Abutting the wall was a mortar floor, which sloped down markedly away from it due to subsidence (perhaps into a hypocaust basement or an earlier feature). The floor was covered by a charcoal-rich occupation deposit which yielded a coin of AD 388–402 (no. 75). This was sealed by demolition rubble which contained finds including a bone die, a copper-alloy spoon and brooch, a whetstone, fragments of glass and a coin of AD 388–402 (no. 65). The wall was cut through by a small pit of uncertain date, sealed beneath dark earth.

### The Firs, Victoria Road

The site of The Firs has long been regarded as being of high archaeological potential. The house was owned by the antiquarian Thomas Bravender, and Beecham records his account of discoveries in this area:

The Firs is on the site of a Roman house, and when the foundations were dug up a portion of a pavement was found with the figure of a bird in the centre. It was left and covered up, and is now about a yard under the tiles of the present hall. Pavements and foundations were also found to the south, west and north, but not on the east side that I remember. From the absence of Roman remains between The Firs and the School [the former Grammar School on Victoria Road] it is possible that there may have been an open space in Roman times. Some large stones and pillars were found a little to the north of The Firs which may have been the remains of a Roman temple at the north-west corner or side of the open space; sufficient, however, has not been discovered to make this more than conjecture. (Beecham 1887, 252)

Given the finds of sculpture that had come from this area Bravender marked this area on his map of Roman Cirencester, a version of which was published in Beecham, as 'Site of Roman Temple?'. Accordingly a trial trench was excavated in the car park of The Firs with maximum dimensions of 8 × 5.2m (see Fig. 20, 1999 Trench 3). Due to a lack of time only the uppermost deposits were exposed. These were cleaned but not otherwise investigated and consequently their stratigraphic relationships were not fully understood. A probable floor surface was cut by a stone-lined drain aligned north-east to south-west. The drain was overlaid by a crudely constructed limestone wall, 1.1m wide, which utilised little mortar. While the wall was on a general north-west to south-east alignment it was not exactly aligned with the street grid. A layer of compacted gravel lay to the north-east of the wall, and this was cut by a single posthole. The surface was overlaid by another layer of sandy gravel containing many fragments of tile. Further to the north in the trench spreads of silt and isolated patches of a possible surface were directly overlain by dark earth at least 0.48m thick. Surface cleaning of the uppermost Roman surfaces produced one coin of the House of Theodosius (no. 59), but the deposits are otherwise undated. They appear to relate to a crudely built late Roman structure, but lack of investigation precludes any further interpretation.

## The finds

### *The coins* by Richard Reece

The coins are not a complete series from the sites in which investigation took place because the excavations were concerned with the later deposits. Judged then as a sample from the later deposits in Cirencester the coins are very much as would be expected. The sequence starts as we have come to expect with a number of coins of AD 345–8, with a few earlier issues. The greatest concentration comes in the years AD 364 to 378, the House of Valentinian, and these coins range from almost fresh to mildly worn. They were therefore not in circulation for long. The latest coins, of AD 388 to 402, the House of Theodosius, are well represented and some of these are in very good condition. The deposits are therefore towards the end of the 4th century AD, or very early in the 5th century AD, but not far away from the year AD 400.

One coin (no. 50) has not been recorded before. This sounds exciting but, due to the complexities of mintmarks in the late Roman issues, within a fairly

clear system, there is nothing surprising in it. Three emperors were striking two main issues with an ever-changing series of mint (batch) marks. At Lyon about AD 374 Valentinian, Valens and Gratian were striking issues with Victory or the Emperor. For the mintmark S/R/LVGP Victory had not been recorded for Gratian up to now. This fills a gap.

1.  Claudius II 268–70 RIC 261. Rev: CONSECRATIO – Altar. T4, u/s.
2.  Tetricus I 270–73 RIC 121. Rev: SALU AUG – Salus standing left. T1, u/s.
3.  Barbarous Radiate 270–90. Obv: legend Tetricus II, portrait Tetricus I. Rev: PAX, Pax standing left. T4, 403.
4.  Barbarous Radiate 270–90. Rev illegible. T1, 104.
5.  Carausius 286–93. Rev uncertain. T4, u/s.
6.  Urbs Roma 330–35. HK 750. Cut Down. Rev: Wolf and twins. T1, 111.
7.  Urbs Roma 330–45. HK copy of 65. Rev: Wolf and twins.
8.  House of Constantine 330–45. Hybrid. Obv: as Urbs Roma HK 51. Rev: as Constantinopolis as HK52.
9.  Constantinopolis 330–45. HK copy as 52. Rev: Victory on prow. T1, 116.
10. Helena 337–40. HK as 104. Rev: PAX PUBLICA. T1, 116.
11. Constantius II 324–30. RIC 7, Heraclea 78. Rev: PROVIDENTIAE CAESS – Gateway. T1, u/s.
12. Constantius II 345–48. HK ? 455. Rev: VICTORIAE DD AUGG Q NN – Two victories with wreaths. T1, 114.
13. Constantius II 345–48. HK as 137. Rev: VICTORIAE DD AUGG Q NN – Two victories with wreaths. T1, u/s.
14. Constantius II 356–61. CK as 77. Rev: SPES REIPUBLICE – Emperor standing with spear and shield. T1, 114.
15. Constans 345–48. HK 140. Rev: VICTORIAE DD AUGG Q NN – Two victories with wreaths. T1, u/s.
16. Constans 345–48. HK 148. Rev: VICTORIAE DD AUGG Q NN – Two victories with wreaths. T1, u/s.
17. Constans 345–48. HK as 148. Rev: VICTORIAE DD AUGG Q NN – Two victories with wreaths. T1, u/s.
18. Constans 345–48. HK 153. Rev: VICTORIAE DD AUGG Q NN – Two victories with wreaths. T1, 111.
19. Constans 345–48. HK 158. Rev: VICTORIAE DD AUGG Q NN – Two victories with wreaths.
20. Constans 337–41. HK 243. Rev: GLORIA EXERCITUS – Two soldiers with one standard. T1, u/s.
21. Constans 348–50. CK 626. Rev: FEL TEMP REPARATIO – Emperor in galley. T2, 201.
22. Magnentius 350–60. CK as 8. Rev: VICTORIAE DD NN AUG ET CAE – Two victories with shield.
23. House of Constantine 350–60. CK copy as 25. Rev: FEL TEMP REPARATIO – Fallen horseman. T1, u/s.
24. House of Constantine 350–60. CK copy as 25. Rev: FEL TEMP REPARATIO – Fallen horseman. T1, u/s.
25. House of Constantine 350–60. CK copy as 25. Rev: FEL TEMP REPARATIO – Fallen horseman. T1, u/s.
26. House of Constantine 350–60. CK copy as 25. Rev: FEL TEMP REPARATIO – Fallen horseman. T1, u/s.
27. Valentinian I 364–75. CK as 96. Cut down. Rev: SECURITAS REIPUBLICAE – Victory walking left with wreath. T1, u/s.
28. Valentinian I 364–75. CK as 300. Rev: GLORIA ROMANORUM – Emperor with standard and captive. T1, u/s.
29. Valentinian I 364–75. CK as 300. Rev: SECURITAS REIPUBLICAE – Victory walking left with wreath. T4, 405.

30. Valentinian I 364–75. CK 300. Rev: GLORIA ROMAN-ORUM – Emperor with standard and captive.
31. Valentinian I 364–75. CK as 481. Rev: SECURITAS REIPUBLICAE – Victory walking left with wreath. T2, 201.
32. Valentinian I 364-75. CK 487. Rev: GLORIA ROMAN-ORUM – Emperor with standard and captive. T1, u/s.
33. Valentinian I 364–75. CK 512. Rev: GLORIA ROMAN-ORUM – Emperor with standard and captive. T1, u/s,
34. Valentinian I 364–75. CK as 512. Rev: GLORIA ROM-ANORUM – Emperor with standard and captive. T1, u/s.
35 Valentinian I 364–75. CK as 525. Rev: GLORIA ROMANORUM – Emperor with standard and captive. T1, u/s.
36. Valentinian I 364–75. CK 1030. Rev: SECURITAS REIPUBLICAE – Victory walking left with wreath.
37. Valentinian I 364–75. CK 1415. Rev: SECURITAS REIPUBLICAE – Victory walking left with wreath. T1, u/s.
38. Valentinian I 364–75. Rev: Illegible. T1, u/s.
39. Valens 364–78. CK as 97. Rev: SECURITAS REIPUB-LICAE – Victory walking left with wreath. T1, u/s.
40. Valens 364–78. CK as 275. Rev: GLORIA ROMAN-ORUM – Emperor with standard and captive. T1, u/s.
41. Valens 364–78. CK as 282. Rev: GLORIA ROMAN-ORUM – Emperor with standard and captive.
42. Valens 364–78. CK 322. Rev: SECURITAS REIPUB-LICAE – Victory walking left with wreath. T1, u/s.
43. Valens 364–78. CK 361. Rev: SECURITAS REI-PUBLICAE – Victory walking left with wreath. T1, u/s.
44. Valens 364–78. CK as 512. Rev: GLORIA ROMAN-ORUM – Emperor with standard and captive. T1, u/s.
45. Valens 364–78. CK 526. Rev: GLORIA ROMAN-ORUM – Emperor with standard and captive. T1, u/s.
46. Valens 364–78. CK 528. Rev: SECURITAS REIPUB-LICAE – Victory walking left with wreath.
47. Valens 364–78. CK 1416. Rev: SECURITAS REIPUB-LICAE – Victory walking left with wreath. T1, u/s.
48. Gratian 367–78. CK as 98. Rev: SECURITAS REIPUB-LICAE – Victory walking left with wreath. T1, u/s.
49. Gratian 367–78. CK as 308. Rev: GLORIA ROMAN-ORUM – Emperor with standard and captive. T1, u/s.
50. Gratian 367–78. CK 363a (as 357 but mm 363). Rev: SECURITAS REIPUBLICAE – Victory walking left with wreath.
51. Gratian 367–78. CK as 529. Rev: GLORIA NOVI SAECULI – Emperor with spear and shield. T1, u/s.
52. Gratian 367–78. CK 1412. Rev: GLORIA ROMAN-ORUM – Emperor with standard and captive. T1, u/s.
53. House of Valentinian 364–78. CK as 96. Rev: SECUR-ITAS REIPUBLICAE – Victory walking left with wreath. T1, u/s.
54. House of Valentinian 364–78. CK as 516. Rev: SECUR-ITAS REIPUBLICAE – Victory walking left with wreath. T1, u/s.
55. House of Valentinian 364–78. Rev: illegible. T1, 111.
56. Magnus Maximus 387–88. CK 560. Rev: SPES ROMAN-ORUM – Gateway. T4, u/s.
57. Valentinian II 388–92. CK as 162. Rev: VICTORIA AUGGG – Victory left with wreath. T1, 111.
58. Valentinian II 388–92. CK 389. Rev: VICTORIA AUGGG – Victory left with wreath.
59. Theodosius I 388–95. CK as 163. Rev: VICTORIA AUGGG – Victory left with wreath. T3, u/s.
60. Theodosius I 388–95. CK as 163. Rev: VICTORIA AUGGG – Victory left with wreath.

61. Theodosius I 388–95. CK 565. Rev: VICTORIA AUGGG – Victory left with wreath.
62. Theodosius I 388–95. CK 1106. Rev: SALUS REIPU-BLICAE – Victory to left with captive, chi-ro left. T1, u/s.
63. Arcadius 388–402. CK 566. Rev: VICTORIA AUGGG – Victory left with wreath. T1, u/s.
64. House of Theodosius 388–402. CK as 162. Rev: VIC-TORIA AUGGG – Victory left with wreath. T1, u/s.
65. House of Theodosius 388–402. CK as 162. Rev: VIC-TORIA AUGGG – Victory left with wreath. T4, 405.
66. House of Theodosius 388–402. CK as 162. Rev: VIC-TORIA AUGGG – Victory left with wreath. T1, u/s.
67. House of Theodosius 388–402. CK as 162. Rev: VIC-TORIA AUGGG – Victory left with wreath.
68. House of Theodosius 388–402. CK as 162. Rev: VIC-TORIA AUGGG – Victory left with wreath.
69. House of Theodosius 388–402. CK as 162. Rev VIC-TORIA AUGGG – Victory left with wreath.
70. House of Theodosius 388–402. CK as 162. Rev: VIC-TORIA AUGGG – Victory left with wreath. T4, u/s.
71. House of Theodosius 388–402. CK as 796. Rev: SALUS REIPUBLICAE – Victory to left with captive, chi-ro left. T1, u/s.
72. House of Theodosius 388–402. CK as 796. Rev: SALUS REIPUBLICAE – Victory to left with captive, chi-ro left. T1, u/s.
73. House of Theodosius 388–402. CK as 796. Rev: SALUS REIPUBLICAE – Victory to left with captive, chi-ro left. T1, 111.
74. House of Theodosius 388–402. Rev: illegible. T4, u/s.
75. House of Theodosius 388–402. Rev: illegible. T4, 410.
76. Uncertain 4th C. Corroded. Rev: illegible.
77. Uncertain 4th C. Corroded. Rev: illegible. T1, 114.
78. Uncertain 4th C. Corroded. Rev: illegible. T1, 116.
79. Uncertain 4th C. Corroded. Rev: illegible. T1, 116.
80. Uncertain 4th C. Corroded and burnt. Rev: illegible. T1, u/s.
81. Uncertain 4th C. Corroded and burnt. Rev: illegible. T1, u/s.
82. Uncertain 4th C. Corroded and burnt. Rev: illegible. T1, u/s.

### *The pottery* by Jane Timby

The four trenches in *insula* IX resulted in the recovery of 883 sherds of Roman pottery, 8 sherds of medieval pottery and 116 sherds of post-medieval wares. The total weight of the assemblage was 12.36kg. The vast majority (728 sherds) was recovered from trench 1. Full details of the pottery can be found in the typescript report (Hirst 2003). The assemblage is fairly typical of that to be expected in later Roman Cirencester. Continental imports, although not prolific partly due to the late date of the groups, are represented by finewares, amphorae and mortaria. A small number of wares dominate the Roman assemblage: Dorset Black-Burnished ware (14% by weight), Oxfordshire products (23%), Midlands shell-tempered ware (12%) and late grey wares (29%). Although comparable late Roman groups of pottery are scarce in Cirencester, the dominance of Dorset Black-Burnished ware and Oxford red-slipped ware appears to be the norm in 4th-century AD Cirencester (CE V, 337–8). The high percentage of Midlands shell-tempered ware is not dissimilar to that recorded from Beeches Road (ibid., table 29) where it accounted for 20% by EVE compared to 17% from the current assemblage. The

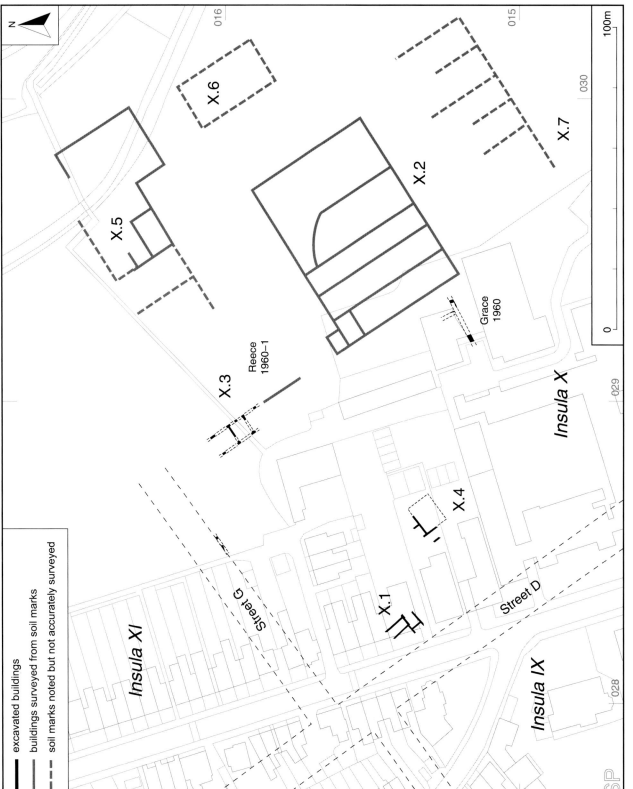

*Fig. 57*   Plan of structures detected by excavation and surface survey in *insula* X (1:1250)

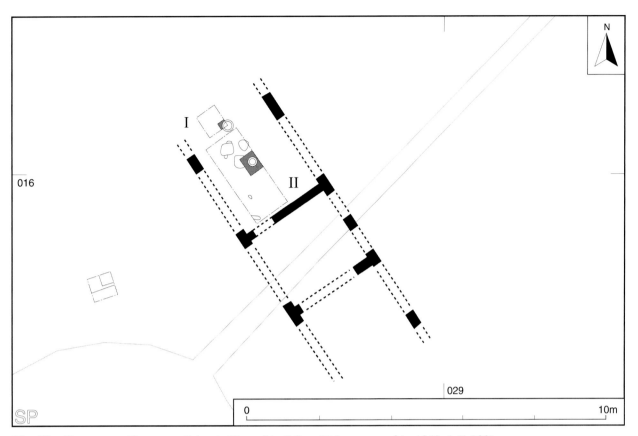

*Fig. 58* Cirencester Grammar School. Plan of building X.3 excavated in 1960–1 (1:100)

absence of any sub-Roman material and the paucity of medieval wares suggest little use of the area after the Roman abandonment until the 18th–20th centuries.

## OBSERVATIONS AND EXCAVATION AT CIRENCESTER GRAMMAR SCHOOL, VICTORIA ROAD, 1960
### by Peter Grace and Neil Holbrook

On the plan of the Roman town contained in CE III four structures are marked within *insula* X (Fig. 57). Buildings X.1 and X.4 were examined in 1895 and 1922 (CE III, 247) while X.3 was excavated by Richard Reece in 1960–1 after the accidental discovery of Roman structures during operations to level part of the Grammar School field for the construction of an access road (Reece 1970; Fig. 58). It is likely that Reece excavated the north-east range of a courtyard house, and that the north-west range of this building fronted onto Street G. Building X.2 is marked at the northern corner of the *insula* and while it is unclear precisely what evidence underpins this designation it is most likely to be observations made by Peter Grace during ploughing of the Grammar School playing field at the beginning of October 1960.

**Observations and excavation in 1960** by Peter Grace

The ploughing was the first stage in the re-grading and levelling of the field, and led to many large pieces of

walling stone and patches of mortar being brought to the surface. After two or three days of frost the soil broke up to reveal numerous defined lines of mortar and rubble, all approximately 0.6m wide, which are best explained as the surface indications of walls lying just below the surface of the field. Once the extent of the surface indications was clearly defined a survey was commenced. Unfortunately limitations of access and time available meant that only two areas (Fig. 57, X.2 and X.5) had been accurately surveyed when ploughing and harrowing unexpectedly commenced once again. The approximate position of two further buildings (here termed X.6 and X.7) were noted but not surveyed in detail. Given the limited resources available (a 66 ft tape, three ranging rods and one sixth form pupil) the accuracy of the survey must be in some doubt. The surface indications suggest the existence of four separate structures, but further examination will be required to determine whether this was indeed the case. In a subsequent ploughing on 10 March 1961 large quantities of dressed stone were brought to the surface. The quantity of Roman artefacts discovered by 'field walking' the wall lines leaves little doubt of their date. Artefacts recovered from the vicinity of the buildings included pottery, tesserae, painted wall plaster, fragments of hypocaust and roofing tile, and two items of special note: a fragment of roofing tile with a graffito AVCXIEX (RIB II.5, 2491.170) and from within X.2 an amphora sherd incised with a graffito of a horse after firing (now in the Corinium Museum).

A new craft block was built to the south-west of X.2. during the summer of 1960 and the foundation trenches were monitored and recorded by the author as and when the opportunity arose. A 0.6m-wide wall which survived three courses high above pitched footings aligned north-east to south-west was found a short distance below the surface. This was abutted by a second wall at right-angles. To the south-west of the latter wall the earliest level encountered was a mortar floor which abutted the wall (natural was not reached). Lying on top of the floor was a fragment of a samian goblet Déchelette form 64 which dates to the 2nd century AD. The floor was overlaid by pure brown clay sealed beneath a mixed clay deposit which was cut by a pit containing coins of Valens (AD 364–78) and a barbarous radiate. The pit was sealed beneath a mixed deposit containing demolition debris. To the north-east of the cross wall an external cobbled surface abutted both walls. It was sealed beneath clean brown clay similar to that found above the mortar floor. One possibility is that the clay might be an alluvial deposit laid down by flooding.

## Discussion

Further archaeological work has occurred in this area since 1960, most notably an evaluation conducted by J.R. Roberts of Gloucestershire County Council in 1988 in advance of the construction of a new playground. The site of the playground overlay the south-western end of Building X.2. Accordingly a trench 25m long by 2m wide was excavated to assess the survival of archaeological deposits in this area. The trench was aligned east–west and was designed to transect the area to the west of the Inner Churn and intersect with the northern corner of X2. A test pit, 2m square, was excavated on the site of a proposed soakaway. Other than a couple of sondages, excavation did not proceed below 0.2m from the current ground surface. Given the restrictions of a single evaluation trench, and the limited permitted depth of excavation, interpretation of the results was difficult. A subsequent note published on the evaluation (Wills 1989, 254) differs in its interpretation of the findings from that presented in an interim typescript report (Roberts 1988). The earliest deposits encountered were of alluvial clay containing flecks of brick and tile which was in excess of 0.7m deep in one of the sondages (excavation ceased at the top of the water table and gravel was not reached). The clays were overlain by thin spreads of limestone rubble which may have formed a platform for the construction of building X.2. Three linear spreads of rubble were found which can be correlated with those plotted by Mr Grace (slight differences in plotted location doubtless being a product of the inevitable inaccuracies in the 1960 survey). Examination of one of the spreads showed that the walls had been thoroughly robbed, and there was a noticeable overall lack of demolition debris within the excavation area. It was suggested that the buildings had been deliberately demolished and much of the larger masonry removed. Alternatively it is possible that the playing fields were subject to terracing and truncation in the 19th century to provide material for the railway embankment which runs along the southern side of the playing fields. One of the latest features on the site was a

ditch on the same alignment as building X.2. It was cut by one of the robber trenches. A subsequent watching brief during the installation of a fence around the playing ground revealed little of significance (Wills 1990, 195).

Overall it is possible to draw some conclusions from the various pieces of work in *insula* X. The alluvial clay presumably accumulated in the early Roman period within the flood plain of the Churn, possibly a result of deliberate reclamation. The edge of the former flood plain must lie a short distance to the north-east of building X.3 as excavation there encountered gravel subsoil overlain by a clay turf line through which 1st-century AD postholes were cut (Reece 1970, 11). Domestic occupation within the *insula* was underway by the mid 2nd century AD at latest, to judge from the date of the levelling deposit laid down prior to the construction of masonry courtyard house X.3. The mosaics within X.4 are also stylistically 2nd century AD (Smith 1975, 273, 280), and stamped tiles of the same date have been recovered from this building (RIB II.5, 2489.21A; .44C; F; G; .49; *Britannia* 31 (2000), 439, no. 22). With regard to the plans of the individual buildings, the apparent large size of X.2, *c.* 62 × 44m, should be noted. This is very large in comparison with other domestic structures in the town (cf. Fig. 18) and a house of this size does not seem credible. One possibility is that at least some of the walls are defining yards or courtyards. Another is that some of the soil marks might represent ditches filled with demolition material rather than the robber trenches of masonry walls. Further investigation of this area through geophysics and excavation will be required before greater clarity can be obtained on the nature, plan and extent of these buildings. Probing and rudimentary resistivity by Reece in 1960–1 to the north-west of his excavation area seemed to indicate that Street G continued to the north-east of Street D for some distance, although it faded out thereafter.

## OTHER MISCELLANEOUS INVESTIGATIONS

### Insula III

**III.3** 33 Querns Lane (see Fig. 17, no. 15). Remains of a building on the Fosse Way frontage recorded during a watching brief are reported under Street Observation B.5 (p. 43).

**III.4** 26 Watermoor Road (see Fig. 17, no. 21). A watching brief recorded the uppermost levels of a previously unrecorded building which has been numbered as III.4. Two parallel walls of solid mortared limestone were found, 5m apart. One was abutted by a wall of less robust construction which was 0.6m wide. Within the angle formed by the walls a dark grey occupation deposit containing patches of burnt clay and charcoal yielded a few sherds of mid 2nd to 3rd-century AD pottery. Traces of a probable external surface were also found. All these features were sealed by demolition rubble containing occasional pieces of tile and a small quantity of 2nd to 3rd-century AD pottery (CAT 1999).

# 5. THE TOWN DEFENCES

## EXCAVATION AND WATCHING BRIEF AT COTSWOLD DISTRICT COUNCIL OFFICES TRINITY ROAD, 2001–2002
### by Annette Hancocks, Martin Watts and Neil Holbrook

### Introduction

Between July 2001 and June 2002 CA carried out a watching brief and excavation prior to the redevelopment and extension of the District Council Offices (see Fig. 17, no. 18). The offices lay just within the projected alignment of the Roman town wall and part of the site was designated as a Scheduled Ancient Monument. As a result of the fieldwork described here, which encountered the town wall at two locations, it became apparent that the defences lay slightly further to the north-east than had hitherto been supposed.

During the design process for the office extension a staged programme of archaeological assessment took place, commencing with a desk-based assessment followed by three field evaluations. Information gained from these preparatory studies, coupled with details of the development proposals, informed the production of a Statement of Archaeological Impact and Mitigation. The adopted design sought to minimise the impact of the development upon important archaeological remains, but where this was unavoidable a programme of fieldwork was proposed to mitigate these effects. Planning permission and Scheduled Monument Consent were granted for the development in 2001, both with conditions requiring further archaeological investigation.

All groundworks were conducted under archaeological supervision, hand-excavation commencing when significant archaeological deposits were encountered (Fig. 59). The foundation for the office extension comprised 54 bored piles. The original design included the construction of a small electricity substation, approximately 2.95 × 2.65m in area, the footprint of which was to be subject to prior archaeological excavation (Fig. 59, trench 1). In the event excavation quickly revealed that remains of the town wall and an external tower lay further to the north-east than had been anticipated. In the light of these discoveries it was decided to move the substation to a new location 5m further north, thus allowing the preservation of the remains. Excavation at the new site (trench 24) did not encounter Roman deposits above the formation level for the substation at approximately 1m below ground level. Roman deposits were excavated, however, in the

area of a soakaway and associated drain run (Figs 59–60, trenches 23 and 28).

As a consequence of the policy of minimising disturbance to archaeological deposits from development, where excavation did occur, it was in narrow trenches. The sequence of deposits encountered in trench 23 was complex, and more than one interpretation is possible. In the following account one interpretation is presented, and this phasing has informed the subsequent analysis of the artefacts. It is considered important, however, to present an alternative interpretation and this is done in the discussion. This should assist readers in coming to their own view.

### Pre-Roman topography

In trench 34 saturated running gravels were located at the base of a soakaway, directly overlaid by post-medieval disturbance. It is conceivable that these alluvial deposits mark the former course of a pre-Roman watercourse, which would not be unexpected given observations at Querns Road (CE V, 10). To the south-west in trench 23 natural comprised compact clay that sloped gently upwards towards the south-west.

### Period 1: Deposits pre-dating the earthwork defences (mid–late 1st century AD)

In the central part of trench 23 (Fig. 61, Section 3) excavation ceased at the level required for the drainage run, and so natural was not reached. The earliest deposits revealed were two successive layers of compact rammed gravel road metalling (414 and 417), in excess of 0.6m thick. It is difficult to establish the alignment of the road with accuracy given the narrow confines of the trench, but it clearly had an essentially north–south orientation and was in excess of 4m wide. Its western edge was defined by roadside ditch 413, which was filled with silty road wash 412 which also lapped up over the side of the metalling. The full width of ditch 413 could not be determined, but it was in excess of 1m. The road surface was cut by a shallow intrusion 419, which is more likely to be a pit than the opposing roadside ditch given that further road metalling lay beyond the limit of the intrusion to the east. The pit was filled with red silty clay 418 which also spread out and covered the uppermost road surface 417, thus marking the disuse of the road. At this point a second pit 420 was dug, filled (by 432) with a similar red clay to 418. Further dumping occurred over the site of the former road and ditch (411, 410, 409, 405, 406,

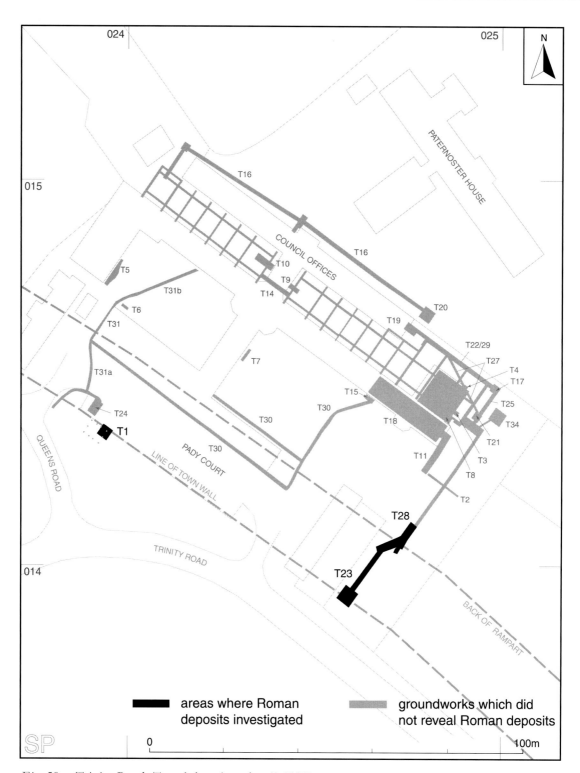

*Fig. 59*    Trinity Road. Trench location plan (1:1000)

407, 408). This mostly comprised clays, although there was also a tip of unworked limestone rubble (407).

### Dating evidence

The pottery is dominated by Savernake ware (TF 6) and local reduced wares TF 5 and 17, together with small quantities of South Gaulish samian. Dumps sealing the early road and ditch (405, 408 and 409) produced good groups of pottery of

likely Flavian date (discussed in detail below). Ditch fill 412 produced only five sherds of pottery, including Dorset Black-Burnished ware and other 2nd-century AD coarsewares, which should probably be regarded as intrusive.

Dump 405: *Pottery* (39sh./1016g). *Coarsewares*: TF A, 5, 6, 12.

Dump 408: *Pottery* (4sh./406g). *Coarsewares*: TF 5, 6, 12.

Dump 409: *Pottery* (58sh./937g). *Samian*: SG, Drag. 15/17, Pre-Flavian; 27, ?Flavian. *Coarsewares*: TF 5, 6, 17, 35.

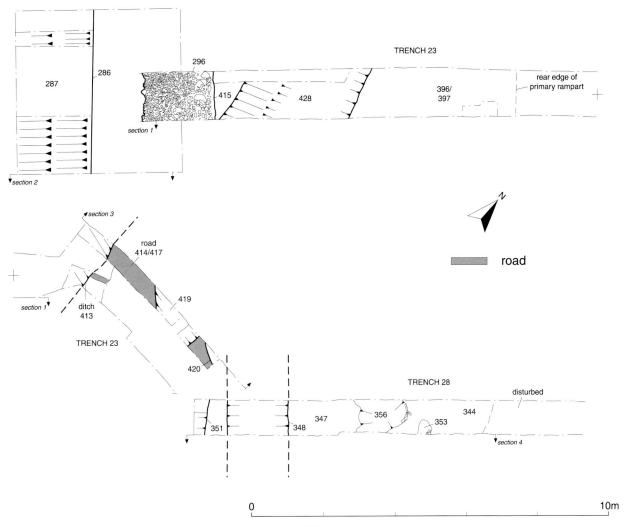

*Fig. 60*    Trinity Road. Plan of trenches 23 and 28 (1:100)

## Period 2: The earthwork defences (mid 2nd century AD)

Firm yellow clay natural (290) was encountered in the south-western part of trench 23 (Fig. 61, Sections 1 and 2). It was covered by up to three layers of clean, firm, red-brown silty clay (285/427/398, 294/433/397, 284/396). This clean material, which is distinct in character from the overlying deposits, can be interpreted with confidence as the rampart of the earthwork defences of the Roman town. The width of the rampart from its tail to the front edge of (later) ditch 286 is 12.75m, and the deposits attained a maximum height of 0.75m. The width is comparable with the rampart on the north-west defences (12.4m; CE V, 76), although the surviving height of 0.75m is surprisingly low. It seems likely that the earthwork bank was originally *c.* 3m high (ibid., 80). While it would be tempting to associate these deposits with the so-called early bank (ibid., 94–6), the pottery appears to favour a mid 2nd-century AD date typical of the town earthwork defences as a whole. Two possibilities might be advanced to suggest why the bank was so low. First, that the bank was never finished, or second that it was subsequently partly

levelled, perhaps to facilitate construction of the town wall.

### Dating evidence

Small quantities of coarse pottery (25 sherds) were recovered from 396 and are broadly dateable to the mid or later 2nd century AD. The earthwork defences are conventionally dated to *c.* AD 140–60 (CE V, 91).

## Period 3: The stone defences and later events (3rd–4th century AD)

### Construction of the masonry defences

At some stage prior to the heightening of the rampart associated with the construction of the stone defences a trench or ditch 428 was dug into the top of the earthwork bank. The feature was 4.6m wide at the top, narrowing to 1.9m at a depth of 1.3m from the top of the cut, 0.5m below the surface of natural. Excavation ceased at this depth, and the trench was not bottomed. The earliest fills exposed were clean re-deposited natural clay 426 and silt 431, overlaid by further clean clays 425, 422, 424 (Fig. 61, Section 1). The trench had a

Trench 23; Section 1

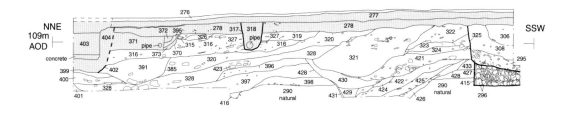

Trench 23; Section 2                          Trench 23; Section 3

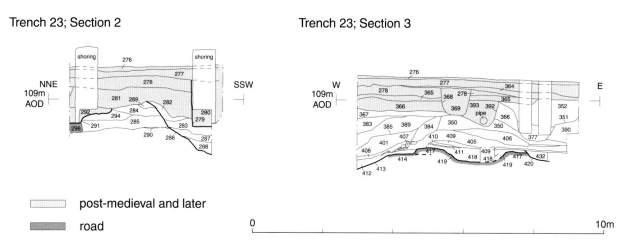

☐☐☐  post-medieval and later

▬▬▬  road

0 ⊢————————————————————————————⊣ 10m

*Fig. 61*   Trinity Road trench 23, sections 1–3 (1:100)

markedly different alignment to the later town wall. Interpretation of this feature is not straightforward. While the profile is consistent with a large ditch it is difficult to understand why such a feature would be cut through the top of the earthwork defences. An alternative explanation is that this feature was dug as the construction trench for the masonry wall. However, before the wall could be constructed to any degree (it is conceivable that footings might have been laid in the trench) there was a change of plan, and the decision was made to construct the wall a short distance further to the south-west on a different alignment. The excavation of the foundation trench on the new wall alignment would have generated a quantity of clean clay which was used to backfill the lower levels of the trench. Support for this interpretation is offered by the fact that the tip lines clearly show that the ditch was filled from its south-western side. The trench was 1.9m wide at the limit of investigation, sufficient to accommodate the foundations of the wall if it was of narrow gauge (*c.* 1.2m wide). It is known from previous work that the wall which was inserted into the front of the earthwork defences was in the first instance of narrow gauge, but for reasons which are still unclear large sections of the circuit were later reduced in their entirety and rebuilt to a wider (2.3–2.7m) specification (CE V, 98).

The construction trench 415 for the re-aligned stone curtain wall was cut through the early rampart and 0.2m into natural. The trench was infilled with four courses of pitched undressed limestone footings (296),

0.6m deep. The footings were 2m wide which, allowing for offsets, suggests that the wall was still of narrow gauge. All the dressed courses of the wall had been robbed, robber trench 325/291 cutting through the rampart and removing the stratigraphic relationship between the rampart heightening and wall construction. Nevertheless it is possible to ascertain the level from which the rampart was heightened due to the marked difference in composition of the heightening dumps compared to the body of the earlier rampart. The first stage of heightening entailed the infilling of the abortive construction trench 428 with mixed clays containing fragments of limestone, charcoal and mortar flecks (429, 430, 421). Following the laying of a distinct layer of pink mortar (324) doubtless spare material from the construction of the wall, further dumps 323, 322, 321 made up the ground behind the newly constructed wall and completely infilled the abortive trench. Further dumps were then tipped onto the sloping rear face of the rampart to extend its height and width. Dumps 328, 423 and 400 contained various tips of large undressed fragments of limestone. Further to the north-east other dumps (?406, 350, 384, 401) were deposited to infill the hollow above the former Period 1 roadside ditch (Fig. 61, Section 3). Some of the rampart dumps included quantities of cattle butchery waste. At this point a ditch (385) was dug into the surface of the rampart (which comprised the upper surface of clay silt 320, although there is no indication of a turf line). Ditch 385 was 2.1m wide and

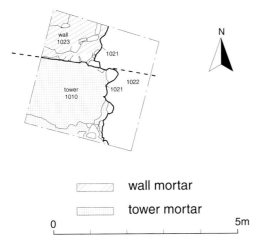

*Fig. 62*    Trinity Road. Plan of trench 1 (1:100)

0.73m deep and must have served to channel rainwater draining off the rampart.

Ditch 385 was infilled with silty clays (391/389 n.i.) before being covered with further layers of rampart heightening. The lowest level 316 contained a dump of flat angular limestone slabs, on average 0.5m square, while other dumps were laid further to the north-east (383, 367, 366, 390). The original profile of the rampart had been truncated by post-medieval levelling.

The inner edge of the innermost ditch 266 of the town defences was found in front of the wall, separated by a 2m-wide berm (Fig. 61, Section 2). The ditch cut the front of the earthwork rampart. It is likely that this ditch is a recut, a small remnant of the fill of an earlier one (289) surviving. The ditch was not bottomed but was in excess of 1.5m deep. The lowest fill 288 contained a number of dressed facing stones from the wall (unlike overlying deposits 287, 283, 282), suggesting that the ditch remained open to this level until the wall was in dereliction.

The masonry town defences were also encountered in trench 1, directly beneath post-medieval layers (Fig. 62). The roughly dressed facing stones of the wall were found, backed by a mortared core. The facing stones were abutted by a mass of coursed undressed limestone rubble, a layer of hard orange-buff mortar 1010 separating the courses. There is little doubt that this is the core of an external tower that was added to the town defences. The facing stones of the eastern side of the tower had been robbed (1021), the robbers also

removing the adjacent stones of the curtain wall. Excavation ceased at this level. Insufficient of the tower was exposed to determine whether it was rectangular or polygonal. The tower lies *c*. 180m north-east of the probable tower located by Baddeley (1922) in Watermoor Hospital Garden.

### Area to the rear of the rampart

In the area to the rear of the rampart in trench 28, excavation did not penetrate deep enough to reach natural. The earliest deposit encountered was yellow clay (354,358) covered by deposits of mortar and small limestone fragments (347,350), perhaps consolidation deposits for a naturally wet area (Fig. 63, Section 4). These layers were cut by ditch 348, 2.2m wide and at least 0.63m deep. It was parallel with the town wall and once again served to collect run-off from the rear face of the rampart whose width can be estimated at 16m. Further north-east irregular scoops 356 and 353 may have been tree boles. Ditch 348 was filled with silts 357 and 349, before all deposits were sealed by a thin layer of silt (343), 80mm thick, perhaps an old turf line or conceivably even an alluvial flood deposit. This deposit was cut by ditch 351 (Fig. 61, Section 3 and Fig. 63, Section 4), which ran along the rear of the rampart back and must have replaced ditch 348. Ditch 351 was *c*. 2.5m wide, 1m deep and was filled with dark brown clays 377/352. These deposits were overlaid by post-medieval make-up 365/331, possibly in origin a very heavily reworked dark earth or medieval cultivation soil.

### Dating evidence

Dating is provided primarily by the pottery, which includes some large and diagnostic groups with appreciable quantities of Central Gaulish samian. Dumps 320, 328 and ditch fill 389 (= 391) each produced large and well-dated pottery assemblages which are discussed in full in the pottery report below (Group 2). Most significant in terms of dating are the coin of AD 117–36, quantities of Central Gaulish samian, and Dorset Black-Burnished ware forms consisting of jars with acute-angled lattice and flat-rimmed bowls. The pottery is unlikely to date later than *c*. AD 200/210 and compares most closely to Cirencester Ceramic Phase 4 (*c*. AD 160–200/10). This is earlier than the conventional dating for the construction of the masonry defences in *c*. AD 240–70 (CE V, 92).

Deposits to the rear of the rampart (levelling layer 350 and ditch fill 349, and rampart dumps 384 and 401) produced

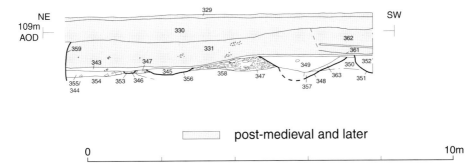

*Fig. 63*    Trinity Road trench 28, section 4 (1:100)

relatively small quantities of pottery. In common with dumps 320, 328 and 389 these are dominated by local reduced wares, particularly (North Wiltshire) grey ware TF 117/98. Savernake ware and local black-sandy wares (TF 5) are present but are probably residual. Most significant in terms of dating among the coarsewares are quantities of Dorset Black-Burnished ware which include flat-rimmed bowls or dishes with burnished lattice decoration typical of the period *c.* AD 120–60. The samian present is a mix of South Gaulish material, which must represent residual material or survivals, and Central Gaulish types of Hadrianic and Antonine date. Amphorae TF 35 (South Gaulish) and TF 40 (South Spanish) are also present in small numbers. Both are broadly dateable to the 1st to 3rd centuries AD. The dating of these groups appears to be consistent and comparable with Ceramic Phase 3 (*c.* AD 100/120–160).

Deposits representing possible secondary heightening of the rampart for the most part produced pottery groups of similar character to those described above. Dumps 316 and 315 and fill 345 of tree bole 356 to the rear of the rampart each produced sizeable groups, dominated by North Wiltshire or Dorset Black-Burnished ware products. The composition of these groups is similar to the smaller groups described above, with the addition of sherds of Oxfordshire whiteware mortaria (dating to no earlier than *c.* AD 140) from each.

Ditch fill 352/377 produced quantities of Oxfordshire red colour-coated ware, including a bowl of Young's C75 or C78, late forms of Dorset Black-Burnished ware and local imitation Black-Burnished ware (TF 118). The group dates to after *c.* AD 270.

### Rampart heightening

320: *Pottery* (163sh./1505g). *Samian*: CG, Drag. 38, 37, 33, 35, all Antonine. *Coarsewares*: TF 5, 6, 17, 17/98, 35, 40, 74, 90, 95/98.

328: *Pottery* (204sh./1666g). *Samian*: CG, Drag. 18/31, Hadrianic/Antonine; Drag. 31, 33, Antonine. *Coarsewares*: TF 17/98, 5, 74, 6, 40, 106, 85.

401: *Pottery* (79sh./838g). *Samian*: SG, Drag. 18, 37, Flavian. CG Drag. 35, Trajanic; Drag. 18/31, Antonine. *Coarsewares*: TF 5, 6, 9, 17/98, 40, 74.

384: *Pottery* (32sh./411g). *Samian*: SG, Drag. 37, Flavian; CG Drag. 18/31, Hadrianic. *Coarsewares*: TF 5, 6, 17, 17/98, 95/98, 40.

389 (= 391): *Pottery* (321sh./4562g). *Samian*: CG, Drag. 38, Late Antonine; Drag. 37, 33, 18/31, 18/31r, 31r, Antonine. *Coarsewares*: TF A, 5, 6, 17, 17/98, 35, 40, 67, 74, 85, 90, 94, 95, 95/98, 106, MARB.

394 (= 391): *Coin*: *denarius* of Empress Sabina, AD 117–36.

383: *Pottery* (29sh./369g). *Samian*: CG, Drag. 36, Antonine. *Coarsewares*: TF 5, 6, 9, 17/98, 40, 67, 74, 90, 95/98.

### Possible later heightening of rampart

316: *Pottery* (696sh./5273g). *Samian*: CG, Drag. 38, Late Antonine; Drag. 27, 37, 33, 18/31, Antonine. *Coarsewares*: TF 5, 6, 17, 17/98, 35, 40, 57, 74, 85, 88, 90, 94, 95/98, 129. *Other*: bone hairpin: Crummy type 2.

315: *Pottery* (74sh./644g). *Samian*: CG, Drag. 36, 37, Hadrianic/Antonine, Antonine. *Coarsewares*: 5, 6, 17, 17/98, 74, 85, 90, 95/98.

### Area to rear of rampart

Levelling layer 350: *Pottery* (17sh./38g). *Coarsewares*: TF 5, 6, 17, 17/98, 74, 40.

Fill 345 of tree bole 356: *Pottery* (110sh./1239g). *Samian*: SG, Drag. 29, pre-Flavian. *Coarsewares*: TF 5, 6, 17/98, 40, 74, 90, 95/98.

Fill 349 of ditch 348: *Pottery* (37sh./349g). *Samian*: CG, Drag. 33, 18/31, 2nd century. *Coarsewares*: TF 5, 6, 17/98, 35, 40, 74, 95/98.

Fills 352/377 of ditch 351: *Pottery* (36sh./227g). *Coarsewares*: TF 17/98, 95/98, 118, 5, 74, 9, 88, 85, 83, 35, 67, 6, 35.

## Period 4: Post-Roman activity

Post-Roman activity comprises the robbing of stone from the town wall, and various post-medieval intrusions and services. The Union workhouse was constructed in 1836.

## The Pottery by E.R. McSloy

Roman pottery amounted to 2703 sherds (28.8kg), recovered from 88 contexts. Small quantities of medieval and post-medieval pottery were also found. The bulk of the Roman pottery derives from dump deposits associated with the construction of the masonry defences, together with occupation to its rear. Condition is mixed, and the overall impression is of a fairly well broken-up assemblage with average sherd weight correspondingly low for a Roman group at 10.6g.

A full appraisal of the dating evidence provided by the pottery and other artefacts has been presented above. In summary, the stratified Roman coarsewares span the period *c.* AD 50/75 to *c.* AD 230/250. There is a clear emphasis on the earlier Roman period, particularly the periods *c.* AD 50–100 and *c.* AD 150–225, which correspond to Cirencester Ceramic Phases 2 and 4 respectively. Additional quantities of 1st-century AD material are present as residual finds and include South Gaulish samian, a terra nigra platter and spouted strainer (Fig. 64, 1). Small quantities of late Roman types occur, frequently re-deposited in post-medieval contexts.

Two pottery groups, selected on the basis of their stratigraphic integrity and intrinsic chronological discreteness, are described below. Recording is according to minimum vessel count (sherd families) and Estimated Vessel Equivalence (EVEs). Quantification was according to sherd count, minimum vessel count (sherd families) and weight per fabric. Attributes such as decoration, use wear evidence, visible residues and any cross-context matches are also recorded for each sherd family.

### Group 1

Period 1 (pre-earthwork defences) dumps 405/8/9 (Tables 11 and 12; Fig. 64). The average sherd weight for Group 1 is high at 23.4g. While this figure is inflated by the dominance of thick-walled Savernake vessels, this group was notable for its lower levels of fragmentation compared to the assemblage overall. Samian is restricted to single examples of a pre-Flavian Drag. 15/17 platter and a Drag. 27 cup of probable Flavian date. Both are South Gaulish (La Graufesenque) products. A single Camulodunum 186 type

**Table 11:** Quantification of Pottery Group 1 (contexts 405/408/409; *c.* AD 70-100) at Trinity Road

KEY: Count = sherd count; Min. vess. = minimum number of vessels; EVEs = estimated vessel equivalents. *Numerical codes relate to Cirencester-type series (Rigby CE I–II; Keely CE III). Codes in parentheses derive from National Roman Fabric Reference Collection (Tomber and Dore 1998).

| Description | Fabric* | Count | Weight (g) | EVEs | Min. vess. | % Min. vess. |
|---|---|---|---|---|---|---|
| *Imported finewares* | | | | | | |
| La Graufesenque samian (LGF SA) | 154a | 2 | 14 | .05 | 2 | 4.2 |
| *Amphorae* | | | | | | |
| Cadiz (CAD AM) | 34 | 1 | 48 | – | 1 | 2.1 |
| *Local wares* | | | | | | |
| Early wheel-thrown black sandy | 5 | 16 | 168 | .82 | 14 | 29.2 |
| Savernake type (SAV GT) | 6 | 75 | 1678 | .61 | 20 | 41.7 |
| Grey with calcareous | 12 | 2 | 406 | 1.11 | 4 | 8.4 |
| Early Wiltshire grey | 17 | 3 | 21 | – | 3 | 6.3 |
| Grog tempered | – | 2 | 24 | – | 2 | 4.2 |
| *Sub-total* | – | *98* | *2297* | *2.54* | *45* | *93.8* |
| **Total** | | **101** | **2359** | **2.59** | **48** | |

amphora fragment dateable to before *c.* AD 120 was also recovered. The composition of the coarsewares, particularly the dominance of Savernake and typically early sandy reduced fabrics and an absence of certain 2nd-century AD forms, supports a Flavian date for the group.

Coarseware forms comprise large Savernake necked storage jars, including examples with diagonal scoring to the shoulder zone, a lid (Fig. 64, no. 4) and bead-rim forms (Fig. 64, no. 5) which compare to examples from Leaholme (CE I, fig. 50, nos 6 and 8) and Savernake Forest (Swan 1975, no. 32). Reduced sandy types (TF 5, 12 and 17), comprise necked jar types which include 'Belgic' characteristics such as cordons (no. 8), girth grooves or a carinated profile (Fig. 64, no. 7). A single platter (Fig. 64, no. 6) in TF 5 compares to examples from late 1st to early 2nd-century AD contexts in the town (CE I, fig. 51, no. 50 and fig. 52, no. 99). Comparable groups in terms of composition and date derive mainly from the area of the Leaholme fort. Absent from this group are the fine oxidised wares which characterise pre-Flavian or early Flavian groups from Cirencester, and in this respect Group 1 compares to material from Site AG II/III, considered to date to *c.* AD 75–95 (CE I, 163).

## Group 2

Period 3 (construction of the masonry defences) dumps 320/328/389 (Tables 13 and 14; Fig. 65). The average sherd weight for this group is relatively low at 11.2g, which suggests that the material has been fairly well broken up. The composition of Group 2 compares most closely to Cirencester Ceramic Phase 4 dating to *c.* AD 160–200/10. Some elements, such as the high representation of black sandy fabric TF 5, might encourage a slightly later date for the group. The higher representation of TF 5 in Ceramic Phase 5 (dating to *c.* AD 200/10–250) than in Ceramic Phase 4 was interpreted as evidence for expansion of the fabric at this time in forms imitating Black-Burnished ware types (CE V, 332–4). Other aspects of Group 2,

particularly the absence of South West white-slipped wares which are common in Ceramic Phase 5, are consistent, however, with an earlier date. It would seem in this case that the abundance of TF 5 is due to the presence of residual material.

The samian from Group 2 amounts to 33 vessels, principally Central Gaulish plainware forms of Antonine date (Table 14). Additional continental finewares comprise a sherd from a probable Argonne-type colour-coated roughcast beaker and a vessel of a form resembling a Drag 18/31 dish in a marbled orange-slipped fabric (Fig. 65, no. 18). The latter, initially identified as a Gaulish import, is probably Caerleon ware (Webster 1993). It is a rare example of the type outside of Wales. Continental coarsewares consist of common amphora types and a Rhône Valley mortarium (Fig. 65, no. 17). Non-local British finewares are represented by a single bag-shaped beaker in Lower Nene Valley colour-coated ware. Local finewares include roughcast-decorated beakers (bag-shaped and indented forms) in North Wiltshire colour-coated ware (TF 85).

The non-local British wares consist almost exclusively of Dorset Black-Burnished ware. Forms comprise cooking pots with acute angle lattice decoration (Fig. 65, no. 13) and flat-rimmed bowls (Fig. 65, nos 11–12). The bulk of the coarsewares comprise North Wiltshire reduced and oxidised wares. The Savernake wares and a proportion of black-sandy TF 5 are likely to

**Table 12:** Samian fabrics and forms in Pottery Group 1 at Trinity Road

KEY: Min. vess. = minimum number of vessels; EVEs = estimated vessel equivalents.

| | | South Gaul (La Grauf.) | |
|---|---|---|---|
| Generic form | Form (Drag.) | Min. vess. | EVEs |
| Cup | 27 | 1 | – |
| Platter | 15/17 | 1 | .05 |

be residual. Vessels in TF 5 imitating a Black-Burnished ware dish (Fig. 65, no. 10) or jar types are representative of the latest phase of production of this fabric, probably in the second half of the 2nd century AD. Forms among the grey ware fabrics TF 17/98 consist primarily of jars, many in imitation of Black-Burnished ware cooking pot types with acute lattice decoration (Fig. 65, no. 14). Oxidised wares include curved-sided bowls (Fig. 65, no. 15) and a flagon of degenerate ring-necked type (Fig. 65, no. 16).

The conventional dating for the construction of the masonry defences is *c.* AD 240–70, significantly later

**Table 13:** Quantification of Pottery Group 2 (contexts 320/328/389; *c.* AD 160–200/10) at Trinity Road

KEY: Count = sherd count; Min. vess. = minimum number of vessels; EVEs = estimated vessel equivalents.
*Numerical codes relate to Cirencester-type series (Rigby CE I-II; Keely CE III). Codes in parentheses derive from National Roman Fabric Reference Collection (Tomber and Dore 1998).

| Description | Fabric* | Count | Weight (g) | EVEs | Min. vess. | % Min. vess. |
|---|---|---|---|---|---|---|
| ***Imported finewares*** | | | | | | |
| Argonne type roughcast (ARG CC) | 57 | 1 | 4 | – | 1 | 0.3 |
| La Graufesenque samian (LGF SA) | 154a | 13 | 61 | .34 | 11 | 3.8 |
| Les Martres-de-Veyre samian (LMV SA) | 154b | 1 | 10 | – | 1 | 0.3 |
| Lezoux samian (LEZ SA2) | 154b | 26 | 476 | 1.65 | 21 | 7.2 |
| *Sub-total* | | *41* | *551* | *1.99* | *34* | *11.6* |
| ***Mortaria*** | | | | | | |
| Rhône Valley (CNG OX) | 67 | 1 | 257 | .15 | 1 | 0.3 |
| Oxford whiteware (OXF WH) | 90 | 1 | 19 | – | 1 | 0.3 |
| *Sub-total* | | *2* | *276* | *.15* | *2* | *0.6* |
| ***Amphorae*** | | | | | | |
| Gaulish (GAL AM1) | 35 | 3 | 27 | – | 2 | 0.6 |
| Baetican (BAT AM2) | 40 | 19 | 1147 | – | 7 | 2.4 |
| *Sub-total* | | *22* | *1174* | – | *9* | *3.0* |
| ***Regional imports*** | | | | | | |
| Dorset Black-Burnished (DOR BB1) | 74 | 113 | 983 | 1.14 | 49 | 16.7 |
| Lower Nene colour-coated (LNV CC) | 81 | 1 | 4 | – | 1 | 0.3 |
| Severn Valley Ware (SVW OX2) | 106 | 5 | 237 | .10 | 4 | 1.4 |
| Caerleon ware | – | 2 | 15 | .11 | 1 | 0.3 |
| *Sub-total* | | *121* | *1239* | *1.35* | *55* | *18.7* |
| ***Local wares*** | | | | | | |
| Early wheel-thrown black sandy | 5 | 118 | 740 | 1.71 | 42 | 14.3 |
| Savernake type (SAV GT) | 6 | 42 | 895 | .53 | 19 | 6.5 |
| North Wiltshire grey | 17/98 | 277 | 2240 | 4.21 | 107 | 36.5 |
| North Wiltshire oxidised | 95/98 | 61 | 599 | 1.32 | 26 | 8.8 |
| North Wiltshire colour-coated | 85 | 2 | 13 | – | 1 | 0.3 |
| *Sub-total* | | *500* | *4487* | *7.77* | *195* | *66.4* |
| **Total** | | **686** | **7627** | **11.26** | **295** | |

**Table 14:** Samian fabrics and forms in Pottery Group 2 at Trinity Road

KEY: Min. vess. = minimum number of vessels; EVEs = estimated vessel equivalents.

| Generic form | Form (Drag.) | South Gaul (La Grauf. ) | | Central Gaul (Les Martres) | | Central Gaul (Lezoux) | |
|---|---|---|---|---|---|---|---|
| | | Min. vess. | EVEs | Min. vess. | EVEs | Min. vess. | EVEs |
| Decorated | 37 | 3 | .06 | 1 | – | 3 | .20 |
| Cup | 33 | – | – | – | – | 4 | .50 |
| | 35 | – | – | – | – | 1 | .04 |
| | 27 | 2 | .04 | – | – | – | – |
| Platter | 18 | 2 | .20 | – | – | – | – |
| Dish | 42 | 1 | .04 | – | – | – | – |
| | 18/31 | – | – | – | – | 6 | .40 |
| | 18/31R | – | – | – | – | 3 | .16 |
| Bowl | 31 | – | – | – | – | 1 | .04 |
| | 31R | – | – | – | – | 1 | .06 |
| | 38 | – | – | – | – | 2 | .25 |
| Misc. | chip | 3 | – | – | – | – | – |

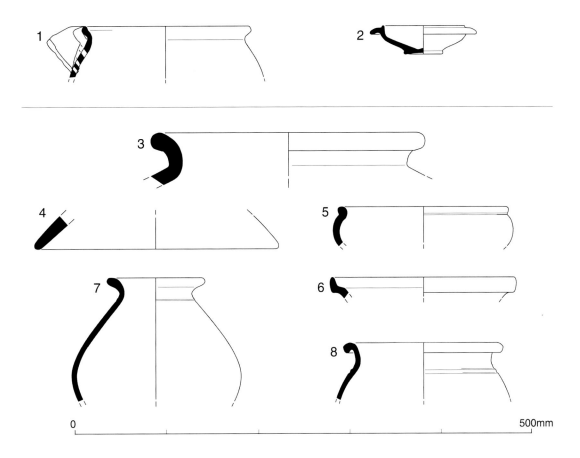

*Fig. 64*   Trinity Road. Roman pottery nos 1–8 (scale 1:4)

than the mid to late Antonine date proposed for Group 2. While it is conceivable that the Group 2 material represents a wholly re-deposited group, and some support for this derives from its poor condition, the absence of anything later than *c*. AD 230 should be noted.

### Illustrated vessels (Figs 64–5)

#### Miscellaneous

1.  TF 9. Spouted strainer. (Residual in) Period 3 layer 316
2.  TF 17. Fine grey ware hemispherical flanged bowl. Period 3 layer 316.

#### Group 1. Period 1 dumps 405/408/409

3.  TF 6. Large necked storage jar.
4.  TF 6. Lid/cover.
5.  TF 6. Bead rim jar/bowl.
6.  TF 5. Platter.
7.  TF 17. Narrow-mouthed jar.
8.  TF 12. Necked jar with cordon.

#### Group 2. Period 3 rampart dumps 320/328/389

9.  TF 5. Carinated bowl, burnished decoration.
10. TF 5. Triangular-rimmed dish (Black-Burnished ware imitation).
11. TF 74. Flat-rimmed bowl.
12. TF 74. Flat-rimmed bowl, burnished arcading.

13. TF 74. Everted-rim jar, acute-angled burnished lattice.
14. TF 98. Everted-rim jar, acute-angled burnished lattice (Black-Burnished ware imitation).
15. TF 95/98. Curved-wall bowl.
16. TF 95/98. Flagon. Vestigial ring-necked form.
17. TF 67b (Rhône Valley mortaria). Bead and hooked flange form.
18. Central Gaulish or Rhineland marbled ware (MARB). Bead-rim dish/bowl.
19. TF 17/98. ?jar with scratched graffito.

### The coins by E.R. McSloy

1.  Period 3 dump 394/389. Empress Sabina, *denarius*, AD 117–36(?). RIC 396.
2.  Period 4 layer 334. Barbarous radiate, AD 270–90. Worn and illegible – reverse from altar?. Diam. 17mm.

### Selected artefacts by E.R. McSloy

#### Copper-alloy object (Fig. 66)

1.  Period 3. Layer to rear or rampart 389. Copper-alloy toilet spoon (Fig. 66). Probably cold forged. Flat, ovoid form scoop, angled slightly upwards. Tapering, round-sectioned handle broken at end. Length 57mm. Toilet spoons or *ligulae* appear to have been made throughout the Roman period. Use for nail manicure, or the extraction of cosmetics from small flasks or similar, has been suggested (Crummy 1983, 59).

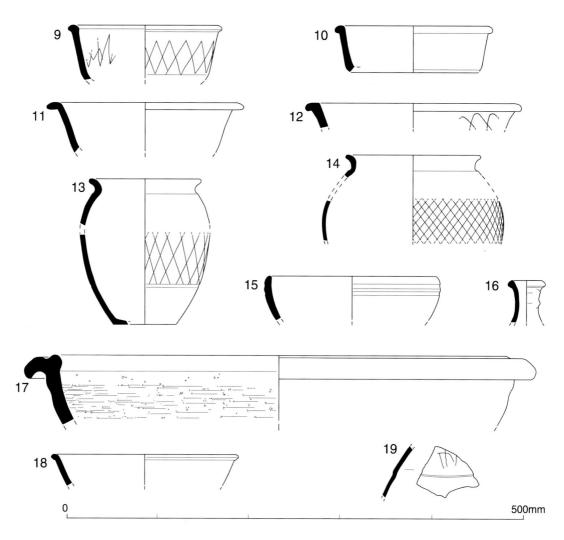

*Fig. 65*   Trinity Road. Roman pottery nos 9–19 (scale 1:4)

### Worked bone hairpins (Fig. 66)

Three bone hairpins were recovered, of which one is very fragmentary and not described. All are identifiable as Crummy's type 2 (pins with 1–3 grooves below a conical head) and dateable to *c.* AD 50–200/250 (Crummy 1979, 157).

2.  Period 4. Layer 1018. Conical head with two grooves below. Shaft tapering to broken tip. Surviving length 78mm.
3.  Period 3. Heightening layer 316. Single-grooved conical head with groove below. Shaft tapering to broken tip. Surviving length 83mm.

### Worked bone needles (Fig. 66)

Bone needles 4 and 5 are of are of the same broad class (Crummy type 1), characterised by a pointed head, and are of similar early Roman date (Crummy 1983, 65–7). They differ in respect of the form of the eye.

4.  Period 3. Heightening layer 316. Figure-of-eight form eye below pointed head. Complete, regular taper to the point which appears worn. Length 128mm.
5.  Period 3. Occupation layer 316. Circular-form eye set within extended pointed head which is expanded outwards and slightly flattened. Shaft is round in section and appears waisted. Surviving length 61mm.

### Objects of shale (*n.i.*)

6.  Period 3. Layer 315. Armlet fragment. Plain, circular form with D-shaped section (faceted inner). Internal diameter *c.* 40–45mm. Thickness 5mm. Armlets of Kimmeridge shale are known throughout the Roman period. The size of this example, which makes it suitable only for a child, is representative of the most commonly encountered plain type (Lawson 1976, 250–2). The angularity of the inner face has resulted from the method of separating the armlet from its core.
7.  Period 3. Layer 400. ?Vessel fragment. Plain rim, slightly curving wall. Diameter *c.* 160mm. Thickness 3mm. Insufficient survives of this vessel to be confident of its form, although a small bowl or platter are most likely.

### Stamped tile (*n.i.*)

8.  Unstratified. Fragment of a box flue-tile, 110 × 100mm, 28mm thick. Stamp is 50mm by 18mm with letters in relief, 12mm high and separated by triangular stops:

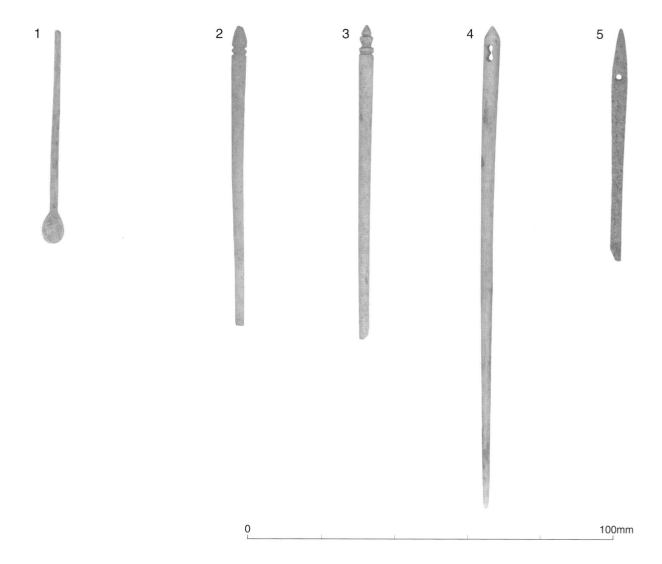

1   2   3   4   5

0                                                                                          100mm

*Fig. 66*   Trinity Road. Copper-alloy toilet spoon (no. 1) and worked bone pins and needles (nos 2–5) (scale 1:1)

V.L.A. The stamp is similar, though from a different die, to previously published examples from Compton Abdale, Withington and Farmington (RIB II.5, 2489.51). This is the first recorded instance of this tile stamp from Cirencester. It has been previously published in *Britannia* 33 (2002), 364.

## Human bone by Teresa Gilmore

Six fragments of disarticulated adult human bone were recovered from three contexts. There was no replication of bone elements and no pathological lesions present.

408 (Period 1): Right acetabulum. Adult. Post-mortem cut on pubis section.
328 (Period 3 rampart): Left ulna, missing proximal and distal ends. Adult.
Left tibia shaft fragment. Adult. Post-mortem cut on distal medial side.
Occipital bone nuchal crest. Adult, probably male.
316 (Period 3 rampart, possible later heightening): Proximal third of the right third metacarpal. Adult.

## Animal bone by Ellen Hambleton

### *Sample size and preservation*

A total of 1991 fragments was recovered by hand from 63 stratified contexts, along with a further 68 unstratified fragments (Table 15). It was only possible to identify 35% of this assemblage (718 fragments) to species level. A full assessment report is contained in the site archive. It did not recommend any further work on this assemblage, and this report therefore provides a short summary of the principal conclusions of the study.

Most of the bone-yielding contexts produced only very small assemblages (half produced fewer than ten fragments each), but four deposits associated with the Period 3 rampart produced large assemblages of more than a hundred fragments. Context 389 (= 391, infill of ditch 385) produced the largest assemblage of bones (445 fragments, 115 of which were identified to species). Possible subsequent rampart heightening (316) produced 416 fragments, while rampart dumps 320 and 328

**Table 15:** Animal bone fragment counts from deposits at Trinity Road

**KEY:** NISP = number of specimens identified to species

|  | Period 3 | | Total | |
|---|---|---|---|---|
|  | **NISP** | **%** | **NISP** | **%** |
| Cow | 350 | 79.2 | 547 | 76.2 |
| Sheep/Goat | 46 | 10.4 | 82 | 11.4 |
| Pig | 36 | 8.1 | 67 | 9.3 |
| Horse | 10 | 2.3 | 15 | 2.1 |
| Dog | 0 | – | 1 | 0.1 |
| Red deer | 0 | – | 6 | 0.8 |
| *Sub-total (identified)* | *442* | | *718* | |
| Bird | 5 | | 10 | |
| Unidentified small mammal | 0 | | 1 | |
| Unidentified mammal | 929 | | 1330 | |
| **Total** | **1376** | | **2059** | |

yielded 110 and 175 fragments respectively. A fifth large assemblage of 120 fragments came from the Period 4 backfill of a post-Roman robber trench 1022, and may well include residual Roman material.

The state of preservation of the faunal remains for each context was assigned to one of five categories ranging from good to poor. Most contexts (55) produced assemblages that were classed as moderate while all other contexts were more poorly preserved. Overall the assemblage can be described as moderately well preserved.

### Species representation and assemblage composition

Among the 718 fragments identified to species (Table 15), the assemblage is dominated by cattle (76%). Sheep/goat (11%) are substantially less abundant than cattle and present in similar quantities to pig (9%). Horse (2%) is present in small numbers, while only one fragment of dog (0.1%) was recovered. Red deer (1%) was the only wild mammal species identified and is represented in the assemblage mostly by antler fragments, although post-cranial skeletal elements were also recovered. Bird remains are also only present in low numbers; of the bird fragments identified to species, the majority belonged to domestic fowl (chicken). One mallard/domestic duck fragment and one fragment of a small wild bird were recovered from Period 4 (post-Roman) deposits.

There is very little variation apparent in the patterns of species abundance between different periods, or indeed between contexts within this assemblage. Cattle are the most abundant species in 88% of all context assemblages (including all the large contexts). High percentages of cattle (66–91%) are apparent in all periods, and a similar pattern of species representation in the Period 4 assemblage is most probably due to the incorporation of a considerable amount of residual Roman material in these later deposits. Only the Period 3 assemblage is of sufficient size or secure enough date to warrant detailed discussion of species representation and assemblage composition.

The majority of the assemblage was recovered from Period 3 contexts attributable to the heightening of the rampart associated with the construction of the masonry defences. These included 442 fragments that were identified to mammal species. The identified assemblage is made up entirely of domestic species of which cattle (79%) by far out number sheep/goat (10%), pig (8%) and horse (2%). Domestic fowl were the only species identified among the bird remains from Period 3. There is a consistent pattern of assemblage composition from the four large groups listed above. All are dominated by the remains of cattle fragments, which make up 69–86% of each assemblage. Sheep/goat is consistently the second most abundant species in all four contexts, making up 8–12% of each assemblage, followed by pig (4–11%). The four assemblages, as well as being dominated by cattle, all share similar patterns of body part representation. Although no quantitative record of element abundance was made as part of the assessment, qualitative observations of these contexts all note the same general composition. Head and feet bones of cattle tend to be particularly well represented in all groups. A relatively high abundance of rib and vertebral fragments was also noted in several instances, although this is to be expected given their numbers in the skeleton. Long bone fragments from the main meat bearing upper limb bones, although present, are much less abundant than other elements. This pattern of body part representation is indicative of a high proportion of primary butchery waste where the discarded, low meat bearing 'waste' elements such as the head, feet and parts of the spine are prevalent, while the main meat bearing parts of the carcass have been removed.

### Ageing and metrical data

The ageing data available from the assemblage are extremely limited. The 49 cattle bones from Period 3 might potentially provide some information concerning the age composition of the cattle in the assemblage if considered in conjunction with the small sample of 13 cattle mandibles from the same period, but even then the sample is insufficient to provide reliable and detailed interpretations of cattle husbandry strategy. General observations made during the assessment noted the presence of both adults and juveniles in the cattle and sheep/goat assemblages. Porous bones belonging to very young infant/neonatal or possibly even foetal individuals were noted in very small numbers for cattle, sheep/goat, pig and also (in one instance) horse.

The number of fragments with the potential to provide metrical data is also very small. No single period assemblage contains sufficient numbers of measurable fragments to warrant any detailed metrical analysis.

### Butchery data

Butchery marks were not quantified as part of the assessment, but general observations were made and occasional specific comments noted. Some knife cut marks were observed, including probable skinning marks on a sheep metacarpal and a cattle 1st phalange.

Also noted were similar fine medio-lateral knife cuts at the proximal end of a pig radius from Period 1. Heavy chop marks from a cleaver or similar heavy bladed tool were generally more common than cut marks within the cattle assemblage. The cattle butchery in the assemblage is characterised by oblique and saggital chops through many long bone epiphyses, probably associated with disarticulation and also probably some marrow extraction. The type of butchery marks evident on the cattle remains appear typical of those observed and discussed in other contemporary deposits at Cirencester, and indeed at several other Romano-British urban sites (CE V, 352–70). Maltby (1989) has suggested that this consistent pattern of butchery is indicative of specialist butchers processing large quantities of cattle carcasses for a market, and that this is what occurred in the centre of Roman Cirencester (CE V, 361). A further indication of large-scale cattle processing is the uneven representation of anatomical parts (ibid., 357), which is a feature of many of the larger Period 3 groups.

## Summary and discussion

The overall composition of the Period 3 assemblages shares similarities with many other urban Romano-British sites in that there are very high percentages of cattle present (King 1978; 1999). The evidence from Trinity Road clearly suggests that cattle provided the main meat component of the diet in Cirencester, which is typical of other Romano-British urban sites (King 1978; 1999). It should be noted, however, that such general patterns fail to take into account the considerable intra-site variability often seen on urban sites, and already demonstrated within Cirencester. Maltby (CE V, 352–70) noted considerable variation in the relative abundance of cattle, sheep/goat and pig among the different assemblages from the town, a feature also borne out by the assemblages from Stepstairs Lane (see above). Maltby (CE V, 354), reporting on a series of assemblages analysed in the early 1990s, categorised the Cirencester material into three main groups based on species representation. The Trinity Road Period 3 assemblage appears most similar to those from previous excavations at Chester Street (3rd–4th century AD), St Michael's Field (2nd century AD) and the Bath Gate cemetery (2nd–4th century AD). These fall into his Type 2 category where cattle fragments typically make up over 75% of the sample and by far outnumber sheep/goat and pig fragments, which each commonly contribute less than 15% or even 10% of identified fragments. Maltby argues that the high proportion of cattle remains in the Type 2 sites reflect the presence of large-scale dumps of waste from specialist 'commercial' butchery activity. For the Period 3 deposit, the assemblage composition in terms of species abundance, body part representation and observed butchery marks is suggestive of carcass-processing waste derived mostly from primary butchery activity. This pattern of assemblage composition and the relatively large size of some of the deposits might suggest that the primary processing activity represented in the Trinity Road assemblage might have been undertaken by specialist 'commercial' butchers. Such activity may have taken place at the edge of town and the resulting waste dumped directly into the rampart, which would have been a suitable location for the disposal of noxious material.

Previous excavations in the centre of the Roman town at Chester Street and St Michael's Field uncovered large dumps of cattle processing waste, which probably represent the waste from large-scale specialist butchery activity associated with a meat market (CE V, 355–6). These 'commercial' dumps are broadly comparable to the large Period 3 deposits from Trinity Road in terms of assemblage composition. This gives rise to the possibility that the Period 3 groups from the rampart dumps might include large-scale cattle butchery waste initially accumulated elsewhere in the town which was then re-deposited in the convenient location of the rampart. It is, however, difficult to determine from the faunal remains alone whether they represent primary deposition or fairly rapidly re-deposited material. Although no quantitative analysis of the butchery marks and element composition was carried out as part of the assessment, the patterns of butchery and body part representation observed from Trinity Road clearly followed similar patterns to those discussed by Maltby (1989; 1994) for dumps of large-scale primary processing waste at Cirencester and other Romano-British towns.

An appreciation of the age and sex profile of animals within an assemblage can improve understanding of animal husbandry strategies, and in particular the issue of how Roman towns were supplied with meat (Maltby 1994). There is some indication from the observations of very small numbers of foetal/neonatal cattle and sheep/goat present in several contexts that at least some of the consumed animals may have been reared in or near the town during the Roman period.

## Discussion

While the investigations at Trinity Road were limited in extent, they have nevertheless provided valuable new information. To judge from the observations in trench 34 it appears that a watercourse passed through the northern part of the site, as had been predicted from previous observations (CE V, 10). It is likely that this was drained in the 1st or 2nd centuries AD as part of the operations to divert the main course of the Churn to pass outside of the line adopted for the north-east defences. To the south-west of the stream course the earliest feature encountered was a road.

While this much is clear, more than one interpretation is possible for the subsequent deposits investigated in trench 23. One problem with the interpretation outlined in the stratigraphic account is that the dumps which constitute the Period 2 earthwork defences only survived to a height of 0.75m, considerably lower than elsewhere on the circuit. An alternative interpretation as the so-called 'early bank' was rejected because of a small amount of 2nd-century AD pottery from the uppermost layer 396. If it is considered that this is later material trampled into the surface of the early bank, then the rejected interpretation could still stand. In this case the sequence invites comparison with that found at Watermoor Hospital Garden 90m to the south-east.

Here a 3.35m-wide road lay immediately behind a rampart that has been interpreted as either the defences of a military annex (CE I, 51) or a late 1st or early 2nd-century AD town defence (CE V, 94–6). Pottery from the infilling of the roadside ditch (AWI 79) and from material sealing the road (AWI 71) at Watermoor Hospital Garden dates to the Flavian period, as do dumps 405, 408, 409 at Trinity Road (CE I, 143–4, 191). While there is no direct evidence for the date of construction of the road at the current site it had certainly gone out of use before the end of the 1st century AD, the time when the main elements of the street grid were being laid out (CE V, 22). It was impossible to accurately determine the orientation of the road within the narrow confines of the trench, but the apparent roadside ditch did appear to run north to south. If this is an accurate guide then it is unlikely that the roads at Trinity Road and Watermoor Hospital Garden are one and the same. This difficulty could be overcome, however, if it is considered that ditch 413 was dug through the road after its abandonment and so does not accurately reflect its true alignment. The character of this pre- or early-Flavian activity remains to be established. It might relate either to a period of military occupation or else be associated with an early phase in the development of the town. In either case the roads surely pre-date the establishment of the formal street grid of the Roman town around the turn of the 2nd century AD, and probably relate to an as yet poorly known period of early civilian activity in the late 1st century AD (Holbrook 2008).

If this alternative sequence is followed it can be argued that cut 428, interpreted as an abortive construction trench for the masonry defences, was in fact a ditch parallel and contemporary with ditch 413. Unfortunately no dating evidence was recovered from the lowest fills of 428. The next event would be the construction of the earthwork defences by infilling of the ditch and construction of a rampart. A problem with this interpretation, however, is the presence in these deposits of mixed clays containing flecks of mortar, fragments of limestone and a distinct layer of pink mortar 324. One might typically expect such material to be associated with the masonry defences. The pottery from these deposits is not necessarily inconsistent with the date of *c.* AD 140–150/160 previously suggested for the earthwork defences (CE V, 91), although the presence of a number of fully Antonine samian vessels perhaps favours a slightly later date. The rampart associated with the masonry defences would then comprise the material considered to be secondary heightening (316 and above).

Neither the interpretation presented in the main account nor the alternative rehearsed here is without difficulty, as each requires an element of special pleading. Only further work will resolve the matter once and for all. We know from previous investigations that the process of building the masonry defences in Cirencester was a complex and probably protracted operation, the intricacies of which still elude us. At Trinity Road the wall as ultimately constructed was of narrow gauge. There is no evidence of later widening as has been found at a number of other places on the

circuit. As more investigations of the town defences are made the heterogeneity rather than homogeneity of the sequence of construction becomes ever more apparent. Wacher's (1998, 41) observations on the difficulty of dating town defences from finds obtained from narrow rampart cuttings are pertinent, and it would be unwise at this stage, especially given the ambiguity of the sequence recovered at Trinity Road, to push this evidence too far.

## EVALUATION AND WATCHING BRIEF BETWEEN SCHOOL LANE AND STEPSTAIRS LANE, 2003–5
### by Tim Havard, Kate Cullen and Martin Watts

In October and November 2003 CA carried out an archaeological evaluation on land off School Lane and Stepstairs Lane. The site straddles the defensive circuit of the Roman town and the evaluation was required to accompany a planning application for the refurbishment of the existing housing estate (CA 2003a) (see Fig. 45). Following the granting of planning permission a watching brief was maintained on all intrusive groundworks during 2005. Archaeological observations in 1971 during demolition of Victorian terraced housing and construction of the existing housing estate identified the alignment of the Roman town wall, including possible internal and external towers. In one trench (CV IV) to the rear of 36 Stepstairs Lane the town wall survived to a height of 2.3m (CE V, 59–62).

The area of the housing estate to be refurbished covered approximately 0.7ha. Sixteen evaluation trenches were machine-excavated to the top of archaeological deposits or natural substrate, whichever was encountered first. This varied from 0.39m to 1.81m below the existing ground level. Where archaeologically significant deposits were encountered during the watching brief, archaeological excavation continued thereafter to the contractor's required dimensions. Evaluation trenches 6, 10, 11, 12, 14 and 16 contained significant archaeological deposits and will be discussed further, along with the most archaeologically significant results from the watching brief. The majority of archaeological deposits encountered were of Roman date, although some evidence for medieval and later stone robbing was also represented. Post-medieval and modern deposits and features are only dealt with briefly within this report.

### The town wall

The compacted pitched limestone footings of the town wall (615) were identified in evaluation trench 6 (Fig. 67) The footings extended beyond the confines of the trench, preventing an assessment of their width, and were sealed by a layer of compacted gravel (614) which contained a large dressed fragment of limestone. This deposit may represent the base of the foundations for the town wall. Further observations were made in this

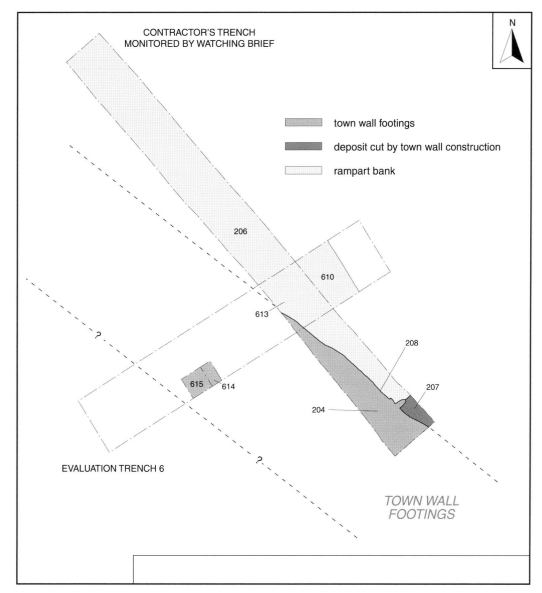

*Fig. 67*   School Lane/Stepstairs Lane. Plan of evaluation trench 6 and trench monitored by watching brief (1:100)

area during the watching brief. A rampart deposit of mixed gravel and sandy clay 207 was cut by limestone wall footings 204. The construction cut for the wall (208) was in excess of 1.3m wide. The footings were visible within the contractor's foundation trench to a height of 0.85m with alternating flat and pitched courses, and extended below the limit of excavation to an unknown depth. Yellow gravel had been placed around the stones, presumably to act as drainage and bonding. The footings were at least 3.2m wide at this point, a dimension and mode of construction consistent with observations made during excavations approximately 800m to the north-west at the Waitrose site (CE V, 69).

### The rampart

The rampart was identified in evaluation trenches 6, 10, 14, 16, and during the watching brief. A single rampart deposit was found within trench 14 overlying natural.

This suggests that the rampart survived to a height of approximately 1.3m in this location. Deposits 610 and 613 within trench 6 correlated well with the previously postulated line of the rampart in this part of the site (Fig. 67). A further deposit of rampart clay (206) was revealed to the rear of the wall during the watching brief. Deposits of silty sands and clays with limestone within evaluation trench 16 were similar to the rampart layers within trench 6 and 1971 trench CV IV (CE V, 59). They exhibited a marked slope indicating that they lay towards the tail of the rampart.

### The defensive ditches

An undated ditch 1104 was observed in evaluation trench 11 cutting the natural substrate 0.8m below the existing ground surface (see Fig. 45). The ditch was aligned north-west/south-east and was at least 0.8m wide and 0.59m deep. It contained a silty fill with occasional fragments of animal bone. This ditch lies inside the line of the town wall and is either unrelated to the town defences or is part of an earlier phase on a slightly different alignment. The ditch in front of the town wall itself was not identified during the course of the works, although undated deposits in evaluation trench 12 tipped down in a manner consistent with the infilling of a substantive feature. The high stone content of one of them is likely to be robber debris infilling the top of the ditch.

## Medieval and later activity

The wall had been extensively robbed in this part of the circuit as only the wall footings survived in evaluation trench 6. Deposits 201 and 202 identified during the watching brief appear to be backfill within the robber trench for the wall. There was a total absence of dressed stones in the various trenches.

## Dating evidence

*Rampart layers 612, 613, 1404, 1603, 1604, 1606, 205, 206*: Individually these layers provide poor dating evidence, mainly consisting of small groups of bodysherds, in coarseware types produced over much of the Roman period. Considered overall, the pottery from these horizons (92 sherds, weighing 629g) represents a broadly consistent group which is similar in date to the much larger groups from the rampart at Trinity Road. Dorset Black-Burnished ware is present in most contexts and provides a *terminus post quem* of *c.* AD 120. The few forms represented consist of jars with acute-angled lattice decoration and a flat-rimmed bowl, all likely to date before *c.* AD 250. Earlier Roman ware types, including Savernake and local black sandy coarsewares (both unlikely to outlast the mid 2nd century AD) occur throughout. Amphora sherds, all of Baetican (Dressel 20) type are also well represented and probably indicate a date of before *c.* AD 250. Other dating indicators include a cornice-rim from a bag-shaped beaker from layer 1603, which is imitative of continental and British colour-coated fineware forms, and probably dates to the second half of the 2nd century AD.

# 6. THE WESTERN CEMETERY

## EXCAVATION AND WATCHING BRIEF ALONG OLD TETBURY ROAD, 2004–6
by Neil Holbrook, E.R. McSloy
and Derek Evans

## Introduction

Between 2004 and 2006 CA carried out two separate investigations along Old Tetbury Road which encountered burials within the western cemetery of the Roman town. In June and July 2004 a small excavation was undertaken to discharge a condition of planning permission for a small residential development 360m outside of the Roman town defences (see Fig. 17, no. 12 and Fig. 68). This site is referred to in this report as Old Tetbury Road. Between October 2004 and January 2006 a watching brief was conducted during groundworks associated with the construction of a new leisure centre on the site of the former cattle market which was 100m nearer the defences. This is referred to as the Former Cattle Market site (Fig. 17, no. 11). Both sites lay immediately south-east of Old Tetbury Road, which probably follows the original alignment of the Fosse Way as it approached the town from the south-west (the course found further to the south appears to be a later Roman re-alignment; CE II, 49; CE V, 14–15). The numbering of burials in this report commences with 1142 so as to continue the sequence for burials to the west of the town started in CE II, 205, MF5 A03–C01. The catalogue number is prefixed by the letter B for inhumation burials and by the letter C for cremations. Deposits of pyre debris which include a small quantity of cremated bone are not designated a burial number as it is assumed that the bulk of the cremated bone was interred elsewhere.

## Old Tetbury Road

### Introduction

The archaeological potential of this site had been demonstrated by an evaluation undertaken by Gloucestershire County Council Archaeology Service in April 2001, prior to the granting of planning permission, which found two truncated cremation burials (Derham 2001). The site lay adjacent to a lodge at the entrance to the former grounds of Querns House, a large ornamental villa built in 1826 on previously vacant land. The grounds of Querns House extended as far as Old Tetbury Road where remnants of the perimeter wall of the estate still survive (CE II, 29–30). Querns House itself now forms one of the buildings of Cirencester Hospital.

The project was initially conceived as a watching brief during the machine excavation of the foundations for the new houses. As archaeological deposits were encountered, however, it became apparent that an excavation would be a more appropriate mitigation strategy, and two discrete areas were examined (Fig. 68). Area A comprised the main development site, and Area B a bus turning area. A modern service trench running along the north-eastern edge of Area A had destroyed all archaeological deposits in this area. Topsoil was removed from both areas by a mechanical excavator to the top of archaeologically significant deposits, sampling of features continuing by hand excavation thereafter.

### Topography and geology

The site lies on ground which rises gently to the west. The height of the natural substrate rose from 99m AOD in Area A to 102m AOD in Area B. The land also falls away slightly to the south into a former valley whose line is now largely followed by the A419 Bristol Road (Fig. 68). The natural substrate was highly variable across Area A consisting of a mixture of limestone brash and firm grey clay, dark silty clays and brown clayey sand. The derivation and interpretation of the silty clays are problematical. They do not occur consistently across the site, but in places can be up 0.65m deep where they appear to be infilling natural undulations in the brash. The clays are totally devoid of artefacts and are cut by Roman features, and are therefore of a different period to the alluvial clays found in Area B and elsewhere which overlay Roman deposits (see below).

### Area A

#### Period 1: Roman (1st to 2nd century + AD)

The Roman activity has been subdivided into four separate phases based upon stratigraphic relationships (Fig. 69).

#### Phases 1 and 2: Land division

The earliest deposit encountered was a 0.1m-thick clayey occupation spread containing domestic waste (125) in the north-eastern corner of the site. This was

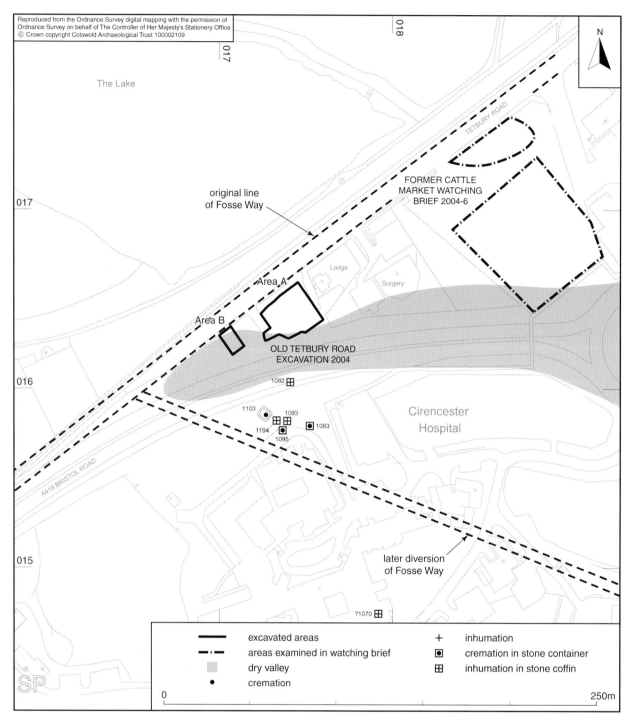

*Fig. 68*    Location of the Old Tetbury Road and Former Cattle Market sites in relation to previous discoveries of Roman burials and the infilled dry valley (1:2000)

superseded by two gullies (collectively termed boundary A). One was laid out at right-angles to Old Tetbury Road and continued beyond the limits of the site to the south-east. A second gully formed at arm from the main land division and cut through 125. Both gullies were heavily truncated, surviving up to 1m wide and 0.3m deep. They typically contained a single silty fill (Fig. 70, Section AA). No other features which could be securely associated with these gullies were identified.

*Phase 3: Flavian cremation activity*

Ditch 1 lay close to the north-western limit of the site. It was heavily truncated by a later wall and its associated construction cut, and obscured in plan by post-medieval make-up layer 106 which was only removed in four small areas. The ditch was 2.25m wide, 0.5–0.8m deep, and contained a series of silty fills (Fig. 70, Section BB). Several fragments of a juvenile sheep were recovered from one of the fills, and this individual

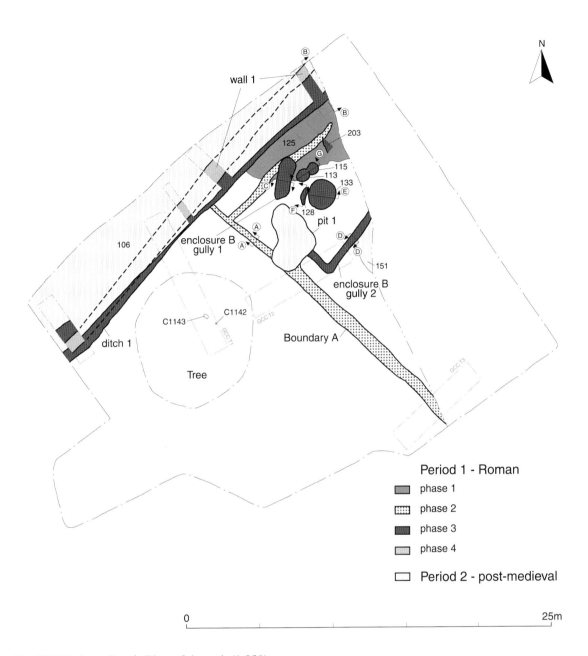

*Fig. 69* Old Tetbury Road. Plan of Area A (1:250)

carcass may have been partially articulated at the time of deposition. The area to the south-east of ditch 1 was at least partially enclosed on two sides by gully 2, 0.5m wide and 0.3m deep (Fig. 70, Section DD). This area is designated as enclosure B. Within enclosure B a gully or elongated pit (gully 1) cut through one of the gullies of boundary A. Gully 1 was *c*. 3m long, 0.9m wide and up to 0.25m deep (Fig. 70, Section CC). To the south-east of it were a number of pits. Pit 133 lay centrally within the excavated area of enclosure B and was roughly circular in plan, 2m in diameter and 0.5m deep (Fig. 70, Section EE). Immediately to the west of this was pit 128 which was smaller and more irregular in plan (up to 1m wide and only 0.15m deep; Fig. 70, Section FF). Both pits contained small quantities of cremated adult human bone and pit 128 also included four fragments of burnt sheep-sized animal bone. Two circular intercutting pits

(113 and 115) to the north-west of pit 133 were up to 0.9m in diameter and 0.25m deep (Fig. 70, Section GG). These two pits yielded good groups of pottery, some of which was heat-altered to varying degrees, suggesting a close association with a cremation pyre. The pits did not produce cremated human bone, but as samples were not collected for sieving it cannot be ruled out that they also contained small quantities of such material. Cross-context joins between pottery sherds from pits 113, 115 and 133 strongly suggest that they were infilled at the same time. The presence of glass droplets and small fragments of copper alloy in pits 133 and 128, along with the relatively small amounts of cremated human bone and the lack of evidence for a burial vessel, suggest that these pit fills contain pyre debris rather than cremation burials per se. The fills of the gullies defining enclosure B were very similar in character to

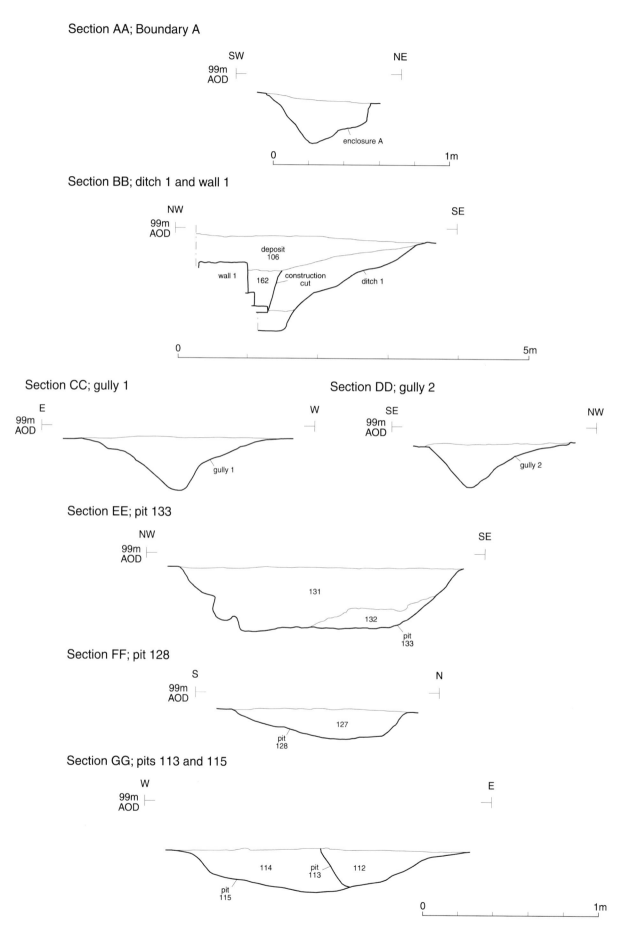

*Fig. 70*   Old Tetbury Road. Sections (1:20 and 1:50)

those of the pits, and also contained burnt pottery sherds of comparable form and date, suggesting that all these features were infilled at the same time. Another pit (203) was found in the northern part of enclosure B. This pit was not visible in plan and was only revealed when a section was excavated across one of the gullies of boundary A (which it partially cut). The pit was up to 0.4m deep and contained abundant fragments of limestone. Its function is unclear.

Two cremation burials were found to the south-west of enclosure B during the 2001 evaluation within an area not subsequently re-examined by the excavation. Burial C1142 was represented by the broken base of a pottery vessel filled with fragments of burnt bone. Burial C1143 lay 0.6m further to the north-west and comprised a small pit 0.32m long by 0.26m wide filled with frequent inclusions of charcoal, fragments of burnt bone up to 10mm in length and a probable iron hobnail. Both cremations were left *in situ* and were not further examined.

### Phase 4: Masonry wall

A masonry wall (wall 1) was constructed above the by now infilled ditch 1, its construction trench cutting into the ditch backfill. Above two courses of footings the wall was 0.75m wide and built from mortar-bonded dressed stones. It survived to a maximum height of 0.7m (Fig. 70, Section BB; Figs 71–2). In form and construction the wall appears typically Roman, although the recovery of a medieval iron spur from the infill of the construction trench raises a question as to its date. On balance a Roman date is preferred (see discussion).

### Period 2: Post-medieval (?early 19th century)

A thin layer (151) up to 0.1m-thick containing crushed oyster shell and charcoal flecks partially overlay gully 2 of enclosure B. The full extent of the deposit was not exposed. Ditch 1 and wall 1 were covered by a clayey make-up deposit 106 up to 0.6m thick which contained 17th- to 18th-century material (Fig. 70, Section BB). This deposit is most likely to be associated with the construction in 1826 of the adjacent estate wall and lodge of Querns House. To the south-east of this deposit an irregular pit (pit 1) cut through Roman deposits.

### Area B

A cremation burial was found close to the south-western edge of Area B cut into the surface of the natural brash (Fig. 73). Burial C1144 lay within a pit (504) which was 0.3m in diameter and heavily truncated to a maximum surviving depth of 0.1m. The cremated bone of a four-year-old child was contained within the base of a Savernake ware jar into which had also been placed a small cup. The cremation was covered by up to 0.9m of silty clay (502) which can be interpreted as an alluvial deposit associated with the infilling of the dry valley to the south-east. The surface of the clay was cut by an undated dry-stone culvert, 0.7m wide and 0.5m high, aligned north-east to south-west.

### Dating evidence

#### Period 1: Phases 1 and 2

Phase 1 deposit 125 did not produce any dating evidence, while small quantities of coarseware pottery from the fills of the phase 2 gullies provide only a broad date. Fabrics include black sandy types TF 5 and 11 and Savernake ware (TF 6), types which are likely to pre-date the middle of the 2nd century AD. Similar dating is supported by the absence of

*Fig. 71* Old Tetbury Road. Possible precinct wall 1 (scale 1m)

*Fig. 72* Old Tetbury Road. Section through wall 1 and ditch 1 (scale 1m)

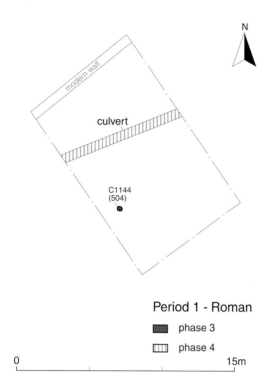

N

culvert

C1144
(504)

## Period 1 - Roman

▨ phase 3

▥ phase 4

0                                        15m

*Fig. 73*   Old Tetbury Road. Plan of Area B (1:250)

Dorset Black-Burnished ware, abundant in Cirencester after *c.* AD 130/50.

### Period 1: Phase 3

Pottery from the fills of Ditch 1 is sparse and abraded, but in character it is comparable with that from boundary A, with material certainly of the period after *c.* AD 150 absent. Pits 113, 115 and 133 within enclosure B produced moderately large groups of pottery, including 30 sherds of South Gaulish samian (Tables 17–18). The samian forms indicate a Flavian date and in the absence of Central Gaulish material the likely date range is *c.* AD 70–100. Cross-context joins of samian and other vessels from each of these features suggest close contemporaneity. Similar dating is also probable for the substantial portion of a flagon of unusual type (Fig. 77, 3) and sherds of Dressel 2–4 wine amphora. The amphora(s), flagon and some of the samian vessels are heat-altered to varying degrees, suggesting incorporation in, or proximity to, the cremation pyre. The fills of gullies 1 and 2 also include burnt sherds of amphora and flagon comparable to material from pits 113 and 115. Other pottery from these gullies consists of earlier Roman coarseware types, including from gully 2 a shouldered bowl in TF 5, a type known from middle or late 1st-century AD deposits in the town (CE I, fig. 54, no. 138).

The pottery vessels associated with Burial C1144 consist of a Savernake ware jar and a carinated bowl in TF 5. A date before *c.* AD 120/140 is suggested for the cremation by the presence of Savernake ware, a type which declines in use beyond the early 2nd century AD. A similar date is likely for the carinated cup.

### Period 1: Phase 4

Foundation fill 139 and masonry 138 of wall A each produced single sherds of Dorset Black-Burnished ware, suggestive of

dating after the early 2nd century AD. A fragmentary iron rowel spur (n.i.), possibly of 14th-century date, was recovered from the infill 162 of the construction trench for the wall (Fig. 70, Section BB). On balance this single item of metalwork is considered to be intrusive from the overlying post-medieval deposit 106 and a Roman date is preferred for the wall (see discussion).

### Period 2

A single abraded Minety ware sherd dateable to between the 12th and 15th centuries was recovered from layer 151. As medieval sherds occurred residually in clearly post-medieval deposits on the site, a post-medieval date for this deposit may also be likely. Levelling deposit 106 and pit 1 produced pottery groups of very similar composition which probably date to the mid 18th century. Most abundant are glazed earthenware sherds with clear (red-appearing) glaze and mottled brown glazed Staffordshire/Bristol-type earthenware. There are occasional sherds of English tablewares in the form of white salt-glazed stoneware and tin-glazed earthenware, and continental imports comprising Frechen and Westerwald stonewares.

## The Former Cattle Market site

### Introduction

When plans for the redevelopment of the cattle market were originally proposed the archaeological potential of the site had been considered to be high. The stone coffin of a child and numerous urned cremations were found during the levelling of the area for the construction of the cattle market in February 1867. There are also references to a second stone coffin, although other descriptions refer to 'a square stone with space for bones' which would fit with other examples in Cirencester of cremations being interred in hollowed-out stone blocks (CE II, 207, MF5 A10–12 nos 1058–62). Three of the cremation vessels survive in the Corinium Museum and date to the 1st and 2nd centuries AD (ibid., fig. 88, nos 1058–1060). Burial 1060 also contained a 1st-century AD pottery lamp. Another stone coffin was discovered on the site in 1983 during levelling for the creation of a car park (ibid., MF5 appendix no. 1141). At least 46 cremations and 8 extended inhumations were recorded in 1960 during salvage recording immediately to the north-east of the cattle market at Oakley Cottage (now Bridges Garage; Reece 1962) (Fig. 74). Given these discoveries an archaeological evaluation comprising the excavation of 30 trenches was undertaken by Oxford Archaeology in 2002 to assess the potential of the site (Oxford Archaeology 2002d). The evaluation revealed a complete absence of archaeological deposits in the central part of the cattle market, although in trench 6 adjacent to Old Tetbury Road a single urned cremation and inhumation were found. Deposits of silty clay were found in trenches 22, 24, 25 and 26 in the southern sector of the site infilling the dry valley.

Following the evaluation planning permission was granted for the construction of a new leisure centre, which commenced in October 2004. CA was commissioned to monitor groundworks, which comprised the

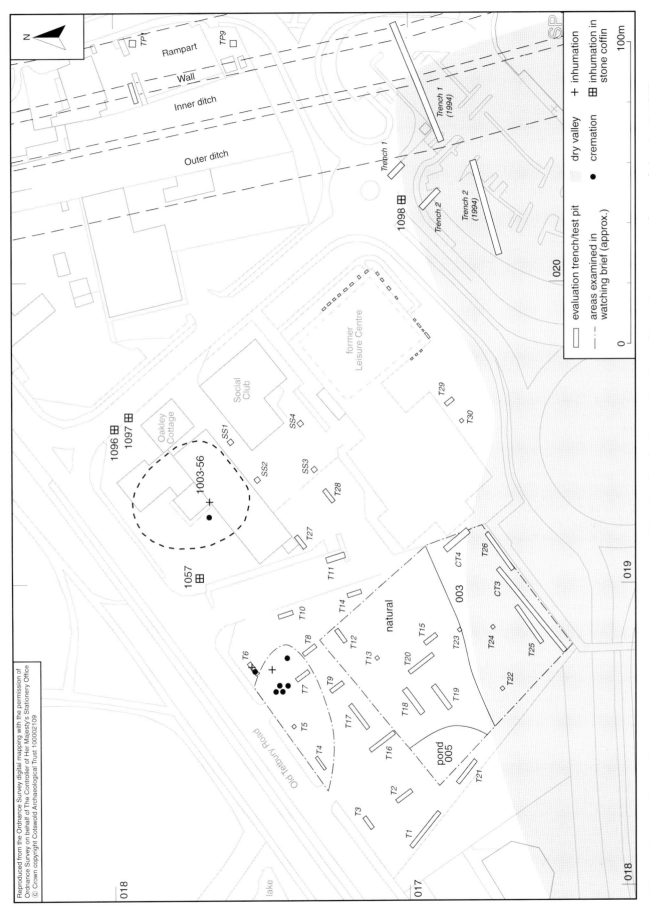

*Fig. 74* Former Cattle Market. Areas examined during the watching brief and other archaeological investigations in and around the site (1:1250)

removal of hard standings and make-up beneath the footprint of the new building and part of its car park, and a few areas of localised deep excavation. Given the survival of Roman deposits in the northern part of the site adjacent to Old Tetbury Road it was hoped to preserve any burials in this area where possible.

### Results

Five cremation burials and one extended inhumation were recorded during the watching brief, as well as clay silt deposits infilling the dry valley to the south. The level of truncation in the central and northern parts of the site resulting from the construction of the cattle market was found to be very high, with the make-up for tarmac surfacings frequently directly overlying natural. Natural comprised limestone brash in a clay matrix above firmer bedrock. The natural ground surface, as revealed following machine stripping, sloped down markedly to the south and west, its height falling from approximately 115.9m AOD in the northernmost part of the site to approximately 111.2m AOD by the southernmost limit of excavation. This slope would originally have been more pronounced as the natural substrate was heavily truncated in the northern part of the site and despite the drop in ground level was not generally exposed to the south where it remained covered by post-medieval topsoil 003 up to 0.8m thick. An exception to this was two deep trenches (Fig. 74, CT3 and CT4), excavated by the contractor, which revealed a thick clayey deposit with frequent limestone inclusions (302/402; n.i.). This material was quite difficult to tell apart from the natural, but was distinguished by its darker colour. In CT 4 the deposit was approximately 2.5m thick and directly overlay limestone bedrock. The base of the layer was not exposed in CT 3. Deposit 302/402 was not recorded

elsewhere on the site, soakaway trenches further to the north revealing only bedrock beneath 0.3m of natural clay brash. Former topsoil 003 had also been entirely removed in the northern part of the site.

Towards the western limit of the site there was a localised dip in the ground level which was filled with grey-blue clay (005) up to 0.3m deep. The full extent of the clay was not revealed, and it was covered by a thin spread of blue clay containing lenses of orange sand (004; n.i.). Both clays are most likely to have been deposited by water action, and the possibilities are that they formed within either a natural watercourse or else a natural or man-made pond. The natural ground level is falling to the south-west and clay was encountered at a depth of almost 1m below the car park surface in evaluation trench 21. The lake within the grounds of Cirencester Park is only short distance away on the opposite side of Old Tetbury Road and it is conceivable that this natural dip was originally occupied by a watercourse draining south-eastwards into the now fully silted-up dry valley. The construction of the lake perhaps led to the drying up of the watercourse, and alluvial deposit 004 was sealed by post-medieval topsoil 003 indicating that the feature had gone out of use by this time. No trace of similar alluvial deposits was found in any of the evaluation trenches in this part of the site, however, and consequently the interpretation as a pond is equally plausible.

At the northern end of the site natural was partially overlain by a patchy brown clay-silt between 80mm and 0.23m deep, probably the remnants of a Roman ground surface as it was cut through by burials C1145–7, C1150 and B1152. It can be equated with the similar deposit found at Old Tetbury Road. In all six human cremation burials (C1145–50) were found buried in pits close to the north-western limit of the site (Fig. 75). Although these burials were found grouped together, there was

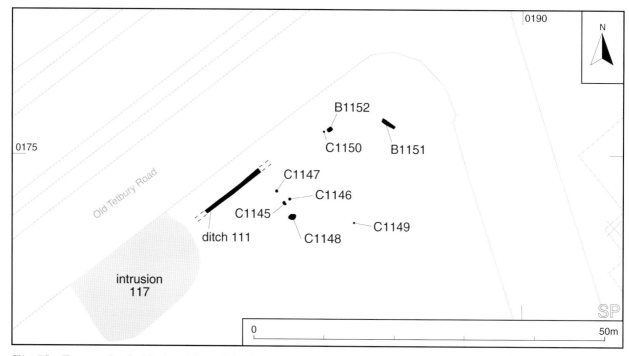

*Fig. 75*   Former Cattle Market. Plan of the burials (1:500)

no obvious pattern to their layout. Each pit was roughly circular in plan and had been severely truncated during the construction of the cattle market so that they only survived to a depth of between 80 and 200mm. This high level of truncation meant that the profiles of the pits were difficult to characterise, but they appeared to be generally U-shaped. The lower portions of cremation vessels survived intact within C1145, C1147, C1149 and C1150. Burial C1148 was interred in a very precisely dug oval-shaped pit 0.7m long, 0.45m wide and 0.13m deep. The pit was filled with dark brown silty clay containing abundant flecks of charcoal and burnt bone, and large sherds of pottery which are probably the remnants of a cremation urn. Burial C1146 comprised a sub-circular pit 0.42m in diameter which was filled with much charcoal, especially around the edges, along with small fragments of cremated bone and sherds of pottery. It is conceivable that this feature represents a highly truncated cremation burial (and thus it has been ascribed a burial number), although alternatively the pit may have been dug for the disposal of pyre debris. Burial C1150 was found and lifted during the evaluation. This was found right on the edge of trench 6 and comprised an irregular cut up to 0.8m wide and 0.34m deep containing a fragmentary pottery vessel partially filled with cremated bone. The upper fill of the cut contained scattered sherds from other vessels which had presumably been disturbed by the construction of the cattle market. Each cremation burial was that of an adult individual, but it was not possible to sex the remains. Quantities of juvenile sheep bone within C1147 and C1148 indicate that a leg of lamb had been placed onto the cremation pyre with the body as part of the funerary rite. Other pyre goods recovered were two heat-affected bone hairpins from C1149, a copper-alloy hook and stud from C1150 and iron nails from C1145–9.

The extended inhumation burial (B1151) of an adult female between 36 and 45 years old was found 4m to the north-east of the cremations. The body lay supine with the hands paced on the pelvis, and was orientated north-west/south-east with the head to the north-west. It had been buried in a well-fitting rectangular grave, 2.2m long and 0.6m wide, which had been severely truncated. Nails found around the skeleton indicated the former presence of a wooden coffin. A second inhumation (B1152) was discovered in evaluation trench 6. The skeleton was cleaned sufficiently to permit basic identification but was not otherwise excavated. The burial was left *in situ* at the completion of the evaluation and it subsequently proved possible to preserve this area within the development. B1152 lay within a shallow rock-cut grave 0.9m long by 0.52m wide. The skeleton was in a very fragmentary condition and most of the bone appeared to have been previously disturbed and partially scattered. The skull had been broken in antiquity and was partially incomplete with both the lower portion of the skull and jaw missing. The body was aligned north-east/south-west and the size of both the grave and the bones exposed indicate that it was a juvenile. An area of modern disturbance (117) to the south-west of the recorded burials has probably destroyed any further burials in this area which had escaped truncation during the construction of the cattle market. A ditch (111), 0.58m wide and up to 0.41m deep, was exposed for a length of 10m running parallel with Old Tetbury Road. The ditch fill contained animal bone but no pottery. While undated it is more likely to be associated with the cattle market than the Roman burials.

## Dating evidence

The dates of the individual burials are discussed below; as a group they appear to date between the later 1st and 3rd centuries AD. The post-medieval topsoil 003 contained eight sherds of earlier Roman coarsewares (TF 9, TF 17 and TF 5) and South Gaulish samian (TF 154a), presumably disturbed from underlying deposits. Quantities of re-deposited Roman and medieval pottery occur alongside post-medieval and later pottery in deposits 118 and 122 associated with the construction of the cattle market in 1867. The latest material in these deposits consists of mottled brown-glazed earth-

**Table 16:** Metalwork and glass from burials and associated deposits at Old Tetbury Road and the Former Cattle Market (quantification by fragment count)

| Feature no. | Pit 128 | Pit 133 | C1144 | C1145 | C1146 | C1147 | C1148 | C1148 | B1151 | Total |
|---|---|---|---|---|---|---|---|---|---|---|
| Sample no. | – | – | <1> | <1> | <2> | <3> | – | <5> | <103–4> | |
| *Metalwork* | | | | | | | | | | |
| Fe nails: 20mm | – | – | – | 1 | – | – | – | – | – | 1 |
| Fe nails: 25–40mm | – | 5 | – | – | – | – | – | – | – | 5 |
| Fe nails: 45–65mm | – | 3 | – | – | 1 | 1 | 1 | – | 5 | 6 |
| Fe nails: shaft/head fragments | 18 | 47 | 14 | – | 14 | – | – | 21 | 4 | 118 |
| Fe hobnails | – | – | – | – | 4 | – | – | 11 | – | 15 |
| Fe sheet/strip fragment | – | – | – | – | – | 1 | – | – | – | 1 |
| *Green glass* | | | | | | | | | | |
| Fully distorted/droplets | 35 | 9 | – | – | – | – | – | – | – | 44 |
| Part distorted tubular | 1 | – | – | – | – | – | – | – | – | 1 |
| Unburnt, thin-walled | 2 | – | – | – | 1 | – | – | – | 1 | 3 |
| *Clear glass* | | | | | | | | | | |
| Fully distorted/droplets | – | 2 | – | – | – | – | – | – | – | 2 |

**Table 17:** Summary of pottery from cremation burials/related features at Old Tetbury Road
and the Former Cattle Market

**KEY:** Count = sherd count; Min. vess. = minimum number of vessels; EVEs = rim estimated vessel equivalents.
*Numerical codes relate to Cirencester-type series (Rigby CE I-II; Keely CE III). Codes in parentheses derive from National
Roman Fabric Reference Collection (Tomber and Dore 1998).

| Context | Fabric* | Form | Count | Min. vess. | EVEs | Weight (g) | Comment |
|---|---|---|---|---|---|---|---|
| **Old Tetbury Road** | | | | | | | |
| **C1144 Pit 504** (505/6) | 6 (SAV GT) | large jar | 17 | 1 | – | 1254 | – |
| | 5 | carinated bowl | 34 | 1 | .20 | 224 | – |
| **Pit 113** (112) | 154a (LGF SA) | 18 | 9 | 3 | .45 | 168 | Includes NAT stamp 4 × burnt |
| | 154a (LGF SA) | 18/31 | 1 | 1 | – | 2 | – |
| | 154a (LGF SA) | 27 | 10 | 5 | .10 | 34 | 2 × burnt |
| | 39 | – | 13 | 1 | – | 132 | burnt; CC 114/131 |
| | flag.fab. | – | 45 | 1 | – | 360 | burnt; CC 114/131 |
| | 11 | platter | 1 | 1 | .06 | 10 | – |
| **Pit 115** (114) | 154a (LGF SA) | Drag. 18 | 4 | 3 | .35 | 36 | one join to 112 |
| | 154a (LGF SA) | Drag. 18R | 1 | 1 | .10 | 8 | – |
| | 154a (LGF SA) | 27g | 4 | 2 | .10 | 34 | 4 × burnt |
| | 39 | – | 34 | 1 | .70 | 180 | burnt; CC 112/131 |
| | flag.fab. | flagon | 27 | 1 | – | 260 | burnt; CC 112/131 |
| | 6 (SAV GT) | – | 2 | 2 | – | 8 | – |
| **Pit 133** (131) | 154a (LGF SA) | Drag. 18 | 1 | 1 | .05 | 2 | – |
| | 39 | – | 46 | 2 | – | 1024 | burnt |
| | flag.fab. | – | 9 | 1 | – | 134 | CC 112/114 |
| | 11 | jar | 8 | 2 | – | 38 | – |
| | 17 | – | 2 | 2 | – | 4 | – |
| *Sub-total* | | | *268* | *27* | *2.11* | *3912* | |
| **Former Cattle Market** | | | | | | | |
| **C1145** (104) | 74 (DOR BB1) | jar | 34 | 1 | – | 128 | as urn; base only |
| **C1146** (107) | 6 (SAV GT) | jar | 1 | 1 | – | 31 | ?Pyre deposit |
| | 9 | ? | 5 | 1 | – | 34 | Heat–affected sherds |
| **C1147** (108) | 17 | jar | 172 | 1 | 1.0 | 1585 | as urn |
| **C1148** (115) | 6 (SAV GT) | jar | 34 | 1 | – | 420 | as urn? |
| | 5 | ? | 12 | 1 | – | 32 | ?accessory |
| **C1149** (126) | 74 (DOR BB1) | jar | 60 | 1 | – | 120 | as urn; base only |
| **C1150** (610) | 74 (DOR BB1) | jar | 84 | 1 | – | 602 | BB1 ev.-rim jar as urn |
| **Layer 122** | 9 | flagon | 8 | 5 | 1.7 | 333 | TF9 variant |
| | 9 | jar | 1 | 1 | .08 | 5 | – |
| | 9 | ? | 24 | 21 | – | 411 | – |
| | 35 (GAL AM1) | amphora | 1 | 1 | – | 498 | – |
| | 17 | jar | 1 | 1 | .10 | 13 | – |
| | 17 | ? | 2 | 2 | – | 16 | – |
| | 106–9 | bowl | 1 | 1 | .20 | 91 | – |
| | 101–4 | dish | 1 | 1 | .18 | 136 | – |
| *Sub -total* | | | *441* | *41* | *3.26* | *4455* | |

enware of probable 18th-century date, glazed earthenwares
broadly dating between the 16th and 18th centuries and
creamwares dating after *c.* 1780.

### Artefacts associated with the burials and pyre debris by E.R. McSloy

#### Inhumation B1151

Iron nails recovered from the grave fill suggest the
presence of a wooden coffin (Table 16). A small,
unfeatured chip of dark green glass and a small body
sherd of pottery in a coarse grey fabric were also found.

#### Urned cremations

Cremation burials C1144, 1145, 1147, 1149 and 1150
were urned, as probably was C1148 although it had
been much disturbed. In nearly all cases truncation had
resulted in the removal of all but the lowest portions of
the pottery vessels. Non-ceramic artefacts from the
cremations were mostly recovered as a result of the
sieving of soil samples. Details of the vessels associated
with C1150 are taken from E. Biddulph's description
contained within the evaluation report and the sherds
have not been re-examined (Oxford Archaeology
2002d).

Burial C1144 at Old Tetbury Road contained two vessels: a large Savernake ware jar (Fig. 77, no. 1), the upper portion of which had been removed by truncation, and, placed inside, a carinated cup (Fig. 77, no. 2) in local black-sandy fabric (TF 5). The form of this vessel, which is derived from late Iron Age ('Belgic') vessels, would seem to be previously unknown in this fabric. Similar forms in Severn Valley ware date to the mid 1st and 2nd centuries AD (Webster 1976). As almost all of the cremated bone came from the base of the larger vessel this suggests that the smaller vessel functioned as a true accessory, and not as a primary container within a protective secondary vessel, comparable to amphora burials known elsewhere (Barber and Bowsher 2000, 106–9). Burial C1148 also included the lower portion of a Savernake type ware jar and sherds from a vessel of uncertain class in TF 5. The pottery from this deposit probably also derives from a disturbed urned cremation and an accessory vessel. Once again a date before the mid 2nd century AD is likely. The occurrence of an accessory vessel inside the primary container is unusual in Roman Britain and cremation burials in south-west England with more than one pottery vessel are rare, unlike the south-east (Philpott 1991, 30–42). At Oakley Cottage Cremation XG of a young adult male had a ring-necked flagon accompanying the cremation urn (Reece 1962, 63).

Three of the burials were accompanied by Black-Burnished ware (TF 74) vessels (Table 17). All appear to be jars, but the degree of truncation of the vessels precluded more detailed classification, with the exception of the vessel containing C1150 which dates to between the mid 2nd and earlier 3rd centuries AD. The upper fill of the cremation pit contained sherds from another Black-Burnished ware jar and sherds in grey, oxidised (orange firing) and sandy whiteware fabrics. Broader dating, between the middle of the 2nd and 4th century AD, is proposed for the heavily truncated vessels with C1145 and C1149. Burial C1147 included the larger part of a jar in a local (North Wiltshire) reduced ware fabric (Fig. 78, no. 1). The survival to full profile of this vessel is presumably the result of deposition within a deeper cut, or the collapse of the vessel long before the levelling of the site. Dating for this vessel, despite its level of completeness, is broadly from the earlier 2nd to 3rd century AD.

*Non-ceramic artefacts*

A small hook and a tiny stud, both made of copper alloy, were recovered from the processed residues of Burial C1150. The hook may originally have been part of a brooch but it could equally, together with the stud, have come from a small box. Iron carpentry nails were recovered from seven of the cremation burials (Table 16). They are presumably pyre goods derived from the coffin or the bier which were collected with the human remains and placed within the urn. The abundance of nails makes it less likely that they all derive from the burning as fuel of reclaimed structural timbers on the pyre. Where identifiable the nails are of typical Roman carpentry form (Manning's 1985, 134 type 1b). Nails

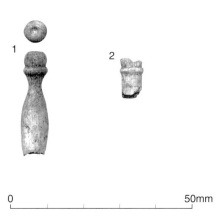

*Fig. 76* Former Cattle Market. Fragments of worked bone pins associated with burial C1149 (scale 1:1)

are frequent finds in Roman cremation deposits (Evans and Maynard 1997, 190). Hobnails retrieved from C1146 and 1148 and fragments of two heat-affected worked bone hairpins from C1149 indicate that at least some of the deceased may have been clothed or adorned at the time of cremation. The bone hairpins from C1149 are fragmentary, but appear to be of a fairly unusual type which is not easily placed within Crummy's typology. They are perhaps closest to her Type 5 pins, considered to date to after *c.* AD 250 (Crummy 1979, 162). The swollen shaft form exhibited by no. 1 also appears to be a feature of 3rd or 4th-century AD bone pins (ibid., 157). A closer match for the head form of no. 1 can be found among metal pins of Cool's Type 21 (Cool 1990, 170), a type which is unfortunately not reliably dated.

*Illustrated pins* (Fig. 76)

1.  Cremation C1149 (fill 127). Worked bone (heat-affected): head and upper portion of probable hairpin. Head features cup-like and spherical moulding with circular depression at the top. The shaft is of shouldered form with a pronouncedly constricted neck. Surviving length 27mm; diameter at shoulder 7.5mm.
2.  Cremation C1149 (fill 127). Worked bone (heat-affected): small fragment from the junction of shaft and head. Narrow cordon, with expanding (?conical or spherical) moulding above. Surviving length 11mm; diameter at neck 5.5mm.

**Table 18:** Summary of the samian forms at Old Tetbury Road. All material is South Gaulish (La Graufesenque) (quantification by minimum vessel count)

| Form | Pit 113 (112) | Pit 115 (114) | Pit 133 (131) | Total |
|---|---|---|---|---|
| Drag. 18 | 3 | 3 | 1 | 7 |
| Drag. 18R | – | 1 | – | 1 |
| Drag. 18/31 | 1 | – | – | 1 |
| Drag. 27 | 5 | 2 | – | 7 |
| **Total** | **9** | **6** | **1** | **16** |

### Pyre debris

The interpretation of the features within enclosure B at Old Tetbury Road rests primarily on the quantities of cremated bone retrieved, identification of pyre goods and other aspects of the artefact assemblage. Cross-context pottery links between pits 133 and 113/115 indicate the close contemporaneity of the features, and the uneven distribution of material between them, particularly in the case of the samian, may be suggestive of deliberate selection or placement (Tables 17–18).

### Pottery

Estimation of the number of vessels represented is rendered difficult by the poor condition of the pottery. The vessel count expressed in Table 17 is almost certainly an overestimate of the actual total. Much of the pottery has clearly been subjected to high temperatures. This is most evident in the discoloura-tion, surface loss and powdery feel of the amphora and flagon fabrics. The samian is affected to a lesser degree, with only some patchy discolouration evident. The most striking aspect of the group is the abundance of continental wares and the virtual absence of locally produced coarsewares. The composition of this group, which contrasts distinctly with contemporary domestic groups from Cirencester (CE V, 327–9), is almost certainly a reflection of the nature of the deposit. Strong emphasis is evident from the forms represented (wine amphorae, flagon, cups and platters) on the consump-tion of food and drink, and it is highly likely that the group represents evidence for feasting associated with the funeral rites. The samian was almost entirely confined to pits 113 and 115 (Table 18) and consists of plainware platters and cups. Estimation of the number of amphorae present in this group was made particularly problematic by the condition of the sherds and identification as Dressel 2–4 type is based upon their distinctive bifid-handles (Fig. 77, no. 4). This type of amphora occurs in Britain throughout the 1st century AD and typically contained wine. It was manufactured at a number of continental and British locations, but as the sherds have been much affected by heat, identification of fabric is difficult (Peacock and Williams 1986, 105–6). The illustrated vessel (Fig. 77, no. 4), represented by ten sherds from pit 133, is most likely of the early Campanian type (R. Tomber, pers. comm.). The second vessel, dispersed across pits 133 and 113/115, is of a much finer buff/pink-firing fabric which is more typical of Gaulish examples.

Nothing is present within the rest of the pottery to contradict a late 1st-century AD date. The flagon/ amphora (Fig. 77, no. 3) is of unusual type, its form reminiscent of flat-based Gaulish wine amphorae, but with round-sectioned handles. Identification of the fabric of this vessel is once again difficult due to the extent of heat alteration which has resulted in the loss of surfaces and discolouration. The form does not appear to have been encountered previously in Cirencester, the closest parallels occurring in late 1st/2nd-century AD contexts at Colchester (Hawkes and Hull 1947, Camulodunum type 168).

### Samian by P.V. Webster

The Old Tetbury Road site produced only a small amount of samian, all of it from South Gaul and thus of 1st to early 2nd-century AD date. The maximum number of vessels represented was 21, of which 16 were associated with deposits associated with cremation activity (Table 18). The other five vessels are likely to have been disturbed from these deposits. Almost half of the assemblage was composed of the plate forms 18 and 18R. The only other forms represented by more than one vessel was the cup form 27 (seven examples) and dish 18/31 (two). Most notable, even in such a small assemblage, is the total absence of decorated forms.

### Non-ceramic artefacts

Quantities of heat-distorted vessel glass and metal items were recovered from pits 128 and 133, predominantly as a result of the sieving of soil samples (Table 16). No comparable material was retrieved from pits 113 and 115, features from which soil samples were not taken. A few unburnt, or less severely distorted, fragments among the glass indicate the presence of thin-walled fineware vessels. Clear and natural green-coloured glass is represented. The more heavily distorted glass might derive from vessels or other items, such as beads.

Iron nails are abundantly represented in pits 113 and 115. All, where identifiable, are of Manning (1985) type 1b. As with the cremation burials the nails probably derive from a coffin or bier burnt as part of the cremation rite. The occasional presence of cremated bone adhering to a nail and the absence of mineralised wood are further indications of the presence of the nails within the pyre. Copper-alloy items from pit 128 consist of fragments of thin sheet, one with a domed rivet *in situ*, and two detached flattened-domed rivets. They probably represent fittings for a wooden casket or box. Similar fittings adorned a box found in a grave at the Butt Road cemetery in Colchester (Crummy 1983, 85–8).

The fill of pit 107 (designated Burial C1146) at the Former Cattle Market contained small quantities of heat-affected pottery, representing at least two vessels (Table 17). Dating on the basis of the identifiable fabrics is between the mid 1st and mid 2nd centuries AD. The pit contained 20 fragments of iron nails and a small chip (<1g) of colourless glass. As the latter was not heat-affected it probably does not represent pyre goods, but rather a fragment from a disturbed grave good or simply a chance inclusion (Table 16). The burnt and fragmented nature of the pottery, combined with the abundance of charcoal and the very small amount of cremated bone present, is more consistent with this deposit representing pyre debris than a discrete cremation burial. Nevertheless as this interpretation is less certain than for the pits at Old Tetbury Road it was deemed safest to allocate this feature a burial number.

### Discussion

Few cremation burials have been excavated and analysed in Cirencester since Reece's (1962) publication of 45 urned burials from Oakley Cottage. Consequently those reported here are of some interest. While the dating of the burials has been hindered by the levels of truncation there are some indications that their date span may be relatively broad. Certainly the burials discovered at the Former Cattle Market do not represent a discrete cluster of burials, but rather the survivors from a more sizeable cemetery largely removed by levelling in 1867. The majority of cremation burials appear to have been interred within single vessels, with Dorset Black-Burnished ware cooking pots used most commonly. Burials containing more than a single vessel might belong to relatively early phase of cemetery use. The focus for cremation burial appears to be between the later 1st and late 2nd or early 3rd century AD, based mainly upon the evidence of the dates ascribed to the Dorset Black-Burnished ware cooking pots. There is some suggestion that burial continued into the later 3rd century AD on the basis of hairpin fragments from C1149. A few 3rd or 4th-century AD cremations utilising Black-Burnished ware jars have been found elsewhere in the Bath Gate cemetery (CEC II, 97). Bone hairpins, similar to those with C1149, have been recovered from other Romano-British cremations. Those at Ospringe, Kent, and Colchester contain solely hairpins, but they are more common in association with other artefacts such as brooches, beads or glass vessels (Philpott 1991, 128–32). Hobnails are most frequently found in cremations in the South-East of England, although they occur in smaller numbers farther afield (ibid., 165).

Exact parallels for the distribution of pyre goods found in the pits at Old Tetbury Road (and, if it is not a formal cremation burial, pit 105/C1146 at the Former Cattle Market) are not readily forthcoming, a reflection that such deposits have to date been infrequently recognised in Romano-British cemeteries. Of the three cremation burials found in the Bath Gate cemetery, two were urned and one was unurned (CE II, 97–100). The latter (Burial 293) was found in a large pit full of burnt

material containing small fragments of bone, a description which is consistent with pyre debris. At the eastern cemetery of London pyre debris was typically found in shallow spreads, samples from which produced an abundance of artefacts and cremated bone (Barber and Bowsher 2000). More closely comparable in terms of feature morphology are the late Iron Age pyre-related features, including pits, found at Westhampnett, West Sussex, and Baldock, Hertfordshire (McKinley 1997, 57; 1993). The composition of the almost contemporary pyre deposits in the London eastern cemetery compare in many respects to those from within enclosure B, particularly in the abundance of pyre goods. Importantly, however, they differ in that multiple individuals were represented there, suggesting that those deposits were composed of accumulations from successive cremations, rather than a single event. Comparison of the pottery from the London deposits against contemporary domestic assemblages revealed differences which reflect in part what is seen here in Cirencester. A higher incidence of amphora and cup/beaker forms was interpreted in London as evidence for the consumption of alcohol associated with feasting at the funeral (Barber and Bowsher 2000, 67–8).

## Other pottery by E.R. McSloy

Small quantities of Roman and later pottery were recovered from non-funerary deposits at the Former Cattle Market, and a small group meriting some further comment derived from levelling deposit 122 associated with the construction of the market (Table 17). In addition to small quantities of later Roman and post-medieval pottery, a number of sherds in a distinctive flagon fabric were recovered. Their fresh condition suggests that they have been disturbed from a discrete Early Roman deposit. The most significant aspect of this group is the presence of large sherds in an oxidised fabric which in some instances exhibit signs of over-firing and bloating. The comparative abundance of

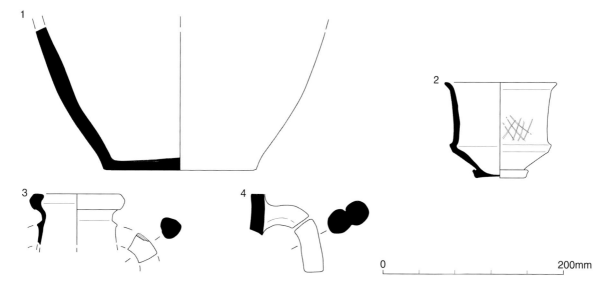

*Fig. 77* Old Tetbury Road. Late Iron Age and Romano-British pottery (scale 1:4)

vessels of this type in this one deposit is unusual, and when combined with the condition of the sherds, suggests a group of wasters or perhaps kiln seconds. The fabric compares in most respects with TF 9, which is abundant in the town after *c.* AD 70/5 and is considered to derive from a relatively local source (CE I, 154). It differs most from the published description for TF 9 in its apparently greater abundance of calcareous (oolitic limestone) inclusions. Identifiable forms consist of flagons which all appear to be single-handled, ring-necked types, with bulbous bodies and foot-ring bases (Fig. 78, nos 2–3). The forms suggest a date between the mid/later 1st and early 2nd centuries AD and compare with previously published examples in fabric TF 9 (CE I, fig. 55, no. 181).

### Fabric description

TF9 variant. Buff surfaces and margins with blue-grey core. Surfaces are soft and powdery. Fracture is fine. Rare to common round, oolitic limestone (0.5–1mm) and rare red iron oxide (1–2mm). There are frequent voids visible to the surfaces and break resulting from the leaching of calcareous inclusions.

### Illustrated vessels

#### Old Tetbury Road (Fig. 77)

1. Savernake ware (TF 6). Lower portion of a jar which served as an urn. Burial C1144 (504).
2. Black sandy fabric (TF 5). Carinated cup with burnished lattice decoration. Accessory vessel, Burial C1144 (504).
3. Flagon-amphora. Burnt oxidised fabric. The rim form is close to Gauloise-type flat-based amphoras. Pyre deposit within pits 133 and 113.
4. Amphora. Dressel 2–4 type, with bifid handles. Burnt. Pyre deposit within pit 133.

#### Former Cattle Market (Fig. 78)

1. Local/North Wiltshire greyware (TF 17). Necked jar serving as an urn. Burial C1147 (108).
2. Local oxidised flagon fabric (TF 9 variant). Ring-necked flagon. Overfired; possible waster? Re-deposited in post-medieval levelling deposit 122.
3. Local oxidised flagon fabric (TF 9 variant). Ring-necked flagon. Overfired; possible waster? Re-deposited in post-medieval levelling deposit 122.

### Human remains

Three deposits of cremated bone were retrieved from the Old Tetbury Road site in the form of soil samples. Burial C1144 was urned, but severely truncated, and was fully excavated. The deposits of bone from pits 128 and 133 were not complete samples as both pits were only half sectioned. One inhumation (B1151) and five cremation (C1145–9) burials were found during the watching brief at the Former Cattle Market. A further cremation burial C1150 was lifted and examined by Oxford Archaeology during the evaluation, and the analysis by Witkin below is reproduced from the evaluation report (Oxford Archaeology 2002d). A second inhumation B1152 was also found during the evaluation, but as it was not lifted it has not been subjected to analysis.

### Inhumation burial B1151 by Teresa Gilmore

#### Methodology

Sex was determined using morphological criteria and metric variation (Brothwell 1981; Buikstra and Ubelaker 1994; Bass 1995). Adult age was assigned on the basis of the skeletal parts present; dental attrition (Brothwell 1981); sternal rib ends (Iscan and Loth 1984;

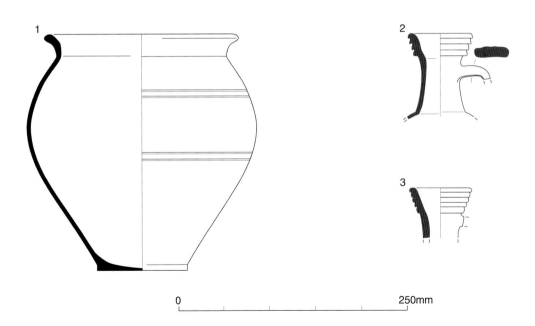

0                                           250mm

*Fig. 78*   Former Cattle Market. Roman pottery (scale 1:4)

Iscan *et al.* 1985) and auricular surface degeneration (Lovejoy *et al.* 1985). Unfortunately no pubic symphyses survived due to the degree of fragmentation. Pathology was determined by macroscopic inspection, using criteria in Manchester and Roberts (1995) and Schwartz (1995). Non-metric variation was determined using criteria in Brothwell (1981). Limited metric analysis was possible due to the fragmentary nature of the remains.

*Preservation and completeness*

Preservation of human skeletal remains depends on a variety of taphonomic factors including size, shape and robusticity of the bones. The conditions after burial can also affect the preservation, including disturbance of the burial, soil characteristics and treatment after excavation. Unfortunately, despite the bone surface being in very good condition, the bones belonging to B1151 were fragmentary, and only a couple of cervical vertebrae survived intact. Overall the preservation was classified as moderate on a five-point scale from excellent to very poor. Approximately 70–75% of the skeleton has survived for analysis (Table 19).

*Age, sex and stature*

A single individual is represented, an adult female between 36 and 45 years old. Stature can be established using any of the long bones, assuming they are complete and fully fused. No long bones survived intact from the burial. In order to gain an idea of stature the right radius, which had a single clean break, was reconstructed and measured. This produced a stature of 154.9cm ± 4.24cm. This is an approximate stature as it was produced from a broken arm bone (the femur and tibia provide the most accurate assessment of stature, whereas the long bones of the arm, in particular the radius and ulna, provide the least accurate assessment).

*Non-metric traits and pathology*

Non-metric traits are examples of normal skeletal variation either related to activity or genetic disposition. Commonly encountered examples are extra bones present in the cranial sutures or wormian bones, squatting facets on the distal tibia, and pronounced ridges on the lateral edges of incisors. Due to the degree of fragmentation the only non-metric trait recorded

from the skeleton was an accessory sacral facet. No cranial or dental non-metric traits were found.

Degenerative joint disease consists of evidence of degradation of joints relating to activity, disease and age. The key features consist of osteophytic lipping (extra bone growth) around the edges of the joint surface, eburnation (polishing) of the joint surface and porosity of the joint surface. The burial demonstrated very little evidence for degenerative joint disease. A total of 5/20 vertebral bodies demonstrated either minor osteophytes or very mild porosity over the surface, mainly on the inferior surface, indicating a degree of physical activity from a young age. The enthesopathies (muscle attachments) on the arm bones and the vertebral arches are pronounced, suggestive of physical activity. Metabolic disease provides evidence of dietary deficiency and stress, predominately during childhood. Cribra Orbitalia, the presence of a fine pitting of the orbital roof, is linked to childhood anaemia and tends to get remodelled as the individual ages into adulthood. It was present in both the left and right orbits of the skeleton.

Dental pathology can be noted in many forms, including calculus (mineralised plaque) to caries and periodontal disease to lines of hypoplasia (temporary cessation of dental development) on the teeth, produced during periods of nutritional stress during childhood. The mandible and the left maxilla were present in the burial, with a total of 29 teeth. Slight calculus was present on 15/29 teeth (52% of teeth present) mainly on the buccal or lingual surfaces. Lines of dental enamel hypoplasia (DEH) were noted on 11/29 (38% of all teeth present). Lines were present on the canines, incisors and first and second premolars, suggesting either periods of dietary or emotional stress, or disease, between two and six years of age.

*Conclusions*

The burial is of a female aged between 36 and 45 years at time of death. Evidence of dietary malnutrition or disease during early childhood is testified by the presence of lines of hypoplasia on the teeth and evidence of iron-deficiency anaemia. The presence of early stages of degenerative joint disease and pronounced enthesopathies indicate a degree of physical activity from a young age. The burial displays consistent features with the skeletons recovered from the Bath Gate cemetery (CEC II). There Cribra Orbitalia was present in 35 of 405 individuals, seven

**Table 19:** Summary of inhumation burial B1151 at the Former Cattle Market

KEY: DEH = dental enamel hypoplasia; DJD = degenerative joint disease

| Grave Dimensions (m) | Coffin? | Preservation | Completeness (%) | Age at death (years) | Sex | Orientation | Body position | Dental pathology | Pathology |
|---|---|---|---|---|---|---|---|---|---|
| 1.86 × 0.6 | Iron nails present suggesting coffin | Good | 70–75% | 36–45 | F | N–S | Extended, supine | Calculus 15/29; DEH 11/29 | Cribra Orbitalia; DJD on vertebral bodies |

**Table 20**: Weights of cremated bone at Old Tetbury Road and the Former Cattle Market

| Bone group | Total weight (g) | Total weight of > 10mm fraction (g) | Fraction % | Total weight of > 5mm fraction (g) | Fraction % | Total weight of > 2mm fraction (g) | Fraction % |
|---|---|---|---|---|---|---|---|
| *Old Tetbury Road* | | | | | | | |
| C1144 | 114 | 10 | 8.8 | 64 | 56.1 | 35 | 30.7 |
| Pit 128 | 56 | 3 | 5.4 | 28 | 50.0 | 24 | 42.8 |
| Pit 133 | 42 | 2 | 4.8 | 20 | 47.6 | 18 | 42.9 |
| *Former Cattle Market* | | | | | | | |
| C1145 | 72 | 1 | 1.4 | 43 | 59.7 | 26 | 36.1 |
| C1146 | 184 | 24 | 13.0 | 97 | 52.7 | 60 | 32.6 |
| C1147 | 904 | 688 | 76.1 | 195 | 21.6 | 14 | 01.6 |
| C1148 | 100 | 8 | 8.0 | 60 | 60.0 | 29 | 29.0 |
| C1149 | 48 | 17 | 35.4 | 23 | 47.9 | 7 | 14.6 |

of which were female. The estimated height of the skeleton falls within the stature range calculated there by Wells of 1.475m to 1.698m. At least 42 of the individuals in the cemetery displayed dental enamel hypoplasia defects similar to those found in this burial. The main teeth to be affected were the canines and the second molars, suggesting nutritional stress between two and four years of age.

### Cremated human bone by Teresa Gilmore

*Methodology*

The cremation burials were retrieved from site in the form of bulk soil samples. The samples were wet-sieved using a 1mm sieve and the cremated remains weighed and separated into 10mm, 5mm and 2mm sieve fractions (Table 20). Each fraction was weighed and the number of identifiable fragments recorded, along with the colour and degree of fragmentation. No duplications of diagnostic bone elements were present in each of the five cremation burials. This would indicate that one individual has been interred in each burial.

*Age and sex*

Sex was determined on adult remains only using standard criteria. Adult age is normally assessed on the basis of the skeletal parts present, but in this assemblage only dental attrition could be used (Brothwell 1981). Pathological features were determined by macroscopic inspection, using criteria in Manchester and Roberts (1995) and Schwartz (1995). It proved difficult to determine the sex of the individuals due to the small quantities of bone present and the high degree of fragmentation. Burial C1147 was the only individual where an attempt could be made to determine sex due to the presence of a left narrow sciatic notch. However as no other key sexual dimorphic traits were present, the burial has been classified as ?Male (Tables 21–22).

Burial C1144 contained a juvenile of around four years based upon the evidence of dental development (Hillson 1996). All the other cremation burials are believed to be adults (older than 18 years of age) as only

fully fused bone fragments of an adult nature were found. The cremated remains from pits 128 and 133 have been assigned an adult age (older than 18 years) based on epiphyseal fusion and the general characteristics of the bone.

*Efficiency of cremation*

An estimation of the efficiency of the cremation process can be gained from analysis of the colour of the cremated bone fragments (fully oxidised bone is white in appearance). Cremation efficiency is related to various factors, the most important being time, temperature and oxygen (McKinley 2000). The majority of the cremated bone was either white or light grey in colour, suggesting a high state of oxidation and a pyre temperature of over $750^\circ$C (Lyman 1994). The cremated material from pits 128 and 133 exhibits high fragmentation, with over 90% of bone being 5mm or smaller in size, and demonstrates some abrasion, suggesting a degree of residuality within the pit fills. Cremated material from Burial C1144 was not abraded but demonstrated a similar degree of fragmentation. Some fragments from C1147 and C1149 are indicative of a lower state of oxidisation. Posterior bone fragments in C1147, such as vertebral neural arches, were dark grey in colour, and some bone fragments from C1149 had a white/light grey exterior but a dark grey interior, indicating a change in the oxidisation level of the bone.

*Weight and skeletal elements represented*

The expected weight range for an adult cremation, based upon observations in modern crematoria, is in the range of *c.* 1000–2400g, with an average of *c.* 1650g (McKinley 1993). In practice on archaeological sites much smaller quantities are normally recovered, as for example at the Romano-British cemetery at Baldock, where the cremation weights were in the range of 1–1599.1g, with an average of 452g for unurned burials (McKinley 2000). The weight range for burials at this site is low at 48–904g (an average of 237g). Burial C1147 has the highest weight (904g), which is slightly

**Table 21:** Summary of cremation burial C1144 and other contexts containing cremated bone at Old Tetbury Road

| Burial/ Bone Group | Context | Sample no. | Vessels present | Colour of cremated bone | Weight (g) | Weight of identifiable bone (g) | Identifiable elements present | Age | Sex | Other material | Comments |
|---|---|---|---|---|---|---|---|---|---|---|---|
| C1144 | 505 | <1> | Double-urned | White/ cream/ light grey | 110 | 10 | Petrous portion occipital crest humeral diaphysis vertebral arch 2 deciduous canine crowns 1 permanent incisor crown 3 molar crowns 1 deciduous M1 7 tooth roots 1 rib midsection long bone frags cranial vault frags | 4 years +/- 1 year | ? | Snails charcoal Iron object slag | fill of external vessel |
| C1144 | 505 | <103> | Double-urned | White/ cream | 3 | 0 | None | ? | ? | Charcoal pottery | soil adhering to the edges of the external vessel |
| C1144 | 506 | <2> | Double-urned | White/ cream | 1 | 1 | Tooth root | ? | ? | Snails charcoal pottery | fill of internal vessel |
| Pit 128 | 127 | – | Un-urned | White/ light grey | 12 | 1 | Molar root incisor root long bone frags | ?adult | ? | Snails charcoal glass mouse humerus | ?actually pyre debris |
| Pit 128 | 127 | <3> | Un-urned | White/ grey | 24 | 1 | Long bone frags 1 M3 root 1 Incisor root | Adult | ? | Snails charcoal glass pottery | ?actually pyre debris |
| Pit 128 | 127 | <7> | Un-urned | White/ light grey/ dark grey | 20 | 1 | Long bone frags tooth root | – | ? | Snails charcoal glass | ?actually pyre debris |
| Pit 133 | 132 | <5> | Un-urned | White/ cream/ light grey | 42 | 2 | Long bone frags proximal foot phalanx head canine tooth root molar root | Adult | ? | Snails charcoal pottery glass | ?actually pyre debris |

**Table 22:** Summary of cremation burials C1145–1149 at the Former Cattle Market

| Cremation burial | Context | Sample no. | Vessels present | Colour of cremated bone | Weight of identifiable bone (g) | Identifiable elements present | Age | Sex | Other material | Comments |
|---|---|---|---|---|---|---|---|---|---|---|
| C1145 | 103 | <1> | Urned | White/ light grey | 1 | Metacarpal head | Adult >18 | ? | Iron nails<br>BB1 pottery | |
| C1146 | 105 | <2> | ?un-urned cremation or pit with pyre debris | White/ light grey | 7 | Molar roots<br>cranial vault<br>thoracic articulation facet | Adult | ? | Snails<br>charcoal<br>small mammal bone<br>glass fragment<br>iron nail<br>pottery | ?pyre debris |
| C1147 | 106 | <3> | Urned | White/ light grey/ dark grey | 138 | Odontoid process<br>5 cervical vertebrae<br>humeral head<br>5 lumbar vertebrae frags<br>sacral frag<br>2 medial cuniforms<br>sciatic notch<br>cranial vault<br>femoral shaft<br>1st metacarpal<br>femoral condyles<br>acetabulum<br>petrous portion<br>tibia shaft<br>incisor tooth root | Adult | ?M | Snails<br>charcoal<br>burnt animal bone<br>iron nail<br>local grey ware pottery | |
| C1148 | 114 | <5> | ?un-urned | Light grey/ dark grey | 8 | Distal femur condyles<br>thoracic vertebral facet | ?adult | ? | Snails<br>burnt animal bone<br>iron nails<br>pottery | Appears to be mainly burnt animal bone |
| C1149 | 127 | <101> | Urned | White with dark grey core | 9 | Cranial vault<br>thoracic vertebral frag,<br>lumbar vertebra body | Adult | ? | Coal<br>snails<br>burnt animal bone<br>bone hairpin<br>iron nail<br>BB1 pottery | |

lower than the expected range for an adult individual from an archaeological site, due to the truncation of the deposit. The other burials weigh significantly less, once again a product of truncation rather than the incomplete collection of bone from the pyre site. The low bone weights recovered from the excavated half sections of pits 128 and 133 suggests that they represent a residue of small bone fragments left behind on the pyre after the larger fragments had been collected for burial elsewhere. Pits 113 and 115 did not have soil samples collected and so it is not known whether they too contained small quantities of cremated bone. As the weights of cremated bone in the burials at Oakley Cottage were not published, no easy comparison can be made between the two sites (Reece 1962).

The high degree of fragmentation resulted in few diagnostic traits being present to permit identification of specific bone elements. Of the bones identified, the majority belonged to the larger skeletal elements, mainly the cranial vault and long bone diaphysis (shafts). Smaller elements identified consisted of tooth roots, tooth crowns and phalangal fragments. Burial C1144 consisted of fragments of long bones, skull, torso and teeth. The presence of the tooth roots suggests that in this case the funeral pyre was raked to collect all the bone for burial within the pottery vessel. The presence of mainly small bones within pits 128 and 133 supports the interpretation that the pyre lay elsewhere and that the larger cremated fragments were hand collected for burial in a different location.

At the Former Cattle Market burial C1147 had the lowest amount of fragmentation, with the majority of the fragments being larger than 10mm. Most of the skeleton is present with the exception of phalanges and tooth roots. This once again suggests that the large fragments were collected by hand from the cremation pyre, leaving behind some of the small bones. The remaining four cremation burials all display a high degree of fragmentation with the majority of fragments present in the 5mm sieve fraction. Burials C1146, C1148 and C1149 appear to demonstrate some evidence of deliberate layering of body elements. Burials C1146 and 1149 consist of elements mainly from the upper body, with skull, vertebra and teeth fragments being present, whilst C1148 contains elements from the lower body such as femora and vertebra fragments. Burial C1145 has so few recognisable fragments and such a low weight that no conclusions can be made about the

deliberate selection of elements for burial. No pathology was noted on any of the fragments of cremated bone, probably a consequence of the highly fragmented nature of the cremated bone and incomplete skeletal recovery.

### Animal remains

Burnt animal bone was recovered as follows: the hind limb of an immature sheep/goat from burial C1147, juvenile sheep bones within C1148, a bird bone from C1150 and four sheep-sized fragments with the cremated material in pit 128. The sheep bone suggests that a leg of lamb was placed onto the pyre along with the body for the funerary rite. Pyre offerings of a leg of lamb are frequently encountered as part of the Roman funerary rite, and at Oakley Cottage five out of the 45 cremation burials had burnt animal bone present (Reece 1962, 65; Philpott 1991, 196–7; Sidell and Reilly 1998). The lamb remains appear to be less calcined than the associated human bone, suggesting that the joint of meat was placed towards the edge of the pyre where the temperature was less than that in the centre. Part of a mouse humerus was found within pit 128, but this is likely to be intrusive and not part of a funerary offering.

### Cremation burial C1150 by AnnSofie Witkin

A sufficient quantity of burnt bone was recovered from the inside of the fragmented vessel and from the fills of the pit to merit full osteological and palaeopathological analysis (Table 23). The cremation consisted of an adult individual of unknown sex. Investigation of the burial ritual concludes that there was no preference in the selection of bone put in the urn for burial. Cremated animal bone and copper-alloy objects were also found with the cremation indicating that these had been present on the pyre.

The cremation burial was subjected to 100% recovery as a whole-earth sample which was subsequently wet sieved. Material from the <2mm fraction was not sorted from the soil residue and was retained en masse. Most of the cremated bone was in good condition, although a few fragments were slightly abraded. This may be due to erosion from acid solution passing through the burial medium. The truncation of the cremation pit may also have contributed to the abrasion of bone fragments.

**Table 23:** Summary of cremation burial C1150 at the Former Cattle Market (excluding unsorted residues)

| Context | Age | Sex | Weight (g) of bone recovered | | | | | |
|---|---|---|---|---|---|---|---|---|
| | | | Skull | Axial | Upper limb | Lower limb | Unident. | Total |
| C1150 (609/613/614) | 20–30 years | Unknown | *10mm fraction* | | | | | |
| | | | 24 | 24 | 37 | 56 | 135 | **276** |
| | | | *5mm fraction* | | | | | |
| | | | 5 | 4 | 4 | 4 | 189 | **206** |
| | | | *2mm fraction* | | | | | |
| | | | – | – | – | – | 5 | **5** |

*Osteological procedures*

The cremated bone from each context was passed through a sieve stack of 10, 5 and 2mm mesh size. The bones from each sieve were weighed and calculated as a percentage of the total weight of the cremation. This allowed the degree of fragmentation to be calculated, which may indicate if the cremated bones had been further processed after the body was burnt. In each of the sieved groups the bones were examined in detail and sorted into identifiable bone groups, which were defined as skull (including mandible and dentition), axial (clavicle, scapula, ribs, vertebra and pelvic elements), upper limb and lower limb. This may elucidate any deliberate bias in the skeletal elements collected for burial. Each sample was weighed on digital scales and details of colour and largest fragment recorded. Where possible, the presence of individual bones within the defined bone groups was noted.

In any cremation the majority of the bones are unidentifiable fragments of long bone shafts and spongy bones. The quantity of the unidentified bone is dependent upon the degree of fragmentation. It is of course easier to identify larger fragments than smaller. Some areas of the skeleton, for example the skull, are easier to identify than other bones. This is a factor which needs to be considered when analysing cremation burials. The estimation of age of a cremated individual is dependent upon the survival of particular skeletal elements indicative of age. In cremations of adult individuals, cranial suture closure (Meindl and Lovejoy 1985), degenerative changes to the auricular surface (Lovejoy *et al.* 1985) and pubic symphysis (Suchey and Brooks 1990) may be used as a general guide.

*Age, sex and pathology*

This cremation contained the remains from one individual. It was not possible to ascertain the sex of the person since none of the sex diagnostic sites survived on any of the fragments. The individual was that of an adult since the femoral head present was fused. However, the sutures present on the cranial fragments were not closed, which suggests that this individual was aged between 20 and 30 years of age.

Pathological lesions may be present on cremated bone, although the lesions seen may be fewer than one

would expect from inhumation burials. The cremated bones present in a burial do not necessarily represent a complete individual and this may hamper the diagnosis of a specific disease. Woven new bone was present on three unidentified long bone fragments. This type of lesion is indicative of an infection of the outer surface of the bones and is known as periostitis. The lesion was active at the time of death.

*Weight of bone, fragmentation and skeletal elements present*

The total weight of this cremation (combined weight of the bones from all the contexts, excluding the small amounts present in the residues) was 487g. This is a relatively low weight and may signify selection of bones for a token deposit. However, the most likely explanation is that it is due to significant post-Roman disturbance. A total of 56.7% of the bone fragments were in the 10mm fraction, and the maximum fragment size was 51.4mm. The level of fragmentation and fragment size of the cremation is within the normal ranges observed, and there is nothing to suggest that any deliberate fragmentation of the burnt bone took place prior to burial (McKinley 1994).

Fragments from all body part groups were present. In general, more bones from the lower limbs were identified than any other body group. This was related to the fragment size since the bones of the legs are thicker and in this instance survived in larger pieces. Since bone from all areas of the skeleton was included in the burial this suggests that there was no preference in the selection of bones included in the cremation.

*Animal bone*

Cremated animal bone was found amongst the burnt human bones. The bones were all from a bird and only a few grams were present. The presence of animal bone in a sample is dependent upon firstly it being collected from the pyre along with the human remains, and secondly the fragments being recognised as animal and not human during analysis. Since the surviving sample sizes show that not all human bone was collected from the pyre, it is likely that not all animal bone was collected either. Moreover, some fragments of unidentifiable animal long bone are also likely to have been overlooked in analysis.

**Table 24**: Charcoal associated with cremated human bone at Old Tetbury Road and the Former Cattle Market
KEY: h = heartwood; s = sapwood (diameter unknown); u = unknown maturity. The number of fragments identified is indicated

| Deposit type | Context | Sample no. | Pomoideae (apple/hawthorn) | *Prunus* (blackthorn) | *Quercus* (Oak) | *Tilia* (Lime) |
|---|---|---|---|---|---|---|
| **Pit 128** | 127 | <3> | – | – | 57h, 64s | 9 |
| **Pit 128** | 127 | <7> | – | – | 32h, 61s | 10 |
| **Pit 133** | 132 | <5> | *cf.* 1 | – | 12h, 34s | – |
| **C1144** | 505 | <1> | – | – | 1s, 1u | – |
| **C1144** | 505 | <103> | *Insufficient charcoal for identification* | | | |
| **C1144** | 506 | <2> | – | – | 1u | – |
| **C1146** | 105 | <2> | – | – | 5h, 102s thin bark | – |

## Charcoal associated with the cremated human bone
by Rowena Gale

A small assemblage of charcoal was recovered from four deposits containing cremated human bone. Species identification was undertaken to assess the character of the wood and timber used in the construction of the cremation pyres. Although the charcoal was generally well preserved, samples 1, 2 and 103 from burial C1144 were extremely small, consisting only of fragments measuring <2mm in radial cross-section. Sample 103 was inadequate for identification. Sample 2 from the fill of pit 105 containing burial C1146, an adult, consisted of well preserved, although rather small, pieces of charcoal mostly <5mm in radial cross-section. Fragments exceeding >2mm in radial cross-section were selected for examination. The samples were prepared using standard methods (Gale and Cutler 2000). Anatomical structures were examined using incident light on a Nikon Labophot-2 compound microscope at magnifications up to x400 and matched to prepared reference slides of modern wood. When possible, the maturity of the wood was assessed (i.e. heartwood or sapwood).

### Results

The taxa identified and context details are presented in Table 24. Classification follows that of *Flora Europaea* (Tutin *et al.* 1964–80). The anatomical structure of the charcoal was consistent with the following taxa or groups of taxa:

Fagaceae. *Quercus* sp., oak.
Rosaceae. Subfamilies:
Pomoideae, which includes *Crataegus* sp., hawthorn; *Malus* sp., apple; *Pyrus* sp., pear; *Sorbus* spp., rowan, service tree and whitebeam. These taxa are anatomically similar.
Prunoideae. *Prunus spinosa* L., blackthorn.
Tiliaceae. *Tilia* sp., lime

Burial C1144 was of a four-year-old child. Associated charcoal was very sparse. Samples 1 and 2 (the fills of the external and internal pottery vessels respectively) contained a few tiny fragments of oak (*Quercus* sp.) and blackthorn (*Prunus spinosa*). The charcoal fragments in sample 103 were too small for identification. Charcoal-rich samples 3 and 7 were collected from pit 128 which contained cremated bone from an adult. The charcoal consisted predominantly of oak heartwood and sapwood, although lime (*Tilia* sp.) was also present. Some of the oak indicated moderate to fast growth rates. Sample 5 from pit 133 which contained cremated bone from an adult also consisted predominantly of oak. A small fragment provisionally named as the hawthorn/ *Sorbus* group (Pomoideae) was also present.

The charcoal from pit 105 containing C1146 consisted entirely of oak, predominantly sapwood. In addition, a few pieces of loose bark, about 1mm in thickness, were recorded and, although unidentified, it seems likely that these originated from the oak. Of the cremation burials found in the watching brief at the Former Cattle Market only C1146 produced significant quantities of pyre material (charcoal). It is clear from the sample examined that the pyre was constructed from oak sapwood, probably mostly fairly young branches or poles; the presence of thin fragments of loose bark supports this suggestion. The charcoal was too fragmented to assess the ages or growth rates of the trees or coppice supplying the fuel. It is difficult to correlate these results with the nails recovered, since it could be anticipated that a coffin, or structural planks, would have been more substantial, with a higher ratio of heartwood, than the juvenile poles/round-wood identified in this deposit.

### Discussion

The association of human bone and charcoal in these cremation deposits implicates the charcoal as pyre fuel debris. That from pits 128 and 133 demonstrated that the pyre structures were constructed mainly from oak, using poles of sufficient maturity to include heartwood. Relatively fast growth rates were noted in some fragments suggesting the trees of origin grew in favourable conditions, such as open or managed woodland. Samples 3 and 7 from pit 128 also included lime. The lime fragments were small and it was difficult to assess the dimensions or the maturity of the wood from which they originated. While lime wood or timber may have been incorporated into the pyre structure, it is also feasible that the wood represents the remains of grave goods placed on the pyre. Traditionally lime wood has been valued for carving and for making small domestic items (Edlin 1949). Similar parameters apply to the small fragment in pit 133, tentatively named as a member of the hawthorn/*Sorbus* group. In view of the paucity of charcoal from C1144 it is not possible to comment on the structure of the pyre, other than to note the use of oak and possibly blackthorn.

An adult cremation requires about one ton of wood or timber for the stout poles of the main framework (McKinley 1994). Infill and kindling can include smallwood or some other readily combustible material. The pyre sites from which the cremated bone found at this site derived were not located, although the evidence from pits 128 and 133 suggests that oak was the preferred, or most readily available, timber. Oak heartwood provides relatively long-lasting, high calorie firewood (Edlin 1949). There was no evidence to suggest the ritual inclusion of evergreen or coniferous species, as is occasionally recorded at Roman sites. For example, yew in cremation burials at Baldock Bypass (Gale unpub. a) and the large Roman cemetery at Westhampnett (Gale 1997), and pine in several contexts in the cemetery at Site 12 on the M6 Toll Road (Gale 2008). In Roman society, as in many other cultures, evergreen species were associated with death and regeneration (Dallimore 1908; Cornish 1946; Cooper 1978).

### Discussion by Neil Holbrook

The evaluation and watching brief at the Former Cattle Market have demonstrated that relatively little now survives of the Roman cemetery in this area. It is possible, however, to reconstruct the original topography of the site to some degree. It would appear that the ground originally rose upwards from the south side of Old Tetbury Road onto a low knoll or ridge before falling away steeply into the dry valley now buried beneath the Bristol Road. Previous work has shown that this 'bowl' was filled with up to 1.5m of clay and silt deposited by seasonal flood waters from a long absent watercourse (CE V, 8–11). As this material overlay and partially infilled the defensive ditches of the town defences, a late or post-Roman date is indicated for this process. The findings in Area B at Old Tetbury Road are useful in that they clearly demonstrate that the deposition of up to 0.9m of silt is later than Burial C1144 which dates to the late 1st or early 2nd century AD. The ground also dropped away to the south-west of the cattle market into a shallow coombe which may once have been occupied by a small watercourse which drained south-eastwards into the larger valley. To the south-west of the coombe the ground rises once more, and excavations at Old Tetbury Road have shown that this area was utilised for burial in the Flavian period.

When the cattle market was constructed in 1867 the summit of the slight knoll was shaved off to make for a more level platform, leading to the discovery and destruction of numerous burials across the central part of the site. The recent work has demonstrated that burials did survive this operation in the north-east corner of the site adjacent to Old Tetbury Road, and it is likely that further burials still exist in those parts of this area which were not disturbed during the construction of the new leisure centre. These may be all that now exists of a once dense area of burial between the original line of the Fosse Way and the northern slopes of the dry valley. Miscellaneous investigations and observations during the construction and demolition of the old leisure centre in 1971 and 2006; the remodelling of Bridges Garage on the former Oakley Cottage site in 1975, and test pits within the grounds of the Social and Services Club in 2001 all produced negative results (CE II, MF5 AO9; CAT 2001a; CA 2007). The burials themselves usefully add to and validate the results obtained under extremely difficult conditions at Oakley Cottage in 1960 (Reece 1962).

At Old Tetbury Road the earliest tangible activity in Area A comprised ditched boundaries at right-angles to the line of Old Tetbury Road, which most likely overlies the original alignment of the Fosse Way. Ditch 1 ran parallel with Old Tetbury Road, but it probably does not represent a side ditch to the Fosse Way given that it was not found in Area B. Ditch 1 cut through the fill of boundary A, although it is conceivable that this relationship could have been a product of the later re-cutting of ditch 1, and the common alignment of boundary A and ditch 1 suggest that the Fosse Way was in existence before the commencement of Phase 2. Following the abandonment of boundary A the site was given over to burial, if indeed this was not already the case in Phase 2, pyre debris from a richly furnished Flavian cremation burial being deposited in pits inside enclosure B. While Burials C1142 and C1143 outside of enclosure B are not closely dated, a Flavian date would also not be inappropriate for C1144 in Area B. The

evidence from enclosure B is important as it testifies to the earliest securely dated civilian burial so far recovered from the town. Some of the cremations discovered at Oakley Cottage, 250m nearer to the town along the line of the Fosse Way, might date to the Flavian period, but precision is not possible as they were interred in coarseware vessels with no fineware accessories (Reece 1962). Some of the cremation vessels at Oakley Cottage certainly date no earlier than the 2nd century AD. The original alignment of the Fosse Way was therefore clearly a focus for 1st and 2nd-century AD cremation burial, and Burial C1144 in Area B shows that this extended for a distance of at least 400m from the line later adopted for the town defences.

As has been noted above, recorded evidence for the deposition of pyre debris is still comparatively rare in Roman Britain, although this is surely a product of the lack of modern detailed investigation at cremation sites rather than a true absence of evidence. At Oakley Cottage, a site which we must remember was hurriedly investigated during the course of its rapid destruction, Reece (1962, 70) noted some small square pits filled with bone and charcoal which he interpreted as pyre debris. The indirect evidence of the pyre sweepings at this site indicate the wealth of this cremation burial, with at least 16 samian vessels, probably two or more wine amphorae and at least one flagon being placed on the pyre along with items of glass and metalwork. The location of the funeral pyre and formal burial spot of the cremation evidenced by the activity in enclosure B appear to have lain beyond the limits of the current excavation area. Cremations of status in the Bath Gate cemetery are recognisable by the use of square blocks of limestone, with a hollow scooped out to take either the ashes or a pottery urn containing the ashes (CE II, 207). Conceivably the bulk of the cremated remains of the individual represented here could also have been treated in this way. At the King Harry Lane cemetery at St Albans, which dates to the first half of the 1st century AD, burials containing burnt pyre goods usually lay in central locations within small ditched burial enclosures (Stead and Rigby 1989; Niblett 1999, 401–2). Enclosure B may not have been dissimilar to these.

Ditch 1 silted up and went out of use at some stage, and wall 1, 0.75m wide, was constructed above it on a similar alignment. The recovery of a small fragment of a medieval iron spur from the infill of the construction trench might suggest a medieval date for the wall, but on general grounds this is hard to accept. The form and construction of the wall are typically Roman, and it is difficult to envisage a context for the construction of a wall of this size in this location in the medieval period. Documentary evidence shows that the land to the south-east of Old Tetbury Road was a rough thorn-covered pasture known as the Querns from before AD 1200, and there is no evidence for any construction on this area until the laying out of Querns House in 1826 (CE II, 27–30). It is therefore more likely that the spur is intrusive from the overlying post-medieval layer 106, in which case a broad date range of 2nd–4th century AD can be proposed for the construction of the wall. The function of wall 1 is debatable. It was of substantial construction and in excess of 25m long, but the absence of any associated features suggests that it may not have been part of a building. One possibility is that the wall defined one side of a walled cemetery or precinct adjacent to the Fosse Way, and that the returns on the wall and (if present) an internal mausoleum, lay beyond the limits of the excavation. Certainly the wall did not exist within Area B. Walled cemeteries are rare but not unknown in Roman Britain (Jessup 1959). They are found predominantly in the south-east of England, and are often adjacent to a road, as for instance at Colchester where a rectangular walled cemetery 11.6 × 8.2m containing cremation and inhumation burials lay 800m outside the Balkerne Gate (Hall 1944). Larger examples include Harpenden, Hertfordshire, where a precinct *c.* 30m square was defined by a stone wall 0.76m wide containing cremation burials surrounding a mausoleum dating to the Hadrianic period (Lowther 1936–8). A much smaller funerary monument has been found in Cirencester on the high ground on the opposite side of the former dry valley to the present excavation on the site now occupied by the Geriatric Hospital. Here a stone-walled enclosure, 6.7 by 6.4m in area, was hurriedly investigated in 1973 (see Fig. 68, 1103). Only the pitched stone foundations of the perimeter walls survived, and inside the enclosure a cremation contained within a Savernake ware jar of late 1st-

century AD date was found (CE II, MF5 B10–11 no. 1103; D11, fig. 89, no. 1103).

An alternative interpretation for wall 1 is that it supported an aqueduct which channelled water from a source on the high ground around Deer Park School north-eastwards into the Roman town. There are a number of problems with this interpretation, however, not least that no trace of any aqueduct channel or wall was found in Area B. The undated culvert found there cut into the surface of the silt which elsewhere in this part of Cirencester dates to the late or post-Roman periods (see above). The culvert is very likely post-medieval, most probably an early 19th-century feature associated with the laying out of the grounds of Querns House. In any case the culvert does not directly align with wall 1. It is also the case that no trace of a wall on this orientation has been found further to the north-east during observations at the Former Cattle Market and Oakley Cottage (including subsequent monitoring during the remodelling of Bridges Garage in 1975; Reece 1962; CE II, MF5 A09). The wall is probably also too narrow to have stood to any great height and to have supported a pipe housed in concrete (it is certainly too slight to have comfortably accommodated a stone-lined channel). Interpretation as an aqueduct is therefore considered unlikely and a precinct wall is preferred pending further evidence.

# 7. MISCELLANEOUS OTHER INVESTIGATIONS BEYOND THE WALLS

## EVALUATION AT
### 157 WATERMOOR ROAD, 2000
#### by Neil Holbrook

A single evaluation trench, 10m long by 1.5m wide, was excavated in a small open area between 157 and 159 Watermoor Road (CAT 2000d). The site lay 120m outside of the Roman town defences and 10m to the north-east of Watermoor Road which is here assumed to overlie the course of Ermin Street (SP 0305 0114; see Fig. 17, no. 22): Natural gravel was encountered in a sondage at 103.7m AOD. It was overlaid by 0.3m of clean silty clay, most likely alluvium deposited from the river Churn (the present course of the Inner Churn lies 20m further to the north-east of the trench). Overlying the alluvium in that part of the trench nearest to Watermoor Road was a thin layer of crushed limestone and silt which may be wash from the surface of Ermin Street. This was sealed by dark brown clay-silt which was found throughout the trench. Articulated human burials were found within this layer, but it was not possible to discern individual grave cuts unless they penetrated into the underlying deposits of road wash or alluvium. The clay-silt contained fragments of

Line of Roman Town Defences

1752
661 ha
1·63

Old Mill House

colluvium filled dry valley    ?Roman surface

0    100m

*Fig. 79*    Queen Elizabeth Road. Location of excavation and dry valley (1:1250)

limestone, animal bone and 15 sherds of pottery which date no earlier than the late 2nd century AD. The surface of this material was cleaned and fragments of approximately nine human inhumation burials on a variety of alignments were found. Some burials clearly cut or overlay earlier ones. None of the burials were lifted. The burials are termed B2037–45 to continue the sequence for the numbering of burials to the south of the town (CE II, 205, MF 5, C01–10). The burials were overlain by up to 0.3m of silt which seems to have been laid down in post-Roman flooding. The silt contained two fragments of post-medieval clay pipe although this might be intrusive from the overlying topsoil. No further archaeological work has occurred at this site.

The evaluation has clearly revealed a small part of the Silchester Gate cemetery. The density and intercutting of the burials and the presence of a seemingly homogeneous 'burial earth' in which it is almost impossible to detect individual grave cuts invite comparison with of the discoveries in the Bath Gate cemetery (CE II, 100–6). The burials extend for at least 15–20m from the projected alignment of Ermin Street, over which distance the height of the underlying natural gravel fell by 0.5m. It is likely that the north-eastern limit of the cemetery was defined by the increasingly boggy nature of the ground as it approached the river.

## EXCAVATION AT
## QUEEN ELIZABETH ROAD, 1999
### by Alistair Barber, Mark Collard and
### Neil Holbrook

Queen Elizabeth Road lies 100m to the east of the Roman town defences, just beyond the eastern ring road (NGR: SP 0325 0147; see Fig. 17, no. 14). Trial trench evaluation in 1999 identified a series of undated pits and ditches sealed by substantial layers of colluvium (Coleman 1999). Subsequently when planning permission was granted for residential development excavation of an area of 0.95ha was required to satisfy a planning condition (CAT 2000e; Fig. 79). The geology of the site consisted of limestone cornbrash overlain by deposits of yellow-blue clay. An unpronounced but nevertheless discernible dry valley aligned north-east to south-west ran through the northern part of the site.

The earliest archaeological activity was represented by 19 fragments of prehistoric struck flint. While the assemblage is generally not diagnostic, it includes two broken blades, a utilised long flake and a finely made scraper which would fit best with an earlier Neolithic date. Ten of the flints were recovered from one discrete scatter, on the gentle north-west facing slope of the dry valley, at the base of the earliest colluvium which overlay natural. Several scattered, truncated, shallow pits and ditches cut into the natural clay. They did not form any coherent plan and did not produce any dating evidence, so it is unclear whether they had any association with the flint scatter. The presence of small fragments of fired clay within the pit fills, perhaps derived from an oven or a wattle and daub building, could suggest the presence of some form of structure within the vicinity of the excavation.

A silty-clay colluvium accumulated within the dry valley, sealing the earliest features. It yielded two sherds of Romano-British pottery and three fragments of tile. The slender dating evidence suggests that the colluvium accumulated during or after the early 2nd century AD. A rough metalled surface composed of small sub-angular pieces of limestone was set into the upper surface of the colluvium. It lay on the edge of the excavation trench and its full extent was not revealed. One residual worked flint, two small fragments of abraded Roman tile and three sherds of heavily abraded Romano-British pottery were recovered from the metalling. Although it cannot be entirely discounted that the Roman material is residual, a date for the construction of the surface during or soon after the early 2nd century AD is possible.

A further deposit of hillwash subsequently accumulated within the dry valley in the northern part of the site, sealing the metalled surface. This colluvium yielded one Roman sherd in its lower horizon but solely post-medieval material in its upper levels. Two post-medieval stone trackways depicted on the 1875 Ordnance Survey map overlay the later colluvium.

While unspectacular the results of this excavation are of some interest. The flint scatter adds to the evidence for earlier prehistoric activity on the eastern margins of the Churn valley near Cirencester, as exemplified by the middle Bronze Age enclosure examined at The Beeches 700m to the north-east of this site (Young 2001; Yates 2007, 40–1). The colluvium that accumulated in the dry valley is likely to date to the Iron Age or early Romano-British period, and presumably testifies to ploughing further up slope at this time. The general absence of Roman remains, save for a few possible features, suggests that this area immediately beyond the town defences was primarily agricultural land at this time, as has been suggested by investigations on neighbouring sites. Cropmarks representing later prehistoric or Romano-British enclosures and linear ditches have been recorded over an area of 5ha at Kingshill, 500m to the south-east of the Queen Elizabeth Road (RCHME 1976; 95, Preston 1; Leech 1977, map 1). A small portion of the cropmark complex was examined by excavation in advance of the construction of the eastern ring road in 1974, revealing a series of linear features containing exclusively Romano-British pottery (Reece 1990, 39–44). Further excavation in 1977 revealed palisade-slots and ditched boundaries of a farmstead occupied in the 1st and 2nd centuries AD. The settlement remains were sealed by a stone-free plough-soil which contained 4th-century AD pottery. Further evidence for the farmstead was detected in geophysical survey and trial trench evaluation undertaken by Archaeology South-East in 2006. This found that the focus of occupation appears to lie 250m south of Queen Elizabeth Road (Hart and Collings 2006). Further features which are probably associated with this early Roman activity were found immediately west of the ring road during evaluation by CA in 1993 (Barber 1993).

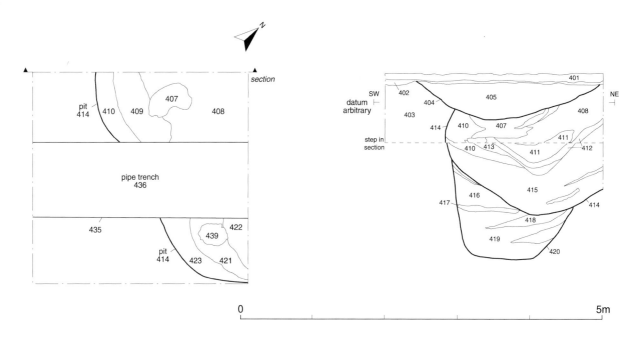

*Fig. 80*     Stratton Watermeadows. Plan and section of pits 414 and 420 discovered in test pit 4 (1:50)

## OBSERVATIONS AT
## STRATTON WATERMEADOWS, 2003
### by Neil Holbrook

Recording was undertaken by CA in 2003 during groundworks associated with essential repairs on the sewer system in and around Cirencester town centre (CA 2003b). In all 25 mechanically excavated trial pits were observed, which varied considerably in size, shape, and depth but were generally *c.* 2m square. Seventeen of these trial pits lay in various roads within the town itself, and in every case archaeological deposits had been disturbed to a depth of at least 2.5m by existing sewer works. Eight trial pits were dug to the north of the town in watermeadows bordering the river Churn, and one of these (trial pit 4) contained archaeological remains which pre-dated ridge and furrow earthworks. In all eight excavations the natural substrate of calcareous gravels was encountered at an average depth of 0.4m below present ground level. This was overlain by mid brown silty clay subsoil averaging 0.25m in thickness, which was in turn sealed by 0.15m of dark brown highly organic topsoil. However, the depths of the subsoil and topsoil varied considerably across the field. Trial pits situated in lower-lying ground which sloped south-eastwards towards the river had thicker layers of subsoil, presumably a result of alluviation. The trial pits on higher ground (including trial pit 4) had significantly less subsoil but a greater thickness of topsoil. Within trial pit 4 (SP 0183 0304), 600m to the north-west of the Roman town defences and 100m to the north-east of Ermin Street, two intercutting pits were found (420 and 414) (Fig. 80). The sewer pipe trench had cut through the pits effectively bisecting them. Pit 420 was 2.3m deep. Its south-west side was nearly vertical, while to the north-

east it had a more gentle concave profile. It contained four main fills (419, 418, 417, 416), all of which contained animal bone and late Iron Age/early Roman pottery. Fills 416, 418 and 419 were a mixture of gravels and sand, but 417 was a lens of charcoal-rich silty clay. Slumping of the sides suggests that the pit was left open and slowly infilled, rather than being rapidly backfilled.

Pit 420 was cut by a second pit, 414, 1.7m deep, with steeply sloping concave sides, and a wide concave base. A thick charcoal-rich layer 415/423 formed the primary fill. This contained quantities of pottery, animal and fish bone, cremated/burnt bone, charred seeds and plant remains, shell, slag, burnt flint, a fragment of a probable iron brooch and ten possible foetal/neonatal bones. This fill was overlain by sands and gravels 410, 412, 411, mixed with re-deposited natural gravel 413, which yielded 17 fragments of animal bone. Above this was a burnt red clay 409 containing further fragments of animal bone beneath mixed gravels and sands 408 and 410 which contained a dump of white clay 407. These fills were cut by a medieval or later furrow 404. Unlike the other pit, pit 414 appears to have been quickly and deliberately backfilled.

### The finds by E.R. McSloy

#### *Pottery*

A total of 95 sherds was recovered (3.14 kg) from the fills of pits 420 and 414 (Table 25). A pre-Flavian date (*c.* AD 50–70) is probable for this group. The condition of the pottery is good with little abrasion apparent and the average sherd weight is high at 33g.

There are ten sherds of handmade Iron Age pottery. Most are of a fairly coarse limestone-tempered fabric, typical of the late Iron Age in this region and

**Table 25:** Quantification of the pottery from pits 420 and 414 at Stratton Watermeadows

KEY: Count = sherd count. *Letter and numerical codes relate to Cirencester-type series (Rigby CE I-II; Keely CE III). Codes in parentheses derive from National Roman Fabric Reference Collection (Tomber and Dore 1998).

| Description | Fabric* | Count | Weight (g) |
|---|---|---|---|
| IA coarse calcareous type | B | 8 | 33 |
| IA calcareous/quartz type | B | 2 | 75 |
| Grog/argillaceous | C | 38 | 777 |
| Savernake type | 6 (SAV GT) | 30 | 1589 |
| Catalan amphora | (CAT AM) | 14 | 628 |
| Romanising quartz-tempered | – | 1 | 13 |
| Samian ?South Gaulish | 154a (LGF SA) | 1 | 1 |
| White-slipped flagon fabric | 9? | 1 | 29 |
| **Total** | | **95** | **3145** |

corresponding to Cirencester fabric TF B. Further material in a harder-fired limestone and quartz-tempered fabric includes typically late Iron Age forms consisting of a round-shouldered bowl with bead rim and a small globular jar with bead rim. The bulk of the assemblage is made up of a grogged/argillaceous tempered fabric. Voids and black coloured streaks in the fabric indicate the presence of organic inclusions. This fabric is generally fine and soft, with a soapy feel and most often fired to a light brown or grey. Forms, all of which are wheel-thrown, include a curved-rim jar, an everted-rim jar or beaker and four or five platters of a devolved Gallo-Belgic form. A finer version of the fabric, which is fired to a pale orange colour, includes a small vessel (?beaker) with short pedestal base and a small jar/beaker with an everted rim. Savernake-type wares constitute the second most commonly occurring type. The fabric is typically hard, grey or grey/brown firing and liberally tempered with coarse grog and in rare instances flint. Forms are restricted to large necked storage jars, one of which features burnished 'zig-zag' decoration to the shoulder. Other types present include single sherds of 'Romanising' coarse quartz-tempered fabric (a platter), a white-slipped buff flagon fabric and a single small chip of South Gaulish samian. Of particular interest are sherds almost certainly from a Catalan amphora of collared Pascual 1/Dressel 1 form. Amphorae of this type, which probably contained wine, are uncommon finds from Britain and are mostly confined to the south coast. A pre-Conquest, late Augustan to Tiberian, date is likely (J. Timby, pers. comm.).

Three vessels display external sooting and two sherds exhibit post-firing 'graffiti' or scratched decoration: a Savernake-type sherd from 415 has a scratched chequer-board or lattice design, and a grog/argillaceous sherd from 417 features a single square or diamond design. The significance of such 'graffiti' is unclear although good parallels exist from Bagendon (Fell 1961, no. 175).

The group is likely to be contemporary with the occupation of the Leaholme fort (which is dated *c.* AD 50/55–65/70; Darvill and Holbrook 1994, 53–4) and displays some similarities, as well as significant differences, to material from the earliest military occupation (CE I, 179–81). The almost complete absence of imported finewares probably indicates that this is a non-military group and is probably associated with domestic activity in the vicinity. The group is closest in character to material from the nearby sites of Bagendon (Fell 1961, 212–57), Ditches, North Cerney (Trow 1988, 64–76) and Middle Duntisbourne (Timby 1999, 329–32).

### The brooch

A fragmentary iron object from fill 415 of pit 420 is almost certainly a portion of the bow and spring attachment of an iron brooch. The form is unclassifiable but most likely to date to the middle of the 1st century AD.

### The environmental samples

Two bulk samples were taken from the charcoal-rich primary fill of pit 420 to assess the presence of biological remains. One 20-litre sample was collected from fill 415 and one 10-litre sample from fill 423. Ten litres of each sample was processed by floatation utilising meshes of 250 and 500 microns for the flot and residue respectively. The dried flots were scanned under a low power binocular microscope for charred plant remains, molluscs and artefacts. The sample from fill 415 contained 35 sherds of pottery and fired clay (31g); 75 fragments of large mammal bone (41g); 20 fragments of small mammal bone (<1g); 10 possible foetal/neonatal bones (3g); a quantity of cremated/burnt bone (17g); 1 fish vertebrae (<1g); a quantity of charcoal (8g); 4 fragments of charred plant remains (<1g); 2 fragments of burnt flint (<1g); 7 fragments from an iron object (1g) and 1 fragment of a copper-alloy object (<1g). The sample from fill 423 contained 19 sherds of pottery (45g); 75 fragments of large mammal bone (58g); 23 fragments of small mammal bone (<1g); cremated/burnt bone (40g); charcoal (23g); 10 charred seeds (<1g); 18 fragments of plant remains (>1g); 1 fragment of shell (>1g); 8 fragments from iron objects (4g) and 2 fragments of slag (>1g). This basic analysis indicates that the pit fill was rich in biological remains.

## Discussion

The discovery of the two intercutting late Iron Age/ early Roman pits in an area where archaeological remains have not previously been recorded is noteworthy. The size and shape of pit 420 suggest that it was originally dug to quarry gravel and that it was backfilled with domestic refuse. The similarities in the pottery finds between the two pits suggest that pit 414 was dug not long after the filling of pit 420. The refuse contained in the pits presumably derives from nearby occupation, and the pottery indicates that this is likely to have been contemporary with that found at Bagendon (Clifford 1961). To date little archaeological work has been done in Stratton, especially in the areas which lie immediately above the floodplain of the Churn. This chance discovery suggests that further investigation of the water-meadows, in particular by geophysical survey, might be worthwhile. It is now clear that late pre-Roman Iron Age activity was not solely restricted to the area of the Bagendon dykes, but was more extensive taking in a variety of other sites such as the hillfort at Ditches (Trow 1988), the rectilinear enclosures at Middle Duntisbourne and Duntisbourne Grove (Mudd 1999, 77–97), and now conceivably a further occupation area at Stratton (Moore 2006, 148–9; Holbrook 2008).

# 8. CONCLUSIONS
## by Neil Holbrook

The investigations reported in this volume demonstrate the steady accumulation of knowledge about the Roman town over the last ten years. Whilst the results may seem in some ways unspectacular compared to previous work, taken in aggregate it is possible to draw some general conclusions from them.

In 1998 a first attempt was made to map the pre-Roman topography and hydrology of Cirencester (CE V, 8–11), and the conclusions drawn there have been largely supported by more recent work. It is now clear that the river Churn was originally braided into two channels on the site adopted for the Roman town, with a slightly higher gravel island lying between. Further evidence for the eastern channel has been found at a couple of locations. At the Waterloo Car Park (see Fig. 17, no. 20) archaeological and geotechnical evaluation in 1998 detected a channel which was c. 1m deep filled with silty alluvial clay which spread beyond its edge (Coleman 1998). The silt was covered by a 50mm-thick layer of clay containing frequent organic inclusions including fragments of decayed wood and leaves. This was sealed beneath a late Roman consolidation deposit which was overlaid by further alluvial deposits, suggesting renewed flooding in the late or post-Roman period. A similar sequence was also recognised in evaluation at 57 Purley Road in 1994 (Fig. 17, no. 13; Ings 1994). Here early Roman occupation was sealed by a build-up of mixed clays containing possible turf lines suggesting a lengthy period of abandonment. The area doubtless remained seasonally wet, and attempts at ground consolidation are represented by a layer of rubble containing 3rd or 4th-century AD pottery. At the Grammar School Field (Fig. 17, no. 9) evaluation in 1988 found alluvial clay containing flecks of brick and tile which probably relates to early Roman reclamation of the flood plain prior to construction of a stone building (p. 92). In the northern part of the town at Coxwell Street Peter Grace recorded a 1m-thickness of silty clay above natural gravels in 1969, which corresponds with previous discoveries in this area (Fig. 17, no. 7; Brown and McWhirr 1967, 195). Deep deposits of silty alluvial clay infilling the western channel were observed in geotechnical works at the Corinium Museum in 2001 and at Trinity Road where saturated running gravels were found (Fig. 17, nos 5 and 18; CAT 2001b; p. 93). The excavation at Stepstairs Lane in the southern part of the town lay just beyond the river channel, but there were evidently problems with flooding there (Fig. 17, no. 16; p. 83). Dumped deposits were laid down to raise the ground level in preparation for the construction of a building, and a series of short-lived ditches which fell out of use in the early 2nd century AD were dug to further drain the site. To the south-west of the town a shallow subsidiary valley which ran into the valley of the Churn has been found, defined to the south by the limestone ridge of the Querns and to the north by the line of Old Tetbury Road and Cirencester Park. It is now largely overlain by the A419 Bristol Road. The valley became choked with sediment laid down by seasonal flood waters in the late or post-Roman periods. One source of this water might have been a small stream which drained southwards into the valley from the area now occupied by the lake within Cirencester Park (p. 116).

The wet, boggy nature of much of the ground later to be enclosed within the walls of Cirencester is now apparent, and Reece (2003) has sought to explain this choice of an outwardly unpromising site as a consequence of a desire on the part of the Roman road surveyors to avoid a putative late Iron Age ritual centre on the rising ground to the north-east of the town. Certainly no trace of prehistoric settlement has been found in any of the excavations within Cirencester, in contrast to recent work to the east of the town. At The Beeches a middle Bronze Age ditched enclosure has been excavated, while at Kingshill evaluation has revealed Bronze Age ring ditches and suggestions of an Iron Age enclosure (Young 2001; Oxford Archaeology 2006b; Yates 2007, 40–1). No evidence of late pre-Roman Iron Age activity has been found in this work, although the discovery of a rectilinear cropmark enclosure adjacent to Tar Barrow is of interest (Holbrook 2008). One interpretation of this monument is that it represents a late Iron Age cremation enclosure, and that the barrows might be of similar date. Further work will be required to substantiate or disprove this theory, and it is encouraging that Dr Peter Guest of Cardiff University is now undertaking a detailed geophysical survey of this area. A single late Iron Age pit was recorded in a watching brief during sewer renewal in Stratton watermeadows on the west side of the river Churn, 600m north-east of the Roman town. The artefacts contained in the pit are likely to derive from nearby, but as yet unlocated, settlement and suggest another focus of activity contemporary with that at Bagendon.

Nothing has been found in the recent excavations to further our understanding of the Roman military occupation, unless the road discovered beneath the rampart of the town defences at Trinity Road dates to this period. The road fell out of use during the Flavian period, and can be added to other observations of short lengths of metalled streets and fragmentary traces of timber buildings which pre-date the laying out of the main street grid of the town. A street beneath the courtyard of the forum was associated with pre-Flavian and Flavian pottery, while another was found at Watermoor Hospital to the rear of an earthen rampart. It was seemingly on a different alignment to that at Trinity Road 90m to the north-west, and pottery from the infilling of the side ditch and overlying its street surface is dateable to *c.* AD 75–85 (CE I, 60–4). Like Trinity Road a length of this street was subsequently buried beneath the rampart of the 2nd-century AD town defences. These three sightings demonstrate the existence of some form of street system within the southern part of Cirencester in the early Flavian period which extended further to the west than the area subsequently enclosed by the defences. This is vital evidence for the period immediately following the abandonment of Cirencester by the military, for Flavian deposits are still remarkably rare in the town. Even allowing for the comparatively few investigations of the earliest levels, where this has occurred it is virtually impossible to demonstrate a Flavian origin for any building which was to form part of the 2nd-century AD town. A large Flavian pit and stone-lined drain were found beneath later town houses at Parsonage Field, and the make-up layers beneath the building at Stepstairs Lane date to the Flavian–Trajanic periods (CE I, 64, 193–4, site AX; Richardson 1962, 160; p. 70). It would therefore appear that further evidence for the earliest civilian occupation of Cirencester should be sought in the Watermoor area. We may also note evidence from Old Tetbury Road for a richly appointed Flavian cremation burial (see below). The evidence from the excavation of public buildings, shops and houses combines to demonstrate that the main infrastructure of the town was not laid out until the first two decades or so of the 2nd century AD (CE V). It may also have been at this time that the town was first equipped with earthwork defences, to judge from a rampart bank which has been discovered at two places in Watermoor which pre-dates the main circuit of the earthwork defences built *c.* AD 140–60 (CE V, 94–6). The picture gained is therefore of the slow development of urban infrastructure in the later 1st century AD, although the Flavian streets and other features in Watermoor hint at some form of urban activity which was replaced by a town designed to a different plan in the early 2nd century A.D. The form and layout of this early 'proto–town' can hardly be comprehended at present (Holbrook 2008).

Observations and investigations of the streets are improving our understanding of the basic layout of the 2nd-century AD town. The discovery of colonnaded porticos flanking either side of Ermin Street at the Bingham Hall and the Foresters Arms is notable. It would now appear that at least 750m of this street may have been so equipped (CE V, 23). The earliest colonnades date to the early Antonine period, but were reconstructed on a number of occasions, and the portico at the Police Station seems not to date before the later 3rd century AD (Wacher 1963, 19–22, fig. 4). There is no evidence that the Fosse Way frontages were provided with a similar level of monumentalisation (no portico was present at 33 Querns Lane for instance; Fig. 19, B.5), which suggests that Ermin Street was always the more significant and prestigious route through the town. The construction of the porticos, if a unified event, can be seen as another element in the 2nd-century AD aggrandisement of Corinium.

Relatively little new information has been forthcoming on the public buildings. The work at the forum has added a few details to the plan of that complex, while the discoveries at Cotswold Mill are tantalising. Masonry walls survived 16 courses high, but little can be deduced of the building plan in this part of the *insula*. It nevertheless remains likely that the walls were part of a public building, most probably the public baths. The new evidence for private houses and other types of buildings is also relatively slender, although the discovery of another richly appointed house furnished with mosaics in *insula* IX is welcome. Further work on the defences at Trinity Road serves to demonstrate just how complex their sequence and development was, and the difficulties of interpretation generated by narrow cuttings (cf. Wacher 1998). It is conceivable that we may have evidence of an abortive construction trench for the masonry wall, which was subsequently built on a slightly different alignment, although unfortunately this interpretation must remain unconfirmed for the time being.

Beyond the walls excavation at Queen Elizabeth Road and evaluation at Kingshill by other archaeological organisations confirms that there was no significant suburban extra-mural activity on this side of the town, and all the evidence points to a rural landscape extending right up to the town defences (p. 133; Oxford Archaeology 2006b). Further traces of a 1st and 2nd-century AD farmstead previously investigated in advance of the construction of Cirencester ring road have been recovered in one of the recent evaluations (Reece 1990, 39–44; Hart and Collings 2006). Whether the origins of this site lie before or after the commencement of Roman activity (military or civilian) in Cirencester is currently unclear. By the later Roman period the farmstead had been abandoned and its site given over to arable to judge from the results of the ring road excavation. Some 3km to the north-east of Cirencester another site, possibly a villa, has recently been recognised from a surface scatter at Wiggold Farm. Artefacts recovered include building tile and pottery which dates exclusively to the 1st and 2nd centuries AD. Investigation of this site by Bournemouth University is planned.

While opportunities to excavate extensive areas of the Roman town have not been available in the last ten years, resources have been found to study some individual deposits in a detail which has not previously been possible. Work in the western cemetery along Old Tetbury Road has revealed both cremation and inhumation burials. Particularly noteworthy has been the identification of pits containing fragments of human bone and heat-affected artefacts set within a small ditched enclosure. These deposits are most plausibly interpreted as sweepings of the residue of a funeral pyre after the bulk of cremated bone had been removed for burial elsewhere. The artefacts suggest that the cremation was richly appointed and of Flavian date. This evidence, albeit indirect, testifies to the earliest securely dated civilian burial so far recovered from the town, and the burial joins the tradition of wealthy cremations found elsewhere in Britain in the 1st century AD (Phillpott 1991, 30–43). The individual must have been a significant member of the first generation of Cirencester townspeople. Many of the other burials investigated proved to be truncated or otherwise disturbed, which has served to reduce their potential for analysis. Nevertheless they add to the assemblages previously reported from the town (Reece 1962; CE II). The lack of ordered planning, so apparent at the Bath Gate cemetery, is also evident in the disposition of the surviving burials at the Former Cattle Market.

The last decade has also seen the widespread and routine application of environmental sampling, both during evaluations and excavations. Despite this work, the environmental record for Cirencester remains patchy. Animal bones are the best studied category of ecofact due to the synthesis published by Mark Maltby in CE V. The further deposits of bone from Stepstairs Lane and Trinity Road reported on by Hambledon usefully add to that work, but do not change its essential conclusions. Palaeobotanical studies have to date been a great weakness in the archaeological record of the town (Van der Veen *et al.* 2007, table 2), and it is pleasing that this volume contains a number of such studies. Analyses of the charred plant remains within a late Roman oven at Stepstairs Lane have shown that it was filled entirely with bread wheat. This is useful, as the chronology of the rise to dominance of naked bread-type wheat over hulled wheats such as emmer and spelt during the 1st millennium AD is still poorly understood (Van der Veen 1994, 205). There is no reason to question the late Roman date of the Stepstairs deposit, however, as while bread wheat is usually the principal form of cereal in post-Roman assemblages, it does occur in reasonable quantities in some late Roman assemblages in southern Britain, including Barton

Court Farm in the Upper Thames Valley (Jones 1986, although *cf.* Campbell and Straker 2003 who suggest that some of the material there may have been wrongly assigned). Analysis of charcoal contained in the cremation-related deposits along Old Tetbury Road has also provided valuable insights into the timber used for the funeral pyre. Despite these advances more work remains to be done on palaeobotany in Cirencester, especially given the potential for waterlogged deposits in and around the relict channels of the river Churn. The recovery and analysis of good assemblages of molluscs and insect fauna that will assist with the reconstruction of environmental conditions should be a priority for the future.

If the last ten years are anything to go by there is every reason to believe that the steady accumulation of knowledge about the Roman and later town will continue in the coming decades, and we should also expect some surprises. Developments to renew or replace building stock erected in the 1960s and 1970s which has not withstood the test of time are currently being planned, and whilst preservation *in situ* of archaeological remains will continue to be the policy objective, opportunities for investigative fieldwork will surely accrue. Resources will also be available to investigate the north-eastern approaches to the town. At the time of writing extensive excavations are just commencing in advance of major housing develop-ments at Kingshill. To judge from the results of the preliminary evaluations these will provide information on the prehistoric occupation of this part of the Churn valley, and provide an opportunity to fully excavate an early Roman farmstead. It will be instructive to ascertain what effect proximity to the town had on the economy and material culture of this site compared to farms further away in the Upper Thames valley and Cotswold uplands. It is also heartening that the eastern periphery of Cirencester is now the focus for two campaigns of research-driven fieldwork. The multi-period archaeological landscape at Wiggold Farm in the parish of Preston is being investigated by Professor Timothy Darvill of Bournemouth University, while the work around Tar Barrows has already been mentioned. Integration of the results of these pieces of work with the results of development-led investigations promises much.

# BIBLIOGRAPHY

Anderson, A.S., Wacher, J.S. and Fitzpatrick, A.P. 2001 *The Romano-British 'small town' at Wanborough, Wiltshire* Britannia Monograph **19**, London, Society for the Promotion of Roman Studies

Anon. (ed.) 1944a 'Report on the conference on the future of archaeology, 1943', *University of London Institute of Archaeology Occasional Paper* **5**

Anon. 1944b 'Proceedings of the Society of Antiquaries', *Antiq. J.* **24**, 171–82

Anon. 1949 'Meetings of the Society 1947–1949', *Trans. Bristol Gloucestershire Archaeol. Soc.* **67**, 422–38

Anon. 1959 'Report of Council, 1958', *Trans. Bristol Gloucestershire Archaeol. Soc.* **78**, 189–91

Arnold, A. and Howard, R. 2007 *St John's Hospital and Chantry, Cirencester, Gloucestershire: Tree ring analysis of timbers* English Heritage Research Department report series **14/2007**

Austin, R. 1938 'New Corinium Museum, Cirencester', *Trans. Bristol Gloucestershire Archaeol. Soc.* **60**, 358–9

Baddeley, W. St. Clair 1922 'The excavation at Cirencester (*Corinium Dobunnorum*) Feb–March 1922, *Trans. Bristol Gloucestershire Archaeol. Soc.* **44**, 101–15

Baddeley, W. St. Clair 1924 *A history of Cirencester* Cirencester, Cirencester Newspaper Company

Barber, A, 1993 *Proposed tree-planting scheme, City Bank, Cirencester. Archaeological evaluation* Cotswold Archaeological Trust typescript report **93121**

Barber, B. and Bowsher, D. 2000 *The eastern cemetery of Roman London: Excavations 1983–90* MoLAS Mon. **4**, London, Museum of London Archaeology Service

Barker, J. 1976 'William and Rebecca George (Powell) and their town house, now Gloucester House, 60 Dyer Street', in McWhirr 1976, 113–125

Bartholomew, D. n.d. (but 1982) *Midland & South Western Junction Railway,* vol. 1, Didcot, Wild Swan Publications

Bass, W.M. 1995 *Human osteology: a laboratory and field manual,* 4th ed., Missouri, Missouri Archaeological Society

Bathurst, W.H. 1879 *Roman antiquities at Lydney Park, Gloucestershire,* London, Longmans

Beecham, K.J.1887 *History of Cirencester* (reprint 1978), Dursley, Alan Sutton

Bewley, R. and Fulford, M. 1996 'Aerial photography and the plan of Silchester (*Calleva Atrebatum*)', *Britannia* **27**, 387–8

Biddle, M. 1974 'The future of the urban past', in P.A. Rahtz (ed.) *Rescue archaeology* Harmondsworth, Penguin, 95–112

Bray, N. 1998 *The Cirencester branch* Usk, Oakwood Press

Brothwell, D.R. 1981 *Digging up bones* Oxford, Oxford University Press

Buckman, J. and Newmarch, C.H. 1850 *Illustrations on the remains of Roman art in Cirencester, the site of antient Corinium* London, George Bell

Buisktra, J.E. and Ubelaker, D.H. (eds.) 1994 *Standards for data collections from human skeletal remains,* Arkansas Archaeol. Survey Res. Sem. **44**, Fayetteville, Arkansas Archaeological Survey

Butcher, S.A. 2001 'Brooches of copper alloy', in Anderson *et al.* 2001, 41–69

CA (Cotswold Archaeology) 2002 33 *Querns Lane, Cirencester, Gloucestershire, watching brief* CA typescript report **02013**

CA (Cotswold Archaeology) 2003a *Land off School Lane and Stepstairs Lane, Cirencester, Gloucestershire. Archaeological evaluation* CA typescript report **03158**

CA (Cotswold Archaeology) 2003b *Thames Water repairs to public sewers, Cirencester, Gloucestershire. Programme of archaeological recording* CA typescript report **03140**

CA (Cotswold Archaeology) 2004 *Forester's Arms, Queen Street, Cirencester, Gloucestershire. Archaeological evaluation* CA typescript report **04002**

CA (Cotswold Archaeology) 2005 *Land to the rear of 3, 5, 5A and 7 Ashcroft Road, Cirencester, Gloucestershire. Archaeological evaluation* CA typescript report **05090**

CA (Cotswold Archaeology) 2007 *St James's Place, Cirencester, Gloucestershire. Archaeological watching brief* CA typescript report **07029**

Campbell, G. 1994 'The preliminary archaeobotanical results from Anglo-Saxon West Cotton and Raunds', in J. Rackham (ed.) *Environment and Economy in Anglo-Saxon England* CBA Res. Rep. **89**, London, Council for British Archaeology, 65–82

Campbell, G. and Straker, V. 2003 'Prehistoric crop husbandry and plant use in southern Britain', in K. Robson Brown (ed.) *Archaeological sciences 99* BAR Int. Ser. **1111**, Oxford, British Archaeological Reports, 14–30

Carne, B. 1995 'Thomas Fulljames 1808–74: Surveyor, architect and civil engineer', *Trans. Bristol Gloucestershire Archaeol. Soc.* **113**, 7–20

Carson, R.A.G. and Kent, J.P.C. 1960 *Late Roman bronze coinage, AD 324–498, part 2* London, Spink

Carson, R.A.G., Hill, P.V., and Kent, J.P.C. 1960 *Late Roman bronze coinage, AD 324–498, part 1* London, Spink

CAT (Cotswold Archaeological Trust) 1997 *Regal Cinema, Lewis Lane, Cirencester, archaeological evaluation* CAT typescript report **97852**

CAT (Cotswold Archaeological Trust) 1999 *26 Watermoor Road, Cirencester, Gloucestershire. Archaeological watching brief* CAT typescript report **991111**

CAT (Cotswold Archaeological Trust) 2000a *23 Victoria Road, Cirencester, Gloucestershire. Archaeological evaluation* CAT typescript report **001174**

CAT (Cotswold Archaeological Trust) 2000b *52–54 Ashcroft Road, Cirencester, Gloucestershire. Archaeological watching brief* CAT typescript report **001200**

CAT (Cotswold Archaeological Trust) 2000c *Land at School Lane/Stepstairs Lane, Cirencester, Gloucestershire: Archaeological evaluation* CAT typescript report **001223**

CAT (Cotswold Archaeological Trust) 2000d *Land adjacent to*

*157 Watermoor Road, Cirencester. Archaeological evaluation* CAT typescript report **001167**

CAT (Cotswold Archaeological Trust) 2000e *Land at Queen Elizabeth Road, Cirencester, Gloucestershire. Archaeological Excavation 1999* CAT typescript report **991118**

CAT (Cotswold Archaeological Trust) 2001a *Cirencester Social and Services Club, Tetbury Road, Cirencester, Gloucestershire. Archaeological evaluation* CAT typescript report **01002**

CAT (Cotswold Archaeological Trust) 2001b *Corinium Museum, Cirencester, Gloucestershire. Archaeological evaluation* CAT typescript report **01078**

CE I: Wacher, J.S. and McWhirr, A.D. 1982 *Early Roman occupation at Cirencester* Cirencester Excavations **I**, Cirencester, Cirencester Excavation Committee

CE II: McWhirr, A., Viner, L. and Wells, C. 1982 *Romano-British cemeteries at Cirencester* Cirencester Excavations **II**, Cirencester, Cirencester Excavation Committee

CE III: McWhirr, A. 1986 *Houses in Roman Cirencester* Cirencester Excavations **III**, Cirencester, Cirencester Excavation Committee

CE IV: Wilkinson, D. and McWhirr, A. 1998 *Cirencester Anglo-Saxon church and medieval abbey* Cirencester Excavations **IV**, Cirencester, Cotswold Archaeological Trust

CE V: Holbrook, N. (ed.) 1998 *Cirencester: The Roman Town defences, public buildings and shops* Cirencester Excavations **V**, Cirencester, Cotswold Archaeological Trust

Clack, T. 2001 *The 150th Anniversary of Holy Trinity Church Watermoor, 1851–2001* Cirencester

Clews, S. 1988 *Cirencester Memorial Hospital: A brief history of the site and buildings* Unpublished report for Cotswold District Council

Clifford, E. 1949 'Mosaic floor at Cirencester', *Trans. Bristol Gloucestershire Archaeol. Soc.* **47**, 381–95

Clifford, E.M. 1961 *Bagendon, a Belgic Oppidum: Excavations 1954–1956* Cambridge, Heffer

Clifton-Taylor, A. 1988 *Cirencester* Cirencester Civic Soc., republished from *Another Six English Towns* (1984), London, British Broadcasting Corporation

Coleman, L. 1998 *Waterloo Car Park, Cirencester, Gloucestershire. Archaeological evaluation* Cotswold Archaeological Trust typescript report **98925**

Coleman, L. 1999 *Queen Elizabeth Road, Cirencester, Gloucestershire. Archaeological evaluation* Cotswold Archaeological Trust typescript report **99999**

Cool, H.E.M. 1979 'A newly found inscription on a pair of silver bracelets from Castlethorpe, Buckinghamshire', *Britannia* **10**, 165–68

Cool, H.E.M. 1990 'Roman metal hair pins from southern Britain', *Archaeol. J.* **147**, 148–82.

Cool, H.E.M. 2001 'The significance of snake jewellery hoards', *Britannia* **31**, 29–40

Cooper, J.C. 1978 *An illustrated encyclopaedia of traditional symbols* London, Thames and Hudson

Cornish, V. 1946 *The churchyard yew and immortality* London, F. Muller

Cosh, S.R. 2007 'A "new" mosaic from Cirencester', *Mosaic* **34**, 12–13

Cosh, S.R. and Neal, D.S. 2005 *Roman mosaics of Britain. Volume 2: South-West Britain* London, Illuminata

Crummy, N. 1979 'A chronology of Romano-British bone pins', *Britannia* **10**, 157–63.

Crummy, N. 1983 *Colchester Archaeological Report 2: The Roman small finds from excavations in Colchester 1971–9* Colchester, Colchester Archaeological Trust

Curle, J. 1911 *A Roman frontier post and its people: The fort at Newstead in the parish of Melrose* Glasgow, Maclehose

Dallimore, W. 1908 *Holly, yew and box* London, John Lane/ Bodley Head

Darvill, T.C. and Holbrook, N. 1994 'The Cirencester area in the prehistoric and early Roman Roman periods', in Darvill and Gerrard 1994, 47–56

Darvill, T. and Gerrard, C. 1994 *Cirencester: town and landscape. An urban archaeological assessment* Cirencester, Cotswold Archaeological Trust

Davies, B., Richardson, B. and Tomber, R. 1994 *A dated corpus of early Roman pottery from the City of London* The Archaeology of Roman London **5**, CBA Res. Rep. **98**, London, Council for British Archaeology

Davis, M.J., Gdaniec, K.L.A., Bryce, M. and White, L. 2004 *Study of the mitigation of the construction impacts on archaeological remains* London, Museum of London Archaeology Service

Derham, K. 2001 *An archaeological evaluation at Tetbury Road, Cirencester, Gloucestershire* Gloucestershire County Council unpublished report

DoE (Department of the Environment) 1990 *Archaeology and planning: Planning policy guidance note 16* London, HMSO

Edlin. H.L. 1949 *Woodland crafts in Britain* London, Batsford

English Heritage 2007 *Piling and archaeology. An English Heritage guidance note* Swindon, English Heritage

Evans, D.R. and Maynard, D.J. 1997 'Caerleon Lodge Hill cemetery, the Abbeyfield Extra Care Society site', *Britannia* **28**, 169–243

Fell, C. 1961 'The coarse pottery of Bagendon', in Clifford 1961, 212–67

Fitzpatrick, A.P. 1997 *Archaeological excavations on the route of the A27 Westhampnett Bypass, West Sussex, 1992. Volume 2: The Late Iron Age, Romano-British, and Anglo-Saxon cemeteries* Wessex Archaeol. Rep. **12**, Salisbury, Wessex Archaeology

Frank, M. 1990 *Cirencester, Gloucestershire* Georgian Group Town Report **4**

Frere, S.S. 1970 'The Roman theatre at Canterbury', *Britannia* **1**, 83–113

Fulford, M. and Timby, J. 2000 *Late Iron Age and Roman Silchester* Britannia Monograph **15**, London, Society for the Promotion of Roman Studies

Gale, R. 1997 'Charcoal', in Fitzpatrick 1997, 77–82

Gale, R. 2008 'Charcoal', in Powell, A.B., Booth, P., Fitzpatrick, A.P. and Crockett, A.D. *The archaeology of the M6 Toll 2000-2003*, Oxford Wessex Archaeol. Mon. **2**, Salisbury, Wessex Archaeology, 177–82

Gale, R. unpublished (a) *Baldock bypass, BAL860, BAL953, BALD04: Charcoal from cremation and domestic contexts in Areas 1 and 4*, unpublished report prepared for the Environmental Archaeology Consultancy (2005)

Gale, R. and Cutler, D. 2000 *Plants in archaeology* Otley, Westbury Publishing and Royal Botanic Gardens Kew

Gerrard, C.M and Johnson, C. 1989 *32–38 Cricklade Street, Cirencester: architectural survey and archaeological watching brief* Cotswold Archaeological Trust typescript report **8901**

Going, C.J. 1987 *The mansio and other sites in the south-eastern sector of Caesaromagus: The Roman pottery* CBA Res. Rep. **62**, London, Council for British Archaeology

GRRC (Gloucester Roman Research Committee) 1930 'Gloucester Roman Research Committee', *Trans. Bristol Gloucestershire Archaeol. Soc.* **52**, 301–3

GSB (Geophysical Surveys of Bradford) 1999 *Cirencester* Unpublished GSB report **99/65**

Hall. A.F. 1944 'A Roman walled cemetery at Colchester', *Archaeol. J.* **101**, 68–90

Hall, A.R. and Kenward, H.K. (eds) 1994 *Urban-rural connexions: perspectives from environmental archaeology* Oxford, Oxbow

Hall, L.J. 1983 *The rural houses of North Avon and South Gloucestershire 1400–1720* City of Bristol Museum Art Gallery Mon. **6**, Bristol, City of Bristol Museum and Art Gallery

Hanf, M. 1983 *Weeds and their seedlings* Ipswich, B.A.S.F.

Hart, D. and Collings, M. 2006 *An archaeological evaluation at Kingshill South, Cirencester, Gloucestershire* Archaeology South-East typescript report

Havard, T. 1999 *Akeman Court, Lewis Lane, Cirencester, Gloucestershire. Archaeological watching brief* Cotswold Archaeological Trust typescript report **991035**

Haverfield, F.H. 1920 'Roman Cirencester', *Archaeologia* **49**, 161–209

Hawkes, C.F.C. and Hull, M.R. 1947 *Camulodunum* Rep. Res. Com. Soc. Antiq. London **14**, London, Society of Antiquities

Heighway, C. 2006 'Gloucester', in Holbrook and Juřica 2006, 211–29

Helbaek, H. 1964 'The *Isca* grain, a Roman plant introduction in Britain', *New Phytologist* **63**, 158–64

Hill, M. and Birch, S. 1994 *Cotswold stone homes: history, conservation, care* Stroud, Alan Sutton

Hillson, S. 1996 *Dental anthropology*, Cambridge, Cambridge University Press

Hirst, K. 2003 *An archaeological investigation in Cirencester, Gloucestershire* Time Team report 03/01

Holbrook, N. 2008 'Cirencester and the Cotswolds: the early Roman evolution of a town and rural landscape', *J. Roman Archaeol.* **21**, 201–19

Holbrook, N. and Juřica, J. (eds) *Twenty-five years of archaeology in Gloucestershire: A review of new discoveries and new thinking in Gloucestershire, South Gloucestershire and Bristol 1979–2004* Bristol Gloucestershire Archaeol. Rep. **4**, Cirencester, Cotswold Archaeology

Hooley, D. 2001 'Copper alloy and silver objects', in A.S. Anderson *et al.* 2001, 75–116

Hull, M.R. 1968 'The Nour 'Nour Brooches', in E. Dudley, 'Excavations in the Isles of Scilly 1962–6', *Archaeol. J.* **124**

Hurst, H.R, Dartnall, D.L., Fisher, C. *et al.* 1987 'Excavation at Box Roman villa 1967–8', *Wiltshire Archaeol. Natur. Hist. Mag.* **81**, 19–51

Ings, M. 1994 *Purley Road site, Cirencester. Stage 2 archaeological evaluation* Cotswold Archaeological Trust typescript report **94205**

Iscan, M.Y. and Loth, S.R. 1984 'Determination of age from the sternal rib in white males: A test of the phase method', *J. Forensic Sci.* **31**,122–32

Iscan, M.Y. Loth, S.R. and Scheuerman, E.H. 1985 'Determination of age from the sternal rib in white females: A test of the phase method', *J. Forensic Sci.* **31**, 990–9

Jackson, R. 1990 *Camerton: The late Iron Age and early Roman metalwork* London, British Museum

James, M.C. 2006 *South Porch/Town Hall at the Parish Church of St John the Baptist, Cirencester* Unpublished report for Michael Drury Architects

Jennings, R.W. 1976 'The Reverend W.F. Powell and the restoration of Cirencester Parish Church', in McWhirr 1976, 158–67

Jessup, R.F. 1959 'Barrows and walled cemeteries in Roman Britain', *J. Brit. Archaeol. Assoc.* 3 ser. **22**, 1–32

Jones, M.K. 1986 'Towards the model of a villa estate' and 'The carbonised plant remains' in D. Miles (ed.) *Archaeology at Barton Court Farm, Abingdon, Oxon* CBA Res. Rep. **50**, London, Council for British Archaeology, 38–42 and MF9

Jowitt, R.L.P. 1951 *Cirencester: A series of illustrations*, London, Batsford

King, A.C. 1978 'A comparative survey of bone assemblages from Roman sites in Britain', *Bull. Inst. Archaeol. Univ. London* **15**, 207–32

King, A.C. 1999 'Diet in the Roman world: A regional inter-site comparison of the mammal bones', *J. Roman Archaeol.* **12**, 168–202

Kingsley, N. 1989. *The country houses of Gloucestershire, volume 1, 1500–1660* Cheltenham, N. Kingsley

Kingsley, N. 1992. *The country houses of Gloucestershire, volume 2, 1600–1830* Chichester, Phillimore

Kingsley, N. and Hill, M. 2001 *The country houses of Gloucestershire, Volume 3, 1830–2000* Chichester, Phillimore

Klitz, M. 1969–70 'A house and its owners: no 33 Dyer Street', *Cirencester Archaeol. Hist. Soc. Ann. Rep. and Newsletter* **12**, 11–13

Laithwaite, M. 1973 'The buildings of Burford: A Cotswold town in the 14th to 19th centuries', in A. Everitt (ed.) *Perspectives in English Urban History* London, Macmillan, 60–90

Lawson, A.J. 1976 'Shale and jet objects from Silchester', *Archaeologia* **105**, 241–75

Leech, R.H. 1977 *The upper Thames valley in Gloucestershire and Wiltshire* CRAAGS Survey **4**, Bristol, Committee for Rescue Archaeology in Avon, Gloucestershire and Somerset

Leech, R.H. 1981 *Historic towns in Gloucestershire: Archaeology and planning* CRAAGS Survey **3**, Bristol, Committee for Rescue Archaeology in Avon, Gloucestershire and Somerset

Leech, R.H. and McWhirr, A.D. 1982 'Excavations at St John's Hospital, Cirencester, 1971 and 1976', *Trans. Bristol Gloucestershire Archaeol. Soc.* **100**, 191–209

Lees-Milne, J. 1962. *Earls of Creation: Five great patrons of eighteenth century art*

Lloyd, D. 2001 *Broad Street: Its houses and residents through eight centuries* Ludlow Civic Soc. Res. Pap. **3**, Ludlow

Lovejoy, C.O., Meindl, R.S., Pryzbeck, T.R. and Mensforth, R.P. 1985 'Chronological metamorphosis of the auricular surface of the illium: A new method for determination of adult skeletal age-at-death', *American J. Physical Anthropology* **68**, 15–28.

Loveridge, G.G. 1977 *Watermoor through the ages* Cirencester

Lowther, A.G.W. 1936–8 'Report on the excavation of the Roman structure at Rothamsted Experimental Station, Harpenden', *Trans. St. Albans Architect. Archaeol. Soc.* **5**, 108–14

Lyman, R.L. 1994 *Vertebrate taphonomy* Cambridge, Cambridge University Press

MacGregor, A. 1985 *Bone, antler, ivory and horn: The technology of skeletal materials since the Roman period* Beckenham, Croom Helm

Maltby, M. 1989 'Urban-rural variations in the butchering of cattle in Romano-British Hampshire', in Sarjeantson and Waldron 1989, 75–106

Maltby, M. 1994 'The meat supply in Roman Dorchester and Winchester', in Hall and Kenward 1994, 85–102

Manchester, K. and Roberts, C.A. 1995 *Archaeology of disease*, 2nd ed. Stroud, History Press

Manning, W.H. 1985 *Catalogue of the Romano-British iron tools, fittings and weapons in the British Museum* London, British Museum Publications

Meindl, R.S. and Lovejoy, C.O. 1985 'Ectocranial suture closure: A revised method for the determination of skeletal age at death based on the lateral-anterior sutures', *American J. Physical Anthropol.* **68**, 29–45

McKinley, J.L. 1993 'Bone fragment size and weights of bone from modern British cremations and their implications for the interpretation of archaeological cremations', *Int. J. Osteoarchaeol.* **3**, 283–7

McKinley, J.L. 1994 'The Anglo-Saxon cemetery at Spong Hill, North Elmham. Part VIII: The cremations', *E Anglian Archaeol.* **69**, 78–120

McKinley, J.L. 1997 'The cremated and inhumed human bone from burial and cremation-related contexts', in Fitzpatrick 1997, 55–74 and 244–53

McKinley, J.L. 2000 'Cremation burials' in Barber and Bowsher 2000, 264–77

McWhirr, A.D. (ed.) 1976. *Studies in the Archaeology and History of Cirencester* BAR Brit. Ser. **30**, Oxford, British Archaeological Reports

McWhirr, A.D. 1988 'Cirencester's contribution to the development of urban archaeology', *Cirencester Miscellany* **1**, 11–16

Moore, T. 2006 *Iron Age societies in the Severn-Cotswolds* BAR Brit Ser. **421**, Oxford, British Archaeological Reports

Mowl, T. 2002 *Historic Gardens of Gloucestershire* Stroud, Tempus

Mudd, A., Williams, R.J. and Lupton, A. 1999 *Excavations alongside Roman Ermin Street, Gloucestershire and Wiltshire. The archaeology of the A419/A417 Swindon to Gloucester Road Scheme* Oxford, Oxford Archaeological Unit

Murphy, P. 1976 *Fruits and seeds from Roman deposits at Ilchester* Unpublished Ancient Monuments Lab. report **2112**

Niblett, R. 1999 *The excavation of a ceremonial site at Folly Lane, Verulamium* Britannia Monograph **14**, London, Society for the Promotion of Roman Studies

Nixon, T. 1998 'Practically preserved: Observations on the impact of construction deposits', in M. Corfield, P. Hinton, T. Nixon and M. Pollard (eds) *Preserving archaeological remains in situ. Proceedings of the London conference of 1st–3rd April 1996* London, Museum of London Archaeology Service, 39–46

O'Neil, H. 1952 'Whittington Court Roman villa, Whittington, Gloucestershire', *Trans. Bristol Gloucestershire Archaeol. Soc.* **71**, 13–87

Oxford Archaeology 2002a *The cinema site, Lewis Lane, Cirencester, Gloucestershire: Archaeological impact assessment and strategy for monitoring and mitigation of proposed development* Unpublished report

Oxford Archaeology 2002b *The Angel Cinema site, Lewis Lane, Cirencester, Gloucestershire: Archaeological evaluation* Unpublished report

Oxford Archaeology 2002c *The cinema site, Lewis Lane, Cirencester, Gloucestershire: Archaeological evaluation. Test pits 11, 12, 13 and 14* Unpublished report

Oxford Archaeology 2002d *Evaluation at Cirencester Cattle Market and Leisure Centre car park* Unpublished report

Oxford Archaeology 2006a *Woolmarket car park, Cirencester, Gloucestershire. Archaeological evaluation report* Unpublished report

Oxford Archaeology 2006b *Kingshill North, Cirencester, Gloucestershire. Archaeological evaluation report* Unpublished report

Paterson, N.M. 2006 *The vernacular architecture and buildings of Stroud and Chalford* Oxford, Trafford Publishing

Peacock, D.P.S. and Williams, D.F. 1986 *Amphorae and the Roman economy* Harlow, Longman

Philpott, R. 1991 *Burial practices in Roman Britain: A survey of grave treatment and furnishing AD 43–410* BAR Brit. Ser. **219**, Oxford, British Archaeological Reports

Price, A. and Viner, D. 1994 'Lock-ups at Cirencester and Bisley: An additional note', *Trans Bristol Gloucestershire Archaeol. Soc.* **113**, 193–4

RCHME 1976 *Iron Age and Romano-British monuments in the Gloucestershire Cotswolds* London, HMSO

Reece, R, 1956 'A note on a small excavation at Cirencester', *Trans. Bristol Gloucestershire Archaeol. Soc.* **75**, 203–4

Reece, R. 1962 'The Oakley Cottage Romano-British cemetery, Cirencester', *Trans. Bristol. Gloucestershire Archaeol. Soc.* **81**, 51–72

Reece, R. 1970 'Cirencester Grammar School, 1960–61', *Trans. Bristol Gloucestershire Archaeol. Soc.* **89**, 11–14

Reece, R. 1976 The Ashcroft site, Cirencester', *Trans. Bristol Gloucestershire Archaeol. Soc.* **94**, 92–100

Reece, R. 1988 *My Roman Britain* Cotswold Studies **3**, Cirencester, Cotswold Studies

Reece, R. 1990 *Excavation, survey and records around Cirencester* Cotswold Studies **2**, Cirencester, Cotswold Studies

Reece, R. 2003 'The siting of Roman *Corinium*', *Britannia* **34**, 276–80

Reece, R. and Catling, C. 1975 *Cirencester: The development and buildings of a Cotswold town* BAR Brit. Ser. **12**, Oxford, British Archaeological Reports

Rennie, D.M. 1957 'A section through the Roman defences in Watermoor recreation ground, Cirencester', *Antiq. J.* **37**, 206–15

Rennie, D.M. 1971 'Excavations in the Parsonage Field, Cirencester, 1958', *Trans. Bristol Gloucestershire Archaeol. Soc.* **90**, 64–94

RIB (Roman Inscriptions of Britain): Collingwood, R.G. and Wright, R.P. (eds S.S. Frere and R.S.O. Tomlin) 1990–5 *The Roman Inscriptions of Britain*, vols I–II Stroud, Alan Sutton

Richardson, K. M. 1962 'Excavations in Parsonage Field, Watermoor Road, Cirencester, 1959', *Antiq. J.* **42**, 160–82

Richardson, K. and Stone, J.F.S. 1951 'The excavation of Iron Age villages on Boscombe Down West', *Wiltshire Archaeol. Natur. Hist. Mag.* **54**, 123–68

Roberts, J.P. 1988 *Glos 9482 Victoria Road, Cirencester. Interim report on archaeological excavations March–April 1988* Gloucestershire County Council unpublished report

Rodwell, W. 1997 *The parish church of St John the Baptist, Cirencester: An archaeological appraisal of the fabric and fixtures* Unpublished report for Parochial Church Council of Cirencester

Rodwell, W. 2000 'Daneway and Lodge Park: The archaeology of two Gloucestershire houses' *Trans. Bristol Gloucestershire Archaeol. Soc.* **118**, 11–32

Sarjeantson, D and Waldron, T. (eds) 1989 *Diet and crafts in towns* BAR Brit. Ser **199,** Oxford, British Archaeological Reports

Schwartz, J. H. 1995 *Skeleton keys: An introduction to human skeletal morphology, development and analysis* New York & Oxford, Oxford University Press

Sear, F. 2006 *Roman theatres: An architectural study* Oxford, Oxford University Press

Sidell, E.J. and Reilly, K. 1998 'Recent evidence for the ritual use of animals in Roman London', in B. Watson (ed.) 'Roman London, recent archaeological work', *J. Roman Archaeol. supp. ser.* **24**, 95–9

Slater, T. 1976a 'The town and its region in the Anglo-Saxon and medieval period', in McWhirr 1976, 81–108

Slater, T. 1976b 'Estate ownership and nineteenth century suburban development', in McWhirr 1976, 145–57

Slater, T. 1976c 'The Cirencester Improved Dwellings Company 1880–1914', in McWhirr 1976, 171–97

Slater, T.R. 1978 'Family, society and the ornamental villa on the fringes of English county towns', *J. Hist. Geogr.* **4.2**, 129–44

Smith, D. J. 1975 'Roman mosaics in Britain before the fourth century', in H. Stern and M. Le Glay (eds) *La Mosaïque Gréco–Romaine II* Paris, Centre Nationale de la Recherche Scientifique, 269–89

Smith, D. 1976 'Medieval timber building: A surviving fragment', in McWhirr 1976, 109–112

Stead, I.M. and Rigby, V. 1989 *Verulamium. King Harry Lane site* English Heritage Archaeol. Rep. **12**, London

Suchey, J.M. and Brooks, S. 1990 'Skeletal age determination based on the os pubis: A comparison of the Acsádi-Nemeskéri and Suchey-Brooks method', *Human Evolution* **5**, 227–38

Swan, V. 1975 'Oare reconsidered and the origins of Savernake ware in Wiltshire', *Britannia* **6**, 37–61

Timby, J. 1998 *Excavations at Kingscote and Wycomb, Gloucestershire* Cirencester, Cotswold Archaeological Trust

Timby, J. 1999 'Later prehistoric and Roman pottery', in Mudd *et al* 1999, 320–65

Thomas, A. 1999 *Cotswold Mill, Lewis Lane, Cirencester, Gloucestershire. Archaeological excavation and watching brief* Cotswold Archaeological Trust report **991087**

Tomber, R. and Dore, J. 1998 *The national Roman fabric reference collection: A handbook* MoLAS monograph **2**, London, Museum of London Archaeology Service

Townsend, A. 2006 *Outline report on the condition of Norman Arch Cottage, Cirencester, Glos* Unpublished report for the Norman Arch Group

Turner, K. 2000 *A narrow Cotswold street: Coxwell Street* Cirencester

Turner, N. 1995 *44 Blackjack Street, Cirencester: Building recording* Cotswold Archaeological Trust typescript report **95222**

Turner, N. 1996 *3 Coxwell Street and 1 Park Street, Cirencester, Gloucestershire: Building recording* CAT typescript report **96422**

Trow, S.D. 1988 'Excavations at Ditches hillfort, North Cerney, Gloucestershire', 1982–3', *Trans. Bristol Gloucestershire Archaeol. Soc.* **106**, 19–85

Tutin, T.G., Heywood, V.H. *et al.* 1964–80 *Flora europaea* **1–5**, Cambridge, Cambridge University Press

Van der Veen, M. 1988 'Carbonized grain from a Roman granary at South Shields, North East England', in H. Küster (ed.) *Der Prähistorische Mensch und seine Umwelt. Festschrift für Professor Körber-Grohne* Forschungen und Berichte zur Vor- und Frühgeschichte in Baden-Württemberg **31**, 353–65

Van der Veen, M. 1989 'Charred grain assemblages from Roman-period corn driers in Britain', *Archaeol. J.* **146**, 302–19

Van der Veen, M. 1994 'Reports on the biological remains', in P. Bidwell and S. Speak *Excavations at South Shields Roman fort*, volume 1, Newcastle, Society Antiquaries of Newcastle upon Tyne/Tyne and Wear Museums, 243–64

Van der Veen, M., Livarda, A. and Hill, A. 2007 'The archaeobotany of Roman Britain: Current state and identification of research priorities', *Britannia* **38**, 181–210

Verey, D. 1970 *Gloucestershire 1: The Cotswolds* Harmondsworth, Penguin

Verey, D. 1973 'Two Victorian architects' work in Gloucestershire', *Trans. Bristol Gloucestershire Archaeol. Soc.* **92**, 5–11

Verey, D. 1976 'The architect and architecture of Watermoor House', in McWhirr 1976, 168–70

Verey, D. and Brooks, A. 1999 *Gloucestershire 1: The Cotswolds*, 3rd edn, Harmondsworth, Penguin

Viner, D. 1976 'The Thames and Severn Canal in Cirencester', in McWhirr 1976, 126–44

Viner, D. 1988 *Cirencester town station: An outline history* Unpublished report for Cotswold District Council

Viner, D. 1994 *Cirencester lock-up and workhouse: A brief history and guide* Cirencester

Viner, D. 2000 'Already a folk memory: Cirencester Excavation Committee 1958–1997', *Cirencester Miscellany* **4**, 31–3

Viner, D. 2006. 'The Cirencester obelisk', *Cirencester Archaeol. Hist. Soc. Newsletter* **45**

Viner, D. and Powell, C. 1991 'Lock-ups at Cirencester and Bisley, with a note on Bibury and Great Barrington', *Trans. Bristol Gloucestershire Archaeol. Soc.* **109**, 207–17

Viner, D. and Viner, L. 2004 *Cirencester a century ago: The Bingham legacy* Chalford, Sutton

Wacher, J.S. 1963 'Cirencester 1962: Fourth interim report', *Antiq. J.* **44**, 9–18

Wacher, J. 1995 *The Towns of Roman Britain*, 2nd edn, London, Book Club Associates

Wacher, J.S. 1998 'The dating of town walls in Roman Britain', in J. Bird (ed.) *Form and fabric: Studies in Rome's material past in honour of B.R. Hartley* Oxford, Oxbow, 41–50

Walls, R. 1985–6 'Langley's Mill, Cirencester', *Cirencester Archaeol. Hist. Soc. Ann. Rep. and Newsletter* **28**, 4–17

Waring, D. 1976 'Conservation of historic buildings in Cirencester', in McWhirr 1976, 198–200

Webster, G. 1959 'Cirencester; Dyer Court excavation, 1957', *Trans. Bristol Gloucestershire Archaeol. Soc.* **78**, 44–85

Webster, P.V. 1976 'Severn Valley ware: A preliminary study', *Trans. Bristol Gloucestershire Archaeol. Soc.* **94**, 18–46

Webster, P.V. 1993 'The post-fortress coarsewares', in W.H. Manning, *Report on the excavations at Usk 1965–76: The Roman pottery* Cardiff, University of Wales Press

Welsford, J. 1987a *Cirencester, a history and guide* Stroud, Alan Sutton

Welsford, J. 1987b *Cirencester in old photographs* Stroud, Alan Sutton

Wilkinson, D. 1985–86 'The Historic/Listed Buildings Record at the Corinium Museum', *Cirencester Archaeol. Hist. Soc. Ann. Rep. and Newsletter*, **28**, 17–18

Wilkinson, D. 1992 *OAU fieldwork manual* Oxford Archaeology, unpublished manuscript

Wills, J. 1989 'Cirencester, Victoria Road School', *Trans. Bristol Gloucestershire Archaeol. Soc.* **107**, 254

Wills, J. 1990 'Cirencester, Victoria Road School', *Trans. Bristol Gloucestershire Archaeol. Soc.* **108**, 194–5

Wills, J. 2006 'The view from the Gloucestershire Archaeology Service', in Holbrook and Juřica 2006, 231–35

Wood-Jones, R. 1986 *Traditional domestic architecture in the Banbury Region* Banbury, Wykham Books

Woodward, A. and Leach, P. 1993 *The Uley Shrines. Excavation of a ritual complex on West Hill, Uley, Gloucestershire: 1977–9* English Heritage Archaeol. Rep. **17**, London, English Heritage

Worsley, G.L. 1956. *Traditional domestic architecture in the Cotswold region* Unpublished thesis, University of Manchester

Yates, D.T. 2007 *Land power and prestige. Bronze Age field systems in southern England* Oxford, Oxbow

Young, C.J. 1977 *Oxfordshire Roman pottery* BAR Brit. Ser. **43**, Oxford, British Archaeological Reports

Young, D.E.Y. 2001 *Excavation of two prehistoric enclosures at The Beeches, London Road, Cirencester* Avon Archaeological Unit unpublished report

Young, R. 1991 'Cement scorned in Gloucester Street, Cirencester', *SPAB News* **12.1**, 16–18

Zeepvat, R.J. 1979 'Observations in Dyer Street and Market Place, Cirencester 1849, 1878 and 1974/5', *Trans. Bristol Gloucestershire Archaeol. Soc.* **97**, 65–73

# INDEX

Entries in bold refer to the illustrations